Letters of Appreciation from U.S. Government Leaders

"I want to take this opportunity to thank [Earl Updike] for [his] book... I look forward to working with [Earl Updike] for a better future for our country."

Al Gore
Vice President of the United States, Washington, DC

"I was happy to see that the Department of Agriculture recently revised the food guide pyramid to encourage plant food consumption. I agree with [Earl Updike] that eating healthy foods is a critical part of health care reform. I think more and more people are beginning to recognize this.

Patricia Schroeder
U.S. Congresswoman, Washington, DC

". . . Our present system of health care delivery is extremely complicated. We currently spend over $800 billion per year on medical care—over 13 percent of our Gross National Product. . . . changes are needed. [Earl Updike's] comments on the importance of prevention are right on target. Much study has proven that preventative health efforts produce both a healthier population and reduce health care expenditures. Making intelligent lifestyle choices is one of the most important factors in this effort, and it is clear that the value of a healthy diet is extremely high."

Dan Schaefer
Member of U.S. Congress, Washington, DC

"I couldn't agree more with [Earl Updike] about the importance of preventative health care and healthful living and eating habits as major contributors to holding down health care costs."

Jim Kolbe
Member of U.S. Congress

"My wife and I have enjoyed [Earl Updike's] book. We have already tried two of the recipes. [His] book will give me a guide as to a better diet."

Harry Reid
United States Senate

"Like [Earl Updike], I believe prevention is key in our attempts to solve the health care crisis in our country. I also believe [Earl] when [he] says that a healthy, fortified diet is the first place to start.

John T. Doolittle
4th District, California, Congress of the United States

"Health care and adequate nutrition for everyone is very much on the minds of all of us these days. [Earl Updike is] making a valiant contribution, and I salute [his] effort."

David E. Skaggs
U.S. House of Representatives, Washington, DC

"This book promises to be insightful, and is timely, since our nation has renewed its concentration on health care. It will be a welcome addition to my library."

Dirk Kempthorne
United States Senate

"By reducing the amount of animal fats and replacing them with fruits, vegetables, and cereals, the result is a diet rich in fiber and protein that reduces the risk of heart disease. Clearly, nutrition education is important for both children and adults to prevent serious health problems and health care costs in the future."

Nancy Landon Kassebaum
United States Senate

"[I thank Earl Updike] for writing and sharing [his] views on health care reform."

Hillary Rodham Clinton
The White House

The Miracle Diet

Easy Permanent Weight Loss

COOKBOOK

Fat Free	Cholesterol Free	High Fiber

ATTENTION

This book has a special new binding that allows it to lie flat so that recipes can be easily read without propping or holding your book. This is an expensive extra that you are not being charged for. If you feel it is valuable, we would love to hear from you. Please contact the distributor.

We thank you for buying this important cookbook that can change your life, bring you new vigor and health and save you lots of money on food in the coming years.

Publisher
Best Possible Health
P.O. Box 54282
Phoenix, Arizona 85078-4282

"For the Best Possible Health"

The Miracle Diet

Easy Permanent Weight Loss

Cookbook

Fat Free	Cholesterol Free	High Fiber

LOOK BETTER ... FEEL BETTER
SAVE MONEY ON FOOD
SAVE MONEY ON MEDICAL / DENTAL
LOSE WEIGHT PERMANENTLY
INCREASE YOUR ENERGY

Earl and Ethel Updike

Foreword by Neal D. Barnard, M.D.
President, National Physicians Committee For Responsible Medicine
Author of "The Power of Your Plate" and "Food For Life."

The Miracle Diet Cookbook
First Printing

Copyright © 1995 by Earl F. Updike
ALL RIGHTS RESERVED.
Cover Design copyright © 1995

For information write to:
Best Possible Health
P.O. Box 54282
Phoenix, AZ 85078-4282

ISBN: 1-887437-01-0
Softback Edition

Distributed by:
Best Possible Health
P.O. Box 54282
Phoenix, Arizona 85078-4282
1-800-922-9681

Be sure to look for "The Miracle Diet—
14 Days To New Vigor and Health"
with the bright yellow cover.
A must for a complete understanding of
The Best Possible Health, Happiness and Thinness.

Cover Design by Wil Crandall

Lithographed in the United States of America

Dedication

To our wonderful children, Lorraine, Jim, Alan, David Sr. and Karen, as well as our eighteen lovely grandchildren and their posterity, with the hope that it will inspire all of them to attain "The Best Possible Health."

Acknowledgments

Thanks to all of the beautiful people in our lives who have encouraged us to write this cookbook which teaches you how to strengthen your body's immune system, prevent degenerative diseases and live a happier life.

May God bless each one of you readers of this book to take responsibility for your own health. This is the only way you can be assured of enjoying the best possible health during your time here on earth.

Quality life without obesity, sickness or disease should be your goal, not just longevity. Your family, friends and neighbors will be blessed by your example.

We thank each person who teaches others by example, because we all teach by what we do. Thank all of you for caring and sharing your convictions of the true principles of health.

"FAT FREE" Definition

The food industry has generally adopted the phrase "Fat Free" to mean 'no added fat.' There is naturally occurring fat in low-fat plant foods such as: Beans (3%), Rice (4%), Corn (8%), Whole Wheat flour (5%), Potatoes (trace).

There is no added fat in any recipe in this book. All plant foods contain some fat even if it is only a trace. There are only five plant foods that contain high fat. They are: Avocados, Nuts, Olives, Coconut and Chocolate, none of which are used in these recipes. Some soy products are high in fat.

RECIPE STATISTICS

We do not spell out Fat grams, cholesterol mg., carbohydrate grams, protein grams or fiber grams because:

- The fat content in these recipes is ideal, averaging between 5 and 10%.
- There is no cholesterol in any recipe.
- Protein will average out at about 10% or less (ideal).
- Complex carbohydrate averages about 80% (ideal).
- These recipes will supply about 40 to 60 grams of fiber per day (ideal).

Foreword

One of the great strides in health research in the last two decades is the discovery of the power of meals made from grains, vegetables, fruits, and legumes to prevent health problems and add years to our lives.

We feel better when we eat well. We think better, work better, and even look better when we take care of ourselves.

In many cases, it is precisely the illnesses that are most resistant to treatment which are most amenable to prevention. The vast majority of heart disease cases are preventable, and existing heart disease is potentially reversible with healthful lifestyle including a plant-based diet. As much as 80 percent of cancer is theoretically preventable. And a whole host of other problems, from the "battle of the bulge" to diabetes, arthritis, osteoporosis, and numerous other problems are best addressed by prevention, which includes, first and foremost, an optimal menu.

In this volume are recipes to put healthful eating to work for you and your family. They are easy to prepare, wonderfully nutritious, and, best of all, delightful for the palate. These are foods that not only keep the body in good running order; they also encourage an exploration of new culinary treats and new ways to prepare old favorites.

Neal D. Barnard, M.D.
President, Physicians Committee For Responsible Medicine
Washington, D.C.
Author, "The Power of Your Plate" and "Food For Life."

Vitamin B¹²

If you are pregnant or nursing, or if you follow this program strictly for more than three years, then take at least 5 micrograms supplemental vitamin B¹² each day.

Caution

The information in this book is meant to educate you regarding better health and happiness. Any decision you make in the treatment of any illness should include the advice of a physician experienced in the effects of dietary change. If you are seriously ill or on medication, do not change your diet without your health care professional's approval.

CONTENTS

The doctor of the future will give no medicine,
but will interest his patient in the care of the human
frame, in diet and in the cause and prevention of disease.
—Thomas A. Edison

INFORMATION
YOU NEED
TO KNOW

THE *NEW FOUR FOOD GROUPS*

Whole Grains	Vegetables	Legumes	Fruit
This group includes bread, pasta, hot or cold cereal, corn, millet, barley, bulgur, buckwheat groats and tortillas. Build each of your meals around a hearty grain dish— grains are rich in fiber and other complex carbohydrates, as well as protein, B vitamins and zinc.	Vegetables are packed with nutrients; they provide vitamin C, beta-carotene, riboflavin and other vitamins, iron, calcium and fiber. Dark green, leafy vegetables such as broccoli, collards, kale, mustard and turnip greens, chicory or bok choy are especially good sources of these important nutrients. Dark yellow and orange vegetables such as carrots, winter squash, sweet potatoes and pumpkin provide extra beta-carotene. Include generous portions of a variety of vegetables in your diet.	Legumes, which is another name for beans, peas, and lentils, are all good sources of fiber, protein, iron, calcium, zinc and B vitamins. This group also includes chickpeas, baked and refried beans, soy milk, tofu, tempeh, and texturized vegetable protein.	Fruits are rich in fiber, vitamin C and beta-carotene. Be sure to include at least one serving each day of fruits that are high in vitamin C—citrus fruits, melons and strawberries are all good choices. Choose whole fruit over fruit juices, which don't contain as much healthy fiber.

PHYSICIANS COMMITTEE FOR RESPONSIBLE MEDICINE • P.O. Box 6322, Washington, D.C. 20015 • (202) 686-2210

This is a "plantarian," not vegetarian program.
plan•tar´•i•an (plan tar´ ian) n. [plant + arian] a person whose basic diet revolves around plants (starches), supplemented with vegetables and fruit.

Put Prevention First

You!—Yes, you personally are the solution to the national health care crisis. Doctors, nurses, hospitals, clinics, insurance companies or governments cannot give you health. Only you can give yourself and your family health by changing your lifestyle and the type of food you eat.

According to the U.S. Surgeon General's Report on Nutrition and Health (1988) most illnesses in America are caused by diet and lifestyle practices and therefore are preventable.

PREVENTION IS NOT EARLY DETECTION AND TREATMENT of heart disease, stroke, breast cancer, prostate cancer, colon cancer, adult diabetes, osteoporosis, high blood pressure, obesity and many other preventable diseases that cause untold pain, misery and 80% of all deaths in America each year.

Prevention is following a "Plantarian" starch-based diet. The positive effects of this program can be enhanced by avoiding tobacco, alcohol, drugs, and by including daily exercise such as walking. Learn to relax and enjoy a positive attitude.

Over three billion people worldwide eat a plant-centered diet, with little added fat, no milk products after weaning, and very few animal foods. These people are comparatively free of heart disease, stroke, breast cancer, prostate cancer, colon cancer, diabetes, obesity, osteoporosis, arthritis and multiple sclerosis. These diseases were responsible for the majority of the $1 trillion in health care costs in 1992. That's 14% of Gross National Product, and it increases 10% each year.

Within six years, health care costs may rise to 20% or more of the GNP and could destroy our entire financial system.

Scientists have long known that you and I as human beings are primates, a class which also includes apes, gorillas and monkeys. Primates are primarily herbivores (plant eaters or **Plantarians**).

Medical scientists have long contended that the standard American diet, consisting of nearly 50% fat, 20% protein (mostly animal), 20% simple sugars and only 10% complex carbohydrate, is the major cause of degenerative diseases.

Animal food and high fat are the wrong fuel for humans. For instance, if you use diesel fuel in a gasoline engine, you will destroy the engine. A plant-centered diet is the correct fuel for man.

It is clear from the worldwide epidemiological studies and a consensus of medical scientists that plants should be our major source of calories for optimum health.

The New Four Food Groups

"The New Four Food Groups" were introduced to the world in 1991 by the Physicians Committee for Responsible Medicine, a large body of medical doctors in the USA. They declare that grain, legumes, vegetables, and fruit are the food (fuel) for man. Meat, chicken, fish, eggs and dairy products are not needed in our diet and in fact, these foods are laden with tons of killer cholesterol and saturated fat contributing to 80% of all deaths in America.

This body of physicians teach: To prevent debilitating and killer degenerative diseases we must immediately change to a **plant-based** intake of calories. Also, stop adding vegetable fat and oils to our diet.

A growing number of nurses, medical doctors, scientists, and other health professionals are adopting a plant-centered food program for the **Best Possible Health.** The American people are now recognizing that an animal-based diet is making them fat, sick and tired. By following the program in this book you will have all the tools to become more attractive and enjoy the best possible health.

The official Food Guide Pyramid, adopted in 1992 by the Department of Agriculture and the Department of Health and Human Services, is a step in the right direction and demonstrates that plant food (whole grains-vegetables-legumes-fruit) is the foundation of a balanced diet. The pyramid reveals that daily 85% of calories should be derived from plants, only about 8% from animal products and only about 3.5% from added fat.

Even though the USDA Pyramid is far superior to the old Basic Four Food Groups (1956), it falls far short of the **Best Possible Health** because meat, chicken, fish, eggs and milk products are full of cholesterol and saturated fat that cause death and disease.

Meat, chicken, fish, dairy and eggs are a known cause of heart disease, stroke, osteoporosis, diabetes, and other diseases. High fat intake from animal or vegetable sources also contributes to many cancers. **Animal foods make you fat, in fact, all fat makes you fat!**

Call or write your Congress man or woman and send them a copy of the solution. You are welcome to copy page 5 and send it with your letter.

Talk to your State Legislators and School Board Members about changing the laws in your state and School District concerning the high fat content and large amount of animal foods in school lunches. The food now being served is not only making children fat, it is making sure that over half of them will die of heart disease long before their time. Twenty-five percent will eventually suffer and die of cancer mostly because of the food they are served.

The Solution to the Health Care Crisis: Education

1. Governments and schools must begin an all-out media blitz and an education blitz to promote and teach the fact that plant-based should become the foundation of our daily diet.

2. Total fat intake must be drastically reduced to 10% of daily calories to prevent and reverse degenerative diseases.

3. Fiber must be increased from 10 grams per day to 40–60 grams per day.

Easy Permanent Weight Loss

Crash diets don't work in the long run as most of you already know. As high as 97% of all people who go on standard fad diets regain all of their lost weight and many dieters will add additional fat. To the experienced dieter, this is not news.

The reason dieters are plagued by such poor weight loss statistics is that they continue to eat a high fat animal-based diet with added vegetable and animal fats.

Several reasons for the failure of high-priced commercial diets include:

1. Dieting by cutting and counting calories doesn't work because you are always hungry. Eventually you will tire of starving yourself and begin to satisfy your natural hunger drive. When you cut calories, your body automatically determines that it is starving to death and begins to more efficiently store the calories you eat. Your body automatically stores fat to use in case of a future famine. After some weeks or months of starvation (dieting, counting

calories) you finally start eating enough to satisfy your hunger drive and you begin to gain weight at an accelerated rate because the body has automatically set up a mechanism to use each calorie more efficiently. (Set Point or Body Regulator). Each time you go through this yo-yo process, the body knows it is starving and gets even more efficient at storing every calorie for use in the next famine. Therefore, the end result is that many people, over a period of years of yo-yo losing and gaining weight, live in frustration and despair while becoming heavier and heavier.

2. Dr. John McDougall says, "Some diets may cause ketosis, a condition that also occurs with several common illnesses resulting in suppressed appetite. These low carbohydrate diets can and do make you sick." He adds, "Cans of protein powders are convenient variations of the low carbohydrate 'make-yourself-sick' diets."[1] When people are ill, they usually lose their appetites until they recover. Isn't it interesting that people will make themselves sick just to lose weight?

3. Diet pills work by suppressing the hunger drive a little, causing a small amount of weight loss, but they are costly and have potentially dangerous side effects.

Ultimately, diet pills, making yourself sick by eating a low carbohydrate, high protein diet, or starving yourself by limiting your calories are ridiculous ways to stay slim.

SOLUTION! Changing your major intake of calories to a starch-based diet supplemented with vegetables and fruit will make you lean and healthy. You will never be hungry because you can eat all the food you desire while slimming to your ideal weight. This

[1]John A. McDougall, M.D., "The McDougall Program" (Plume Books, New York New York 1990) p. 379.

plant-centered way of eating has been proven effective by billions of people throughout the world. Proof of this statement comes by visiting China and the Far East. I have been in the Orient and observed the mounds of plant food eaten by people who stay slim and trim throughout life, even into old age.

Companion Book to this Cookbook

For a complete understanding of the relationship between the type of food we eat and the health we can enjoy, we recommend that you read *The Miracle Diet: 14 Days to New Vigor and Health,* (with the bright yellow cover), the companion book to this cookbook. In *The Miracle Diet* Book you will find the answers regarding the causes of, prevention of, and even cures for the major degenerative diseases that plague affluent America and the Western World.

First you'll learn in detail the cause and cure of excess weight and obesity.

Next you will discover the simple truths of *The Miracle Diet* Program and the amazing healing and change in your body, within just the first two weeks.

You'll be convinced that as primates, we are herbivores by nature and need to change to the proper food fuel.

You will no longer wonder why heart attacks, heart disease and cholesterol kill one-half of all people who die each year in the U.S. You'll learn why nearly all of these deaths can be prevented.

Killer Fat—The dreaded enemy will be discussed in simple language so that any layman can understand and get the fat out of his or her life.

Find out why so many people are allergic to cow's milk and dairy products. You'll learn that milk is basically liquid meat and how it contributes to many diseases. Learn how osteoporosis can be prevented by following *The Miracle Diet.* It is basically not caused by lack of calcium. **It may actually be caused by drinking milk!** Find out the truth about dairy products.

"Don't miss the chapter on "Cancer." It can save your life! Find out how you can prevent many cancers.

Learn how to avoid adult diabetes or even reverse this deadly and destructive disease. Find out why adult diabetes is epidemic in America.

Learn why more than 60 million citizens of the U.S. suffer from high blood pressure.

Discover how antioxidants fight deadly free radicals and strengthen our immune system.

The Miracle Diet: 14 Days to New Vigor and Health not only reveals the cause of major degenerative diseases such as heart disease, stroke, cancer, diabetes, osteoporosis, obesity and many others, but tells you in plain understandable terms how to change for the better.

You'll learn the type of food to eat and how to prepare it. The book outlines what foods to stock in your kitchen, the type of simple cookware that is best and how to use and store foods correctly.

You'll find two week menus and recipes for the folks who don't like to cook.

For those who like to cook and make delicious gourmet meals, menus and recipes are given that delight the palate.

The Miracle Diet: 14 Days to New Vigor and Health explains how to eat healthfully when traveling by auto or air. Appendix One in this companion book lists the percentage of fat, protein and carbohydrate in hundreds of common foods; this is very important to know if you want to be an informed, wise consumer. Appendix Two gives the percentage of fat in many well-known fast foods, also a "must know" in order to enjoy the best possible health. You'll discover a gold mine of important information on health in this companion book written by nutrition and health researcher, Earl F. Updike.

Worldwide scientific medical studies of societies that eat a plant-centered diet reveal that very few of these people suffer from the devastating degenerative diseases that kill up to 80 percent of all Americans who die each year. America and the affluent Western world eat mostly animal products. This high fat diet makes people sick and results in millions of people dying prematurely.[2]

The Miracle Diet: 14 Days to New Vigor and Health (with the bright yellow cover) and the book you are now reading make the perfect combination that will keep you at your ideal weight and teach you how to enjoy The Best Possible Health for a lifetime of thinness, happiness and joy.

About This Cookbook

Cholesterol kills, fat kills and insufficient fiber kills. This has been demonstrated by many scientific studies in America as well as

---

[2]Neal D. Barnard, M.D., *The Power of Your Plate* (Summertown, TN: Book Publishing Company, 1990), 71.

by many worldwide epidemiological medical studies. The purpose of this cookbook is to provide a wide range of recipes that are essentially fat free, cholesterol free and high in fiber.

Plant foods contain no cholesterol, a very low amount of fat, and are very high in fiber. Animal foods—meat, fowl, fish, milk, cheese and other dairy products—are loaded with cholesterol, are very high in fat (mostly saturated), and contain absolutely no fiber.

As I have said before, over three billion people, about 65 percent of the current world population, eat a plant-centered diet. The major degenerative diseases—heart disease, stroke, breast cancer, prostate cancer, colon cancer, diabetes, multiple sclerosis, osteoporosis, arthritis and many other well known diseases—are comparatively unknown among populations which do not eat animals as their major intake of calories.

Japanese People Live Longer

Japan, for example, has the longest life expectancy in the world, averaging nearly 80 years,[3] in spite of the fact they have been Westernizing their diet some in the past 25 years. Many Japanese still basically eat a traditional plant-centered diet based on rice, wheat, corn, potatoes and legumes (beans, peas, and lentils), with lots of vegetables and fruit. Their diet is comparatively low in fat calories, about 10–20 percent, but unfortunately it is increasing.

---

[3]Reported on NBC News broadcast, Sunday morning, June 28, 1992. See also the United Nations Population Division, World Population Prospects: 1992 Revision Advance Annex Tables.

The Japanese are very heavy cigarette smokers; smoking at about two times the U.S. per capita rate. However, the Japanese have a low rate of lung cancer, about one-sixth the U.S. rate. They also have a very low incidence of heart disease, about one-tenth that of Americans. The people of Japan are under heavy stress daily to maintain their "number one" status in world markets. Further, many breathe heavily polluted industrial air. Apparently the plant-centered diet enhances their immune systems and protects them from the many carcinogens found in cigarette smoke and in polluted air. The heavy cigarette smoking, pollution and stress do not seem to cause degenerative diseases to the same extent as in America, where we eat an animal-centered, high fat, high cholesterol diet.[4]

Everyone says, "Cut the fat radically"

The American Heart Association, American Cancer Society, U.S. Department of Agriculture, U.S. Department of Health and Human Services, The National Cancer Institute, The American Dietetic Association and other health organizations are calling for people to cut down on fat consumption. Most all health groups are now calling for Americans to cut fat consumption well below 30 percent. It is virtually impossible to cut your fat consumption to any percentage if you do not know what percentage of fat is in each item of food that you consume.

[4]Earl F. Updike, *The Miracle Diet, 14 Days to New Vigor and Health* (Phoenix, AZ: Best Possible Health, 1995). See also John A. McDougall, M.D., *The McDougall Tapes,* Tape 4, Side A, Cancer Prevention, 1989.

NBC's Today Show featured Dr. Art Ulene's weight loss program for the month of January 1995. He said you must eat less than 20% fat if you want to lose weight permanently. Smart people are cutting out the fat and becoming "Plantarians."

Oprah Winfrey's Spring Training Program

TV's Superstar, Oprah Winfrey, advocates that we radically cut the fat in our diet to 20 grams a day. This amounts to only 10% of 1800 calories per day. Oprah says: "This is changing your life forever." Medical scientific literature has long since proven what Oprah promotes.

Thanks, Oprah, for literally saving lives! Because you influence tens of millions of people, what you are doing will help alleviate years of pain and suffering from degenerative diseases. To top it off, your TV viewers are becoming leaner and more attractive which must bring great joy and happiness into their lives.

On her Friday, April 28, 1995 show, she showed viewers how to clean out their refrigerators and cupboards and get rid of all the fat, unhealthy foods. She showed how to restock their kitchen and pantry with Fat-Free and super-low-fat foods.

In our other book *The Miracle Diet: 14 Days to New Vigor and Health* we give detailed information on healthy food to buy and how to prepare it so it's tasteful and delicious.

For the best possible health, you should eat no more than 10 percent of your total calories in fat each day.[4][5][6][7] On a 1500-calorie-per-day diet with 10 percent fat calories, 150 calories would

[4]Dr. T. Colin Campbell, *The Cornell-China-Oxford Project of Nutrition, Health and Environment,* Cornell University, Division of Nutritional Sciences, Ithaca, NY 14853.
[5]Updike, Appendix One.

come from fat. That equals about 16 1/2 grams of fat, since there are 9 calories in every gram of fat. Compare that with carbohydrates and proteins which have 4 calories per gram each. Twelve grams of fat per day might be even better and would amount to about 7.5 percent of total calories.

Wise Consumers Know Their Numbers

We are constantly bombarded by food manufacturers claims that their products are 93% fat free, or 97% fat free, etc. These claims are misleading in most cases. For example, some turkey hot dogs that claim to be 80% fat free in fact contain 80% fat calories. Fat may be only 20% of the total volume of the product, but fat makes up 80% of the total calories. Unless the food product says "fat free," you had better beware and learn to translate the fat grams into calories.

To find the true percentage of fat in any product, first multiply the number of grams of fat times nine. There are nine calories in every gram of fat. Then divide the number of fat calories by the total calories in the serving to determine the true percentage of fat calories in that product.

Example:

Total calories in a serving = 100

Grams of fat in a serving = 5

5 x 9 = 45 fat calories,

45 divided by 100 = .45 or 45% in fat calories

[6]John A. McDougall, M.D., *The McDougall Plan* (Piscataway, NJ: New Century Publishers, 1983), 89.

[7]Nathan Pritikin, *The Pritikin Program for Diet and Exercise* (NY: Bantam Books, 1979), 9–17.

Don't be misled by many manufacturers of ice cream, cheese, lunch meats, hot dogs, bacon and other foods. They may advertise 80, 90, 95 or even 97 percent fat-free. They may be calculating by total weight of the product or using some other method instead of the percentage of calories of the nutrients.

In 1994 the Food and Drug Administration began requiring all manufacturers to display new nutritional labels on most products. The major value of this new labeling is that it gives you total calories and calories from fat so that you can determine the percentage of fat calories in each serving.

Medical Nutritionists Now Choose Starches

Starches such as whole grains, rice, corn, potatoes and legumes are the FOUNDATION of the human diet according to a consensus of medical nutritionists (see the USDA Food Guide Pyramid).[5]

In the past we have been told that starches make you fat, but medical science now knows that the opposite is actually true. Starches make you thin. It is fat that makes your body fat. Fat should be avoided always. A small amount of fat is in most foods anyway. It is nearly impossible to get less than 5 to 10 percent fat in your diet. Oatmeal, for instance, contains over 12 percent fat; whole wheat flour contains 5 percent fat; potatoes contain less than 1 percent fat. Even lettuce contains 13 percent fat! In fact, your body

---

[5]*The Food Guide Pyramid* announced by the U.S. Dept. of Agriculture, April 28, 1992; and *The New Four Food Groups,* announced by the Physicians Committee for Responsible Medicine, April 8, 1991.

can manufacture nearly all the essential fatty acids it needs from any food. The only exception is linoleic acid, which must be obtained from certain foods. For example, three and one-half ounces of oatmeal per day would provide all the linoleic acid we need.[6]

What Does "Fat-Free" Mean?

A "**FAT-FREE**" food commercially is commonly referred to as a food that has no added fat. If you cook potatoes and do not add any type of fat to them, you could refer to them as "**FAT-FREE**". Similarly, if you make cookies and add no fat to them, they also can be referred to as fat free even though the whole wheat flour you make them with contains 5 percent fat. If you make a salad out of lettuce and many other vegetables all of which contain various, relatively small amounts of fats, you could refer to this salad as fat free, but only if you use a fat free salad dressing. (There are many fat free salad dressings from which to choose.) If, however, you use a salad dressing which contains fat, you could not then call your salad "fat free." Many regular salad dressings contain nearly 99 percent fat and should be avoided. Read all labels.

Remember, a medium potato contains about 80 calories; a large potato about 150 calories; and a cup of brown rice is only about 200 calories. They don't make you fat. What makes you fat is the animal food you may ladle onto it like butter, sour cream, or 100% fat, that

---

[6]Nathan Pritikin, *The Pritikin Program for Diet and Exercise* (NY: Bantam Books, 1979), 14.

has been squeezed from plants, called margarine.

The only plant foods that are high in fat calories are avocados (88% fat), olives (98% fat), nuts (75% to 92% fat), coconuts (92% fat) and milk chocolate (56% fat); some soy bean products are also high in fat. These plant foods should be limited if you want to enjoy the **best possible health.**

We repeat: fat should always be avoided. As you eliminate fat from your diet you will soon lose the taste for it and no longer enjoy the taste and texture of fatty foods.

Herbivores versus Carnivores

Contrary to popular belief, human bodies are made like herbivores (plant eaters), not like carnivores[7] (animal eaters). One would have a difficult time making a comparative case for humans being carnivores in any form. On the other hand, it can easily be shown by comparison that human bodies are made like other known herbivores. For example:[8][9][10][11]

1. Human bodies resemble those of other primates (apes, chimpanzees, monkeys and gorillas) more closely than they do any other animal.[12] Primates are primarily plant eaters and they don't smother their wonderful plant food with grease and oil.

[7]Funk and Wagnall's New Encyclopedia #5, p. 314.

[8]John A. McDougall, M.D., *The McDougall Newsletter,* Vol. 5, No. 5, Sept./Oct. 1991.

[9]McDougall and McDougall, 37–38.

[10]Julian M. Whitaker, M.D., *99 Secrets for a Longer Healthier Life* (Phillips Publishing Inc., 7811 Montrose Rd., Potomac, MD 20854), 2–4.

[11]John Robbins, *Diet for a New America* (Stillpoint Publishing, Bos 640, Walpole, NH 03608), 258–260).

[12]Webster's Ninth New Collegiate Dictionary, "Primate: any of an order of mammals comprising man together with the apes, monkeys," p. 934.

2. Humans, like all herbivores, have flat teeth for grinding plant food. Carnivores have sharp teeth all the way to the back of their mouths for ripping and tearing flesh.

3. Carnivores have a liver that will excrete nearly 100 percent of all cholesterol that they ingest from the flesh they eat. However, all herbivores, including humans, have a liver with a limited capacity to excrete excess cholesterol. If humans or other herbivores eat more cholesterol than their liver can excrete, the retained cholesterol can eventually kill. Animal saturated fat can also kill.

4. Humans have a long, convoluted gut like other herbivores have in order to digest plant food. Carnivores, on the other hand, have a very short gut for the digestion of flesh and animal food.

5. Humans have enzymes in their intestine that digest complex carbohydrates; carnivores do not have these enzymes.

6. We have alpha amylase, an enzyme in our saliva that digests complex carbohydrates. This enzyme is not present in carnivores.

A sidelight to further illustrate the difference between herbivores and carnivores is that most herbivores, including humans, sip water and sweat through their pores while most carnivores lap water and sweat through their tongues.[13]

It has been said that the only way humans resemble carnivores is that, in affluent America and the Western world, they eat like carnivores!

---

7 8 9 10 11 12 13Dr. Marc Sorenson, *Megahealth* , National Institute of Health Publisher, 1992, Chapter 7, "Herbivorous By Design," 312–331.

13Whitaker, 2–4. See also McDougall et al, 37–38.

Standard American Diet—Hazardous to Health

The standard American diet is made up mainly of animal food loaded with cholesterol and fats, as well as too many salts, sugars, white flour, refined grains, food additives, added vegetable fats, concentrated chemical preservatives, drugs and residual pesticides from livestock production.

A large percentage of American adults are overweight and suffering from unnecessary degenerative diseases. As a result, medical costs are becoming burdensome for everyone because of rising insurance rates and taxes to fund public medical programs.

It doesn't have to be this way. A growing number of health professionals are promoting new dietary standards. Complex carbohydrates (carbohydrates plus fiber), which are found only in plant foods, have been widely supported as providing the proper basis for our diet. However, in spite of this exploding scientific knowledge, most of us continue to get most of our calories from rich animal foods like meats, chicken, fish, eggs, milk, cheese, ice cream, cottage cheese, sour cream, and other products derived from animals. We consume too many simple carbohydrates such as sugar, honey, fructose and syrups, which have had the fiber removed. Simple carbohydrates should be limited because they are empty calories which burn too quickly, many times causing wide swings in our blood sugar levels.

In Asian countries, obesity is nearly unknown, Why? The Asians who remain slim for an entire lifetime live on a diet consisting mostly of rice, wheat, potatoes, corn, and other starchy vegetables. They shun greasy, fatty flesh and animal milk products.

What happens when they move to America and adopt our eating habits? They get fat like many lifelong Americans.

If you want to lose weight, do what billions of people throughout the world do: eat a diet consisting mainly of plant foods.

Superior Health of Seventh-Day Adventists

Seventh-Day Adventists are the best example of any major religious group in America as far as nutrition and health is concerned. JAMA, the Journal of the American Medical Association, has published two studies in 1992 that statistically prove that Seventh-Day Adventists live longer than the general population of America.

Approximately 50 percent of the Seventh-Day Adventist population in California follow a lacto-ovo vegetarian diet (plant food plus milk and eggs). This Adventist population has been found to have an age-adjusted prostate cancer mortality rate that is only 30 percent that of men in the general population.[14] There was a statistically significant decrease in the risk of cancer for men with relatively higher consumption of legumes and citrus fruit, and an increased risk seen for those with a higher total consumption of meat products, particularly fish. Seventh-Day Adventists (male and female) have overall significantly lower rates of mortality from

[14]Phillips, R.L., "Role of Life-style and Dietary Habits in Risk of Cancer Among Seventh-Day Adventists," *Cancer Research,* 1975; 35: 3513–3522. See also Millo, P. et al, "Cohort Study of Diet, Lifestyle, and Prostate Cancer in Adventist Men," *Cancer* 1989, 64: 605–612.

most major chronic diseases, including coronary artery disease and cancers, compared to the general American population.[15]

In a 1985 medical study on diabetes, Dr. David Snowden of the University of Minnesota and Dr. Roland Phillips of Loma Linda University reported data on 25,698 Seventh-Day Adventists over a 21 year period. They found that plant-eaters were significantly less likely to die from diabetes-related causes than meat-eaters.[16]

William P. Castelli, M.D., the director of the Framingham Heart Study, the longest running heart study in the world, offers the Seventh-Day Adventists as an example of quality of life as well as longevity. He says, "Their philosophy calls for a vegetarian (and therefore low cholesterol) diet, regular exercise and abstention from alcohol, caffeine and tobacco products." Dr. Castelli points out that Seventh-Day Adventist men outlive other Americans by seven years, and their women by five years. He goes on to state that "they have only 15 percent of our heart-attack rate and 40 percent of our cancer rate."[17]

Most Seventh-Day Adventists are not total plantarians. Many Adventists admit they could and should follow an even better diet with much less fat and few, if any, animal products. This would give them an even more impressive record of health and longevity. Since Seventh-Day Adventists put more emphasis on nutrition than any other religious group in America or in the Western world, they are a good example of a people that teach the value of nutrition to obtain better health, quality of life and longevity.

[15]Snowden, D., et al, *Diet, Obesity and Risk of Fatal Prostate Cancer,* American Journal of Epidemiology 1984, 120 (2): 244–250. See also Prostate Cancer A Preventable Disease, Physicians Committee for Responsible Medicine Update News, Spring of 1992, Vol. 8, No. 1.

[16]David Snowden and R.L. Phillips, *Does a Vegetarian Diet Reduce the Occurrence of Diabetes?* Am J Public Health, 1985; 75: 507–517.

[17]*Castelli Speaks from the Heart,* AARP Bulletin, May 1992, Vol. 33 No. 5, p. 16.

All Grain the Staff of Life
(Mormon Teachings: Word of Wisdom)

Mormons have a code of health called the Word of Wisdom. Their philosophy calls for abstention from tobacco, alcohol, tea and coffee as well as the following food healthcode:

"And again, verily I say unto you, all wholesome herbs [**plants**] God hath ordained for the constitution, nature, and use of man— every herb [**plant**] in the season thereof, and every fruit in the season thereof; all these to be used with prudence and thanksgiving.

"Yea, *flesh* also of *beasts [animals]* and of the *fowls* of the air, I, the Lord, have ordained for the use of man with thanksgiving; nevertheless *they [animals and fowls]* are to be used *sparingly*; and it is pleasing unto me that *they* should *not* be used, *only* in times of *winter*, or of *cold*, or *famine*.

"All *grain* is ordained for the use of *man* and of beasts, to be the *staff of life*, not only for man but for the *beasts* of the field, and the *fowls* of heaven, and all *wild animals* that run or creep on earth; and *these [beasts, fowls, and wild animals]* hath God made for the use of man *only* in times of *famine* and *excess* of *hunger*.

"*All grain* is good for the *food* of *man*; as also the *fruit* of the vine; that which yieldeth fruit, whether *in* the ground or *above* the ground—."[18] (emphasis added)

Dictionary Definitions:

"*Staff of life*" is defined in the dictionary as a "staple of diet."

"*Staple*" is defined as "the sustaining or principal element; something used, needed, or enjoyed constantly."

"*Sparingly*" means "barely, slightly, meagerly or sparsely."

18Doctrine and Covenants Section 89: 10–16.

In interviews, most Mormons admit they eat meat, chicken and fish on a regular basis. Many say they need to change. Mormon Church President, Ezra Taft Benson, perhaps said it best, "We are an overfed and undernourished nation, digging an early grave with our teeth, and lacking the energy that could be ours. . . . We need a generation of people who eat in a healthier manner."[19]

Our Children

On April 8, 1991, the government for the first time laid out specific recommendations on how children, two years old and up, should join adults in following a low-fat, low cholesterol diet, saying it could reduce their risk of heart disease later in life. That proves the need to change.

Healthy people have been eating a Plantarian diet for centuries. The Bible records that 2500 years ago, Daniel said to the commander of the officials, *"Give us nothing but vegetables to eat and water to drink. Then compare our appearance with that of the young men who eat the royal food, and treat your servants in accordance with what you see. So he agreed to this and tested them for ten days.*

At the end of ten days they looked healthier and better nourished than any of the young men who ate the royal food. So the guard took away their choice food and the wine they were to drink and gave them vegetables instead."

Daniel 1 The Bible, New International Version (1984)

It is exciting to see the change taking place in America as more and more people are eating a plant-centered diet.

[19]Ezra Taft Benson, "In His Steps," Ensign Magazine (Sept 1988).

New Four Food Groups

The Physicians Committee for Responsible Medicine, a nationally based group of thousands of doctors, announced to the world on April 8, 1991, that meat and dairy products should be dropped from the "Basic Four Food Groups." Instead of the traditional dietary groupings of meat, dairy products, grains, fruits and vegetables (a concept which promoted the health of certain industries at the expense of the health of individuals) this medical group proposes the "New Four Food Groups:" **whole grains, legumes, vegetables and fruit.**[20]

The Committee points out that the meat and dairy groups are the principle sources of cholesterol and saturated fat, and as such the biggest culprits in raising blood cholesterol. They say that meat and dairy products are simply not necessary in the human diet. Nutritional requirements, including protein (the average American eats two to five times as much protein as is needed), zinc, calcium and iron, can be met on a plant-based diet. Legumes—beans, peas, lentils, are the new basic food grouping; all are good sources of fiber, protein, iron, calcium, zinc and B vitamins.

This report was critical of the government's call on Americans just to cut back on, but not omit, foods high in cholesterol and fat. The New Four Food Groups guide does not rely on any admonition to use particular foods in moderation, since all of the foods in the New Four Food Groups guidelines can be consumed without restrictions. According to the Committee, the tools used to teach Americans good nutrition should be changed to reflect the mounting evidence that diets high in fat and low in fiber increase the risk of heart disease, cancer, obesity and diabetes.

[20]*Arizona Republic,* April 9, 1991, p. A1, A4. See also Denver Post, April 9, 1991, p. 1A, 8A.

The committee members said the new groupings would encourage Americans to perceive cereals (whole grains), legumes, vegetables and fruits as essential, and milk or a piece of meat as a non-essential "extra" to a meal.[21]

The Power of Your Plate and *Food For Life* are new books by Neal D. Barnard, M.D.,[22] president of the Physicians Committee for Responsible Medicine. These books reveal convincing evidence that animal products and added fat create disease, heart-artery problems, diabetes, and cancer, to name just a few. Three-fourths of all deaths in America each year are now caused by these degenerative diseases. (Note: A 1988 study by the surgeon general said diet-related diseases account for 68 percent of all deaths in the United States. While different studies may not agree on the exact statistics, all figures are relatively high and range between 68 to 80 percent.)

Dr. Barnard quotes from many noted medical scientists, all of whom attribute the cause of the serious diseases in America to the type of foods we eat, which are mostly animal products, all types of fats, and very little fiber. Dr. Barnard's books are important contributions to the growing evidence that we must change our diets from mostly animal foods, to mostly plant foods (The Staple of Diet), if we are to enjoy the best possible health. The challenge is to get started now with change for the better.

[21]*Arizona Republic,* April 9, 1991, p. A1, A4. See also Denver Post, April 9, 1991, p. 1A, 8A.

[22]Dr. Barnard is Associate Director for Behavioral Studies at the Institute for Disease Prevention of George Washington University School of Medicine, where he has conducted research into programs that help change eating habits. *The Power of Your Plate* is available from the Physicians committee for Responsible Medicine, P.O. Box 6322, Washington, DC 20016, for $10.95 plus $1.95 mailing and handling.

The New Four Food Groups will prove to be the most important scientific medical disclosure for "The Best Possible Health," in the twentieth century.

The New Four Food Groups was announced April 8, 1991, by the Physicians Committee for Responsible Medicine, P.O. Box 6322, Washington, D.C. 20016. (202) 686-2210

THE NEW FOUR FOOD GROUPS

Whole Grains	Vegetables	Legumes	Fruit
This group includes bread, pasta, hot or cold cereal, corn, millet, barley, bulgur, buckwheat groats and tortillas. Build each of your meals around a hearty grain dish—grains are rich in fiber and other complex carbohydrates, as well as protein, B vitamins and zinc.	Vegetables are packed with nutrients; they provide vitamin C, beta-carotene, riboflavin and other vitamins, iron, calcium and fiber. Dark green, leafy vegetables such as broccoli, collards, kale, mustard and turnip greens, chicory or bok choy are especially good sources of these important nutrients. Dark yellow and orange vegetables such as carrots, winter squash, sweet potatoes and pumpkin provide extra beta-carotene. Include generous portions of a variety of vegetables in your diet.	Legumes, which is another name for beans, peas, and lentils, are all good sources of fiber, protein, iron, calcium, zinc and B vitamins. This group also includes chickpeas, baked and refried beans, soy milk, tofu, tempeh, and texturized vegetable protein.	Fruits are rich in fiber, vitamin C and beta-carotene. Be sure to include at least one serving each day of fruits that are high in vitamin C—citrus fruits, melons and strawberries are all good choices. Choose whole fruit over fruit juices, which don't contain as much healthy fiber.

PHYSICIANS COMMITTEE FOR RESPONSIBLE MEDICINE • P.O. Box 6322, Washington, D.C. 20015 • (202) 686-2210

The Food Guide Pyramid
A Step in the Right Direction

On April 28, 1992, the U.S. Department of Agriculture formally adopted The Food Guide Pyramid.

The meat and dairy producers opposed any change from the old Basic Four Food Groups. A New York Times article by Marian Burros in the spring of 1992 quoted Jeannine Kenny, legislative representative for the National Milk Producers Federation. She said: "The industry would have preferred anything but the Pyramid . . . The Pyramid gave a very negative image. It appeared to rank food." Mark Armentrout, chairman of the food policy committee of the National Cattlemen's Association, was quoted as saying, "Something is a better alternative than the Pyramid."

The New York Times article also quoted the medical scientific community: "The Health and Human Services Department regards reducing fat as the most important message, as did a report by the surgeon general in 1988."

"The strongest focus in the Surgeon General's Report is that dietary fat is the single most important factor related to chronic disease," said Dr. Rachel Ballard-Barbash, a medical officer in the division of cancer prevention and control at the National Cancer Institute. She went on to say that, "At the Agriculture Department the nutritionists were certainly aware that the *consensus* was that dietary fat was of paramount importance." She also said that "the emphasis was in terms of *disease prevention.*"

Dr. John A. McDougall, in his book, *The McDougall Plan,* asked the question, "Are the meat and dairy industries brainwashing us?" His answer is, "Yes! . . . For nearly 50 years all schools in America have been teaching our children and adults that about 50 percent of our total calories should come from animals such as meat, dairy products and eggs." McDougall goes on to say, "The food industry has infiltrated the educational system. On the classroom wall hung a large and beautiful poster depicting the Four Basic Food Groups. Since this was school, where, of course, only truth was taught, we opened our minds to this colorful instructional aid. If we had read the small print at the bottom of the chart, we would have learned that this poster was actually a powerful advertising tool supplied by the National Dairy Council, Kellogg's, Del Monte, Pillsbury, McDonald's, or some other industrial interest. Using these food groups as guidelines, parents feed their families what they assume to be a balanced diet. And look at the results: rotting teeth found in epidemic proportions among our children, obesity, constipation, acne, and high blood pressure."

The new U.S. Department of Agriculture Food Guide Pyramid is replacing the old Basic Four Food Groups as the official nutritional guideline for teaching all school children and adults in the U.S.A. The Food Pyramid clearly reveals that 80 to 85 percent of all our calories must come from PLANT FOOD (starches, whole grains, vegetables, legumes and fruits). This is a giant step forward to assure the best possible health for all Americans. Fats, oils, and sweets should be used SPARINGLY according to the Pyramid Food Guide (a combined total of only 7 percent of daily calories). That leaves a very small amount of our total calories to come from animals (meat, poultry, fish, dairy and eggs), probably less than 10 percent of total calories. Although not as strict as the New Four Food Groups, clearly the Food Guide Pyramid is a step in the right direction. Many medical scientists now say that meat and dairy products are non-essential to health and can and do cause severe and fatal illnesses.

FOOD GUIDE PYRAMID
A Step in the Right Direction
US Department of Agriculture, April 28, 1992.

The total servings in the Food guide pyramid is 26. Twenty servings are included in the plant food portion and six in the animal food portion. Because beans and nuts are plant food but included in the same portion allotted to animal food, we have allowed two of those servings to be included as beans and nuts. That leaves only four servings of animal food or 8–10%. The total of twenty plant servings in the foundation of the pyramid and two servings of plant food in the animal section comes to 80–85%.

Fats, oils and sweets are to be used SPARINGLY. Approximately $3^1/2\%$ added sweets and $3^1/2\%$ added fats.

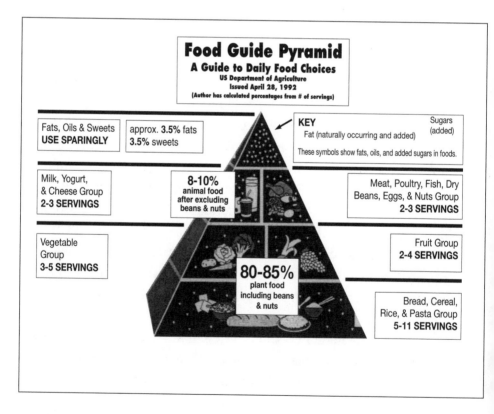

Gains Are Being Made

The good news is that we see the giant food companies recognizing the future markets for their products. In the Kraft Foods quarterly financial report published July 1990, the lead story was entitled, "Fat-Free: The Next Generation." The article states: "Every company has to ask itself, every day, 'What do our consumers want?'

"At Kraft General Foods, we think we've found one answer: fat-free foods. KGF Chairman and CEO Michael A. Miles said recently that the company is 'on the leading edge of one of the food industry's biggest new product opportunities in years.' Indeed, with non-fat foods in seven product categories, and more on the way, the company is aggressively working to keep its lead.

"Fat and cholesterol now top the list of America's dietary concerns. Our fat-free products have the same good taste and texture consumers expect from our regular products."

CBS News reported that in 1994 alone there were 1400 new fat-free and low-fat food items introduced into the market place.

Hundreds of fat-free and cholesterol-free new products are now available, such as salad dressings, non-fat cheese products, non-fat yogurt, non-fat cottage cheese, non-fat sour cream, nonfat frozen desserts, ice cream without fat or cholesterol, and fat-free and cholesterol-free baked goods such as cakes and cookies. Just make sure you read all labels carefully to be sure each product is fat-free and cholesterol-free before buying.

Many food companies are jumping on the non-fat, no cholesterol band wagon. Health Valley Foods, based in California, is a very progressive company interested in your health. Their products are becoming available in supermarkets as well as in health food stores. Look for new, healthy products. Ask your supermarket to stock more and more no-fat, no-cholesterol food products. If there were more requests, supermarkets would carry all types of natural whole grains, whole grain flours, and other basic items that are now found mostly in health food stores.

Fred Meyers Superstores now carry a full line of Natural Health Foods such as: whole grains, flours, beans, peas, lentils, rice, corn, pastas and many other bulk items. They also carry Fat Free soy milk and rice milk.

Fred Meyers is our favorite supermarket.

What Can You Do to Help?

In addition to asking store managers to carry more healthy products, write or call manufacturers and tell them you want products with little or no fat, no cholesterol and low sodium. Each one of us can make a difference as we demand better labeling and healthful foods.

Write or call your national and state elected representatives and urge them to vote for laws that mandate easy and concise access to this vital information on each food item. New national labeling laws are in effect, but they fall far short of informing the consumer of the exact percentage of fat in every food item. To be able to know the percentage of fat we are consuming everyday the percentage of fat must be on each label. Fresh meat, chicken and fish suppliers are not even required by law to list what nutrients their products contain. Contact your lawmakers in Washington, D.C. and request that the government begin implementing "The New Four Food Groups." For more information write: Physicians Committee for

Responsible Medicine, P.O. Box 6322, Washington, D.C., 20015, or telephone (202) 686–2210.

Talk to elected school board members, school superintendents, principals and teachers about teaching up-to-date and better nutritional principles. The "New Four Food Groups" of WHOLE GRAINS, LEGUMES, VEGETABLES AND FRUIT should be presented to all students. The percentage of nutrients (fat, protein and carbohydrate) in the foods we eat should be taught to all students. Charts listing all common foods should be on the walls of classrooms so students from first grade on up through high school can learn to be informed consumers.

Food items sold in school cafeterias should have the percentages of nutritional ingredients listed clearly so students and teachers could know exactly what they are eating. Many school lunches are full of high-fat, high-cholesterol, and low-fiber foods. Parents can change the lunch program by demanding low-fat, high- fiber, plantarian foods like rice, potatoes, corn, beans and a variety of grains.

The Best Possible Health

If we in America were to follow a plant-based eating program very few of us would suffer from major diseases such as atherosclerosis, heart disease, high blood pressure, stroke, diabetes, diet-related cancers, osteoporosis, urinary disease, arthritis, or obesity. Few of us would be bothered by minor, yet painful, diseases such as diverticulitis, hiatus hernia, appendicitis, gallstones, hemorrhoids, kidney stones, varicose veins, and constipation, all of which are associated with the low-fiber, high-fat, cholesterol-laden animal foods.[23] [24] [25] [26] [27]

In countries where people follow the principles of a plant-based diet, there are virtually none of these diseases. The Chinese are a prime example. In China, people eat approximately 80 percent complex carbohydrates, 10 percent fat, and 10 percent protein, the very combination contained in a variety of grains, legumes (beans, peas, lentils), vegetables, and fruits. This seems to be the ideal percentage of calories for good health. Most Chinese people eat very little flesh or animal food of any kind, and dairy products are virtually unknown. The main source of calories in most of China is starches—rice, potatoes, beans, corn, wheat, barley, oats, and other grains, supplemented with vegetables and fruits.[28] [29] [30] [31] [32] [33]

In stark contrast is sick America eating approximately 45 percent of total calories in fat, 15 to 20 percent in protein, and 20 to 25 percent in (mostly refined) simple carbohydrates, probably only 15 percent complex carbohydrates. In addition, we eat from 300 to

[23]H. Trowell, *Definition of Dietary Fiber and Hypotheses That It Is a Protective Fact in Certain Diseases,* Am J Clin Nutr 29:417, 1976.

[24]D. Burkitt, *Some Diseases Characteristic of Modern Western Civilization,* Br Med J 1:274, 1973.

[25]D. Burkitt, *Dietary Fiber and Disease,* JAMA 229: 1068, 1974.

[26]Nathan Pritikin, *The Pritikin Program for Diet and Exercise* (NY: Bantam Books, 1979), 364–386.

[27]Neal D. Barnard, M.D., *The Power of Your Plate* (Summertown, TN: Book Publishing Company, 1990), 7–10, 13–18, 51–55, 69, 73–96, 117–139.

[28]Dr. T. Colin Campbell, *The Cornell-China-Oxford Project of Nutrition, Health and Environment,* Cornell University, Division of Nutritional Sciences, Ithaca, NY 14853, Ph. (607)255–1033.

[29]Anne Simon Moffit, *Research News Science,* May 4, 1990, Vol. 1, 248.

[30]Jane Brody, *China's Blockbuster Diet Study,* Saturday Evening Post, Oct. 1990, 30–32.

[31]Bonnie Liebman, *Lessons from China, Nutritional Action Health Letter,* Center for Science in the Public Interest, Dec. 1990, Vol. 17, No. 10, 1, 5–7.

[32]Jane Brody, *Huge Study of Diet Indicts Fat and Meat,* Science Times, The New York Times, May 8, 1990.

[33]Nathaniel Mead, *The Champion Diet,* EastWest, Sept. 1990, 44–50, 98, 99, 102, 104.

1000 milligrams of cholesterol a day, all of which comes from animal flesh and other animal products. The majority of our calories come from animal flesh (meat, fish, and fowl), other animal foods (milk, cheese, ice cream, cottage cheese, sour cream, butter, eggs, and so on), and added vegetable fats.

Fat content is not the only problem. Animal foods contain no fiber, which is absolutely necessary to maintain proper health. Animal foods are the only foods that contain cholesterol, which is the basic cause of atherosclerosis, the destruction of the inner lining of the arteries and blood vessels. Atherosclerosis leads to heart attacks, strokes, aneurysms, kidney diseases, and many other degenerative conditions. Animal foods are our main source of saturated fat. Our livers make even more cholesterol from saturated fat.

Is it any wonder why so few of us fall within the ideal weight range? The answer is obvious. We are eating the wrong food—rich animal food and added fats, both vegetable and animal. Many people blame sugar. The average American eats 135 pounds of simple carbohydrates (sugars) each year. But sugar isn't the major cause of obesity. It should be limited because it is only empty calories taking the place of complex carbohydrates. The real cause of obesity is our high fat intake, which comes from animal products and added vegetable fats. Fats taste sweet. Perhaps that's why we consume nearly 50 percent of our total calories as fat.[34 35 36 37 38 39]

[34]Nathan Pritikin, *The Pritikin Program for Diet and Exercise* (NY: Bantam Books, 1979), 9, 11, 28, 35.

[35]Julian M. Whitaker, *Reversing Heart Disease* (NY: Warner Books, 1985) 73, 79.

[36]John A. McDougall, M.D., and Mary A. McDougall, *The McDougall Plan* (Piscataway, NJ: New Century Publishers, 1983), 34, 63, 116–122.

The Politics of Nutrition

The politics of nutrition is well-known among nutritional and medical scientific experts in America. Many books, magazines and newspaper articles have been written about this problem. You will find many of these listed in our companion book *The Miracle Diet, 14 Days to New Vigor and Health.* Many more articles on the politics of nutrition are coming forth each month.

In spite of the politics and powerful influences from The Beef Council, Dairy Council, food manufacturers and the medical and pharmaceutical industries, the truth about what type of food we should eat is emerging rapidly.

Most scientists now agree that a plant-centered diet is the best food for man as it is for all other herbivores.

This book, "The Miracle Diet Cookbook," provides you with the information and recipes to enjoy "The Best Possible Health," save up to 50% on your grocery bills, and save many future doctor and dental expenses.

Prevention of disease is the only way we can ever control health care costs. Prevention of disease must be the buzz-word of the future if we are ever going to enjoy the "Best Possible Health" and the happiness and joy that goes with individual and family health.

[37]*Newsweek,* July 30, 1990, p. 59, last paragraph.
[38]Susan S. Lang, *The World's Healthiest Diet,* American Health, Sept. 1989, p. 105–107, 110, 112.
[39]Neal D. Barnard, M.D., *The Power of Your Plate* (Summertown, TN: Book Publishing Company, 1990), 73–96.

Soy Milk

Soy products contain some fat but no cholesterol, because plants contain no cholesterol. Fat Free soy milk is now available.

To make skim soy milk buy the Lite soy milk which contains 1% fat and mix 1 part soy milk to 3 parts water. This makes what can be classified as virtually fat free milk. If you want a thicker milk use less water.

Rice Milk

Rice Milk contains some plant fat but can be broken down one part rice milk to two or three parts water for a virtually fat free product in cooking. Fat-Free rice milk is now available.

Health food stores carry these products. Many supermarkets also have these milks. They have a long shelf life before opening.

Defatting

To defat chicken broth, beef broth or bouillon cube mixtures, chill in refrigerator or freezer until fat congeals on top. Remove fat with a spoon. Fat-free chicken broth is now available in most markets; ask your grocer. Swanson makes a Fat-Free Chicken Broth. Non-animal broth stock alternatives are available in health food stores.

Milk & Dairy Products

You should read chapter seven in the companion book *The Miracle Diet, 14 Days to New Vigor and Health* to be better informed about the effects of milk and dairy products on your health.

We use no dairy products in the recipes in this cookbook. You may choose to use skim, no fat cow's milk products in your cooking instead of Fat Free soy milk or Fat Free rice milk. Skim milk products are basically free from fat but do contain a small amount of cholesterol in most cases.

Typical examples:

Skim milk	5 mg cholesterol per 8 oz. serving
Fat Free yogurt	5 mg cholesterol per 4 oz. serving
Fat Free cottage cheese	5 mg cholesterol per 4 oz. serving
Fat Free cheese	5 mg cholesterol per 1 oz. serving
Fat Free sour cream	0 mg cholesterol

Healthful, Helpful Hints

Now there is *BEANO, The Gas Preventer.* According to advertising the product "prevents the gas from beans and cabbage, peas, broccoli, eggplant and many others." All the people we know say it works. We have tried it and like it.

Some herbal books recommend ginger as a gas inhibitor. Try one-quarter to one-half teaspoon ginger in a half glass of water before meals. It really works.

Limit your salt intake. Most nutritional scientists agree that we eat far too much salt in America. (Refer to Chapter 11, *The Miracle Diet, 14 Days to New Vigor and Health.*)

Rosarita Foods and other companies now make Fat-Free refried beans. Corn chips like Tostitos and California Bakes and potato chips like Louise's are baked, not fried and contain no added fat. Try them—they are delicious and are available in supermarkets. Other food companies make Fat Free or no fat added products.

Many companies make fat-free yogurt and ice cream if you choose to eat dairy products.

Caution: Fat Free yogurt, ice cream, cookies, and cakes contain mostly simple carbohydrates (sugars). We believe simple carbohydrates should only be a minor part of your total calorie intake if you want maximum weight loss and the best possible health.

Check all labels and ask questions at restaurants before you eat food. Be an informed consumer. Don't be fooled by 97% Fat Free or "light" on the label. Do your math calculations.

Applesauce, prune juice, or corn syrup can be substituted in place of fat in most of your favorite recipes that call for added fat.

Today's the Day

The key to change is getting started. Try going cold turkey. Give up all animal foods and added fats. For at least two weeks eat all the plant food you want—never remain hungry. Stay with the Plantarian recipes in this cookbook. After two weeks you'll feel so much better that you will want to extend your plant-centered program for two more weeks—and on and on. In addition to feeling better you'll probably lose a few pounds.

Most likely, after you have been on the Miracle Diet program for one month, you'll have lost the taste for rich animal food and added fat. You are no longer addicted to animal food and fat.

Many people prefer the technique of cutting down gradually. This alternative may work better for you. Begin by having one Plantarian meal a day. After a week or so add another entirely plant-food meal each day. In a few weeks make all your meals plant-based meals except for an occasional feast day. Feast days are only special occasions like Thanksgiving, Christmas, birthdays, etc. Don't let feast days become daily, weekly, or even monthly habits.

Many people have said that animal-foods and added fats are addicting, so take stock of yourself and see if you feel addicted to animal-foods and fat.

Here is your chance to permanently change to a healthier, happier way of life permanently. Never again will you need to "diet."

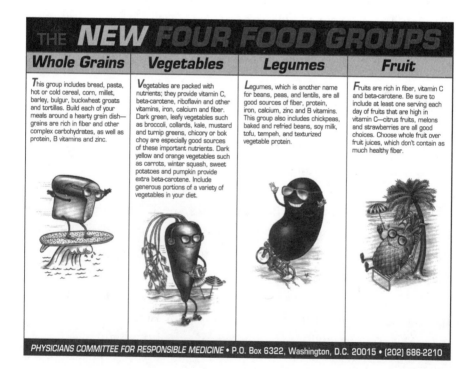

THE NEW FOUR FOOD GROUPS

Whole Grains	Vegetables	Legumes	Fruit
This group includes bread, pasta, hot or cold cereal, corn, millet, barley, bulgur, buckwheat groats and tortillas. Build each of your meals around a hearty grain dish—grains are rich in fiber and other complex carbohydrates, as well as protein, B vitamins and zinc.	Vegetables are packed with nutrients; they provide vitamin C, beta-carotene, riboflavin and other vitamins, iron, calcium and fiber. Dark green, leafy vegetables such as broccoli, collards, kale, mustard and turnip greens, chicory or bok choy are especially good sources of these important nutrients. Dark yellow and orange vegetables such as carrots, winter squash, sweet potatoes and pumpkin provide extra beta-carotene. Include generous portions of a variety of vegetables in your diet.	Legumes, which is another name for beans, peas, and lentils, are all good sources of fiber, protein, iron, calcium, zinc and B vitamins. This group also includes chickpeas, baked and refried beans, soy milk, tofu, tempeh, and texturized vegetable protein.	Fruits are rich in fiber, vitamin C and beta-carotene. Be sure to include at least one serving each day of fruits that are high in vitamin C—citrus fruits, melons and strawberries are all good choices. Choose whole fruit over fruit juices, which don't contain as much healthy fiber.

PHYSICIANS COMMITTEE FOR RESPONSIBLE MEDICINE • P.O. Box 6322, Washington, D.C. 20015 • (202) 686-2210

For a complete explanation of the cause of degenerative diseases and how to change your lifestyle to prevent or reverse disease — read Earl Updike's companion book (with the bright yellow cover).

"THE MIRACLE DIET —
14 DAYS TO NEW VIGOR AND HEALTH."

For a complete explanation of the cause of
degenerative diseases and how to change your
lifestyle to prevent or reverse disease — read
Earl Updike's companion book (with the
bright yellow cover).

"THE MIRACLE DIET — 14 DAYS TO NEW VIGOR AND HEALTH."

"For the Best Possible Health"

The Miracle Diet

Easy **Permanent Weight Loss**

Fat Free | Cholesterol Free | High Fiber

- Look better . . . Feel Better
- Save Money on Food
- Save on Medical / Dental Bills
- Lose Weight Permanently
- Increase Your Energy

- Eat all you want
- Never be hungry
- Lose up to 10 lbs per month
- Learn how Fat makes *you* Fat
- Avoid the killers Cholesterol and Fat!
- Become a Plantarian

14 days to New Vigor and Health

Earl F. Updike

Forward by
Neal D. Barnard, M.D.
President of the National
Physicians Committee for
Responsible Medicine

MAIN DISHES

NOTES

1. Tamari is soy sauce.

2. Remember, the higher the altitude, the longer the beans and rice have to cook.

3. Any recipe requiring beans is better if the beans are soaked overnight.

4. Beans produce much less gas if soaking water is poured and replaced.

5. FAT: There is no need to list the grams of fat or calories of fat in these recipes because there is no added fat and the plant ingredients are well within the 10% fat range, which is ideal.

6. There is no need to list the total calories in these recipes because you don't need to count calories.

7. Your weight loss will begin whenever you start following a plant-based diet. Protein content of a plant-centered program, overall, will be about 10%, which is ideal.

8. Complex carbohydrate calorie intake will be, overall, about 80% using these recipes, which is ideal.

Pizza

(also a good Chip Dip Sauce)

2 c. onions, diced
1 Tbsp. garlic, minced
1 can (28 oz.) tomato sauce
1 tsp. basil
1/2 tsp. oregano
1/2 tsp. salt (optional)
1/4 tsp. pepper
1/8 tsp. Tabasco sauce
1/8 tsp. fennel seed
1/4 tsp. thyme leaves

In a medium bowl, mix all ingredients.

Make pizza crust (see recipes in bread section), spread out in pizza pan, and add sauce.

Topping suggestions include bell peppers, green chilies, onions, mushrooms, and other vegetables of your choice.

Note: This makes enough sauce for 2 pizzas. If making only 1 pizza, store leftover sauce, covered, in refrigerator.

Preparation time: 20 minutes
Servings: sauce for 2 pizzas
(about 3 cups)

Pinto Beans
(Cooked in pressure cooker)

4 c. dry pinto beans (soak overnight, then pour water off and rinse)
2 onions, chopped
1/2 tsp. garlic powder
1 1/2 Tbsp. salt (optional)
1/2 c. catsup
1/4 tsp. black pepper

Bring presoaked beans to boil, then pour off water. Rinse and place in pressure cooker with approximately 2 inches water above beans.

Bring up pressure on pressure cooker, and turn heat to medium-low; cook for 1 1/2 hours.

Turn off heat and allow pressure to escape on its own. (Never fill pressure cooker over 3/4 full with food or liquid.)

Add all remaining ingredients.

Simmer, covered, stirring occasionally, until flavors have blended.

Preparation time: 15 minutes
Bean soak: overnight
Cooking time: about 2 hours
Servings: 12

Legumes—beans, peas, lentils, are the *new* basic food grouping. They are all good sources of fiber, protein, iron, calcium, zinc and B vitamins.

Pinto Bean Chili

(Spicy Style)

2 c. dry pinto beans
4 c. water
1 large sweet onion, chopped
2 garlic cloves, minced
1 can (28 oz.) tomatoes with
   juice, chopped
1 can (4 oz.) chopped green
   chilies
2 carrots, shredded
1 Tbsp. chili powder
1 Tbsp. ground cumin
1 Tbsp. dried oregano
1 Tbsp. paprika
2 tsp. salt (optional)
1/2 tsp. cayenne pepper

Sort and rinse beans. In a large kettle, bring beans and water to a boil for 2 minutes.

Remove from heat and let stand 1 hour, covered.

Return to boil; reduce heat and simmer 1 hour.

Add remaining ingredients.

Simmer, covered, stirring occasionally, until beans are tender and flavors have blended, at least 1 hour.

Preparation time: 20 minutes
Soaking time: 1 hour
Cooking time: 2 hours or more
Servings: 12 to 15, or 3 1/2 quarts

Chili Beans
(Mexican Style)

4 c. dry pinto beans
10 c. water
2 bell peppers, chopped
4 yellow onions, chopped
4 garlic cloves, minced
4 stalks celery, chopped
2 c. tomato sauce
2 cans (16 oz.) tomatoes,
chopped, or stewed
tomatoes
1/2 c. chili powder
3 tsp. ground cumin
1/2 tsp. crushed red pepper
1/4 tsp. cayenne pepper

Sort and wash beans; place beans and water in a large kettle.

Bring to a boil, cover and boil 2 minutes.

Remove from heat and let stand 1 hour.

Return to a boil, reduce heat and simmer 1 hour.

Add remaining ingredients and simmer an additional hour.

Serve over cooked, brown rice, if desired.

Freeze all leftover chili for a quick meal later.

Preparation time: 20 minutes
Soaking time: 1 hour
Cooking time: 2 hours or more
Servings: 8 to 10

Chili with Celery and Beans

2 Tbsp. water
1 c. green bell pepper, chopped
1 c. onion, chopped
1 tsp. garlic, minced
4 c. celery, thinly sliced
1/4 c. chili powder
2 tsp. ground cumin
1 tsp. salt (optional)
1 can (16 oz.) tomatoes,
    crushed
1 can (16 oz.) red kidney
    beans, drained
1 can (8 oz.) tomato sauce
4 c. cooked brown rice
    (optional)

In a large saucepan, cook pepper, onion and garlic in water until crisp tender, about 5 minutes.

Stir in celery, chili powder, cumin and salt; cook and stir 1 minute.

Add crushed tomatoes, kidney beans and tomato sauce; simmer, covered, until celery is crisp tender and flavors are blended, about 15 minutes.

Serve over rice, if desired.

Preparation time: 20 minutes
Cooking time: 20 to 25 minutes
Servings: 4 without rice, 8 to 12 with rice

Beans with Rice

1 c. cooked beans (any variety)

1 c. cooked brown rice

Mix beans and rice in a microwave-safe bowl.

Heat in microwave oven for 3 minutes.

This makes an excellent quick meal and cuts down on the high protein of beans alone.

For variety, add catsup, hot sauce, red pepper or other seasonings.

Serve with a tossed vegetable salad or several raw veggies and whole wheat bread or cornbread for a complete meal.

Preparation time: 2 to 3 min.
Cooking time: 3 minutes
Servings: 1 to 2

Red Beans and Rice
(Spicy Style)

1 lb. dry red kidney beans
2 tsp. paprika
1/2 to 1 tsp. cayenne pepper
1 tsp. black pepper
2 bay leaves
1 tsp. ground cumin
1 qt. water
2 to 3 tsp. salt (optional)
1 1/2 c. celery, chopped
1 1/2 c. onion, chopped
2 garlic cloves, minced
1/2 tsp. hot pepper sauce
3 Tbsp. fresh parsley, minced
3 c. cooked brown rice

Sort and rinse beans.

In a large Dutch oven or kettle, place all ingredients except parsley and rice.

Bring to a boil; reduce heat and simmer, covered, 3 to 4 hours or until beans are tender.

Stir occasionally, adding water as needed to make a thick gravy.

Just before serving, remove bay leaves and stir in parsley.

Serve over rice.

Preparation time: 20 minutes
Cooking time: 3 to 4 hours
Servings: 8 to 10

Black Beans and Brown Rice

2 Tbsp. water
1 medium onion, chopped
1 can (16 oz.) stewed
 tomatoes
1 can (15 oz.) black
beans,undrained
1 tsp. dried oregano
1/2 tsp. garlic powder
Salt to taste (optional)
1 1/2 c. instant brown rice,
uncooked

In a large skillet, heat water and cook onion about 5 minutes.

Add the tomatoes, beans and seasonings.

Bring to a boil. Stir in rice; reduce heat and simmer 5 minutes.

Let stand 5 minutes.

Preparation time: 10 minutes
Cooking time: 15 minutes
Servings: 6 to 8

Hoppin' John

This is a plantarian version of a traditional dish of the Deep South. Serve it with cornbread and tangy coleslaw for a down-home meal.

2 Tbsp. water
1 c. onions, chopped
1 garlic clove, minced
2 c. ripe, juicy tomatoes, chopped, or
1 can (16 oz.) tomatoes, chopped
1/2 tsp. dried basil
1/4 tsp. dried thyme
3 c. cooked brown rice (2/3 c. dry)
2 c. cooked blackeyed peas (3/4 c. dry)
Salt to taste (optional)
Freshly ground pepper to taste

Heat water in a very large skillet and saute onions over a very low heat until translucent.

Add garlic and continue to saute until onions are golden. Stir in tomatoes, basil and thyme; cook until tomatoes have softened a bit, about 5 minutes.

Add rice and blackeyed peas and season to taste. Stir well.

Simmer, covered, for 15 minutes. If mixture seems dry, add a bit of water or cooking liquid from peas.

Serve at once.

Preparation time: 15 minutes
Cooking time: 30 minutes
Servings: 4 to 6

Green Bean Casserole

1 c. onion, chopped
1 c. celery, chopped
1/2 green pepper, chopped
1/2 c. water
1 can (16 oz.) stewed
   tomatoes
2 1/4 tsp. sugar
1/2 tsp. salt (optional)
1/4 tsp. pepper
1/8 tsp. ground cloves
   (optional)
1 bay leaf
4 c. cooked green beans, or
   canned, drained
1 c. soft whole wheat bread
   crumbs

Saute onion, celery, and green pepper in water until tender, 5 minutes.

Add remaining ingredients and place in a 2-quart casserole.

Sprinkle with bread crumbs. Bake, uncovered, at 350 degrees for approximately 30 minutes.

Remove bay leaf.

Preparation time: 20 minutes
Baking time: 30 minutes
Servings: 6

Molasses Glazed Beans

2 c. dry great northern or
   navy beans
5 c. water
1 1/2 tsp. salt (optional)
1 small onion, chopped
1/4 c. brown sugar
1 tsp. dry mustard
1/2 c. molasses

Sort and wash beans.

Put beans and water in a large saucepan and heat to boiling.

Boil 2 minutes; remove from heat, cover and let stand 1 hour. Add salt, if desired.

Cover and boil gently 1 hour. Add remaining ingredients and more water, if needed for cooking.

Stir gently to mix.

Cover and boil gently 1 hour more to blend flavors.

Uncover toward end of cooking, if needed, to thicken liquid.

Preparation time: 15 minutes
Bean soak: 1 hour
Cooking time: 2 hours or more
Servings: 6 to 8

Maple Baked Beans

1 lb. dry navy beans
4 qts. water, divided
1 medium onion, chopped
1 c. maple syrup or maple-
    flavored syrup
1/2 c. catsup
1/4 c. barbecue sauce
5 tsp. cider vinegar
1 tsp. prepared mustard
1 tsp. salt (optional)
1/2 tsp. pepper

Sort and rinse beans; place in a 4-quart Dutch oven.

Cover with 2 quarts cold water. Bring to a boil for 2 minutes.

Remove from heat, cover and let stand 1 hour.

Drain and rinse beans. Return to Dutch oven; cover with remaining water.

Bring to a boil; reduce heat and simmer 30 to 40 minutes.

Drain and reserve liquid. In a 2 1/2-quart casserole or bean pot, combine beans with remaining ingredients.

Bake, covered, at 300 degrees for 2 1/2 hours.

Stir occasionally; add reserved bean liquid if necessary.

Preparation time: 15 minutes
Bean soak: 1 hour
Cooking time: 40 minutes
Baking time: 2 1/2 hours
Servings: 10 to 12

Black Bean Cornmeal Cakes (Polenta)

1 c. dry black beans
3 c. water
1 small onion, chopped
3 Tbsp. water
5 c. defatted chicken stock
1 1/2 c. cornmeal

Sort and wash beans.

In a medium saucepan, cover and boil beans in 3 cups water for 2 minutes.

Remove from heat and soak 1 hour.
Return to boil, reduce heat and simmer until beans are tender, about 1 hour. Cool, drain and chop; set aside.

In saucepan, saute onion in 3 tablespoons water until onion is transparent.

Add chicken stock and bring to a boil.

Slowly add the cornmeal, stirring constantly.

Stir in the black beans and mix well.

Cook over low heat until liquid is absorbed.

Pour into sprayed shallow baking pan and allow to cool before refrigerating for 3-4 hours until firm.

To serve, cut into squares or desired shapes and brown in a skillet or grill which has been lightly sprayed with nonstick spray.

Preparation time: 15 minutes
Bean soak: 1 hour
Cooking time: 1 hour and 45 minutes
Refrigeration time: 3 to 4 hours
Servings: 12 to 14

Enchilada Sauce

1/4 c. water
1 large onion, chopped
4-5 garlic cloves, crushed
1 can (4 oz.) chopped green
   chilies
1 can (28 oz.) tomatoes,
   chopped
1 tsp. basil
1/8 tsp. ground cumin
1/2 tsp. ground oregano
1 c. water
2 Tbsp. low sodium tamari
   (soy sauce)
3 Tbsp. cornstarch
1/4 c. water

Place 1/4 cup water, onion, and garlic in large saucepan. Saute about 5 minutes.

Add tomatoes along with the green chilies and spices. Simmer 15 minutes.

Mix the tamari in 1 cup water; add to the tomato mixture.

Dissolve cornstarch in 1/4 c. water and add to the tomato mixture, stirring well.

Simmer about 10 minutes longer over low heat, stirring occasionally.

Serve with vegetable or bean enchiladas (see following recipe), whole grains, or pasta.

Preparation time: 15 minutes
Cooking time: 35 minutes
Servings: 5 cups sauce

Bean Enchiladas

May be prepared ahead of time and refrigerated. If so, add 15 minutes to your baking time.

5 c. enchilada sauce or
  Mexican hot sauce
  (see recipes)
12 soft corn tortillas
3 c. refried beans (see
  recipe) or no fat
  refried canned beans
1 bunch green onions,
  chopped
1/2 lb. mushrooms,
  chopped (optional)
2 tomatoes, chopped
  (optional)
1 c. frozen corn (optional)

Heat the sauce until just warm.

Thaw the corn tortillas until soft.

Prepare remaining ingredients of your choice.

Take 1 cup of the sauce and spread over the bottom of a 9 x 12 baking dish. Place to one side.

Take one tortilla at a time and spread 1 tablespoon sauce over it.

Spread some refried beans down the middle of the tortilla, sprinkle on some of the green onions, and any options you choose.

Roll up the tortilla and place in the baking dish, seam side down.

Repeat until all of the tortillas are used. Pour the remaining sauce over them.

Bake at 350 degrees for 30 minutes.

Preparation time: 15 minutes
Baking time: 30 minutes, just prepared 45 minutes, refrigerated
Servings: 12 tortillas

Bean Burritos

Corn tortillas
Cooked pinto beans (see recipe), drained and mashed
Mexican hot sauce (see recipe)
Cilantro leaves
Green onions, minced
Lettuce and tomatoes, diced

Place a tortilla on plate. Put a layer of beans and hot sauce over tortilla; sprinkle cilantro and green onions over beans and sauce.

Roll up tortilla and warm, if desired.

After heating, place on warm plate, add a little hot sauce and top with lettuce and tomatoes.

Preparation time: 10 to 15 minutes
Baking time: 10 to 15 minutes
Servings: variable

Variation:
Cooked blackeyed peas or pinto beans
Cooked brown rice
Corn, drained (fresh or canned)
Onion, sliced
Tomatoes, chopped
Green pepper, cut in strips
Salsa (see recipe)

Mexican Red Bean Stew

1 c. water
3/4 c. celery, chopped
3/4 c. green pepper,
  chopped
1 c. onion, chopped
2 garlic cloves, minced
1 can (28 oz.) tomatoes,
  chopped
2 cans (15 oz.) red kidney
  beans, drained
1/4 c. raisins
1 Tbsp. red wine vinegar
1 1/2 tsp. chili powder
1 1/2 tsp. parsley
3/4 tsp. basil
3/4 tsp. oregano
3/4 tsp. ground cumin
1/2 tsp. ground allspice
1/8 tsp. pepper
1/8 tsp. bottled hot pepper
  sauce
1 bay leaf

Heat water in a Dutch oven; add celery, green pepper, onion and garlic; saute 5 minutes.

Stir in the remaining ingredients.

Bring to a boil; then reduce the heat and simmer covered for 1 hour or until tender.

Uncover and simmer an additional 30 minutes or until the stew is the desired consistency.

Remove bay leaf before serving.

Preparation time: 15 minutes
Cooking time: 1 hour and 35
  minutes
Servings: 6

Chili

2 1/2 c. dried pinto, navy
    or great northern beans
1 c. brown rice
7 1/2 c. water
2 green peppers, chopped
3 onions, chopped
1 Tbsp. low-sodium soy
    sauce
1 can (28 oz.) tomatoes,
    chopped, or
2 c. fresh tomatoes,
    chopped
6 garlic cloves, crushed
3 tsp. chili powder
1 tsp. cumin (optional)
1 c. corn kernels

Note: Soaking beans overnight cuts down on cooking time. Or, you may wish to bring beans and water to a boil, cover and boil 2 minutes; remove from heat and let stand 1 hour. Then add remaining ingredients except corn and simmer 1 hour, then continue as above.

Place beans, rice, and water in a large pot.

Cover and cook over fairly low heat, about 1 1/2 hours.

The vegetables, spices, and tomatoes can be prepared while the beans and rice are beginning to cook.

After 90 minutes, add remaining ingredients except corn kernels to the pot.

Cook 2 more hours; uncover during the last 30 minutes of cooking and add the corn.

Can be cooked longer than 3 1/2 hours if desired.

Makes excellent leftovers; spoon into pita bread or over corn chips.

Preparation time: 30 minutes
Cooking time: 3 1/2 hours
Servings: 8

Black Bean Tostados

Corn tortillas (crisp in oven)
2 c. dry black beans
4 c. water
1 can (14 oz.) beef broth, defatted
1/2 tsp. garlic powder or 1 garlic clove, crushed
1 tsp. cumin
1/2 c. onion, finely chopped
Dash salt (optional)
Option: Use canned no fat black beans

Sort and wash beans. In a large saucepan, place beans in water.

Cover and bring to a boil for 2 minutes.

Remove from heat and let soak 1 hour to overnight. Drain water so it just covers beans.

Add beef broth and seasonings. Return to boil, cover and simmer 1 hour.

Makes about 5 cups cooked beans.

When beans are tender, layer tostada as follows, using a small amount of toppings, as desired:
10 to 12 corn tortillas
5 c. black bean mixture
2 c. shredded lettuce
1 1/2 c. tomatoes, chopped
1/3 c. fresh cilantro, snipped w/scissors
2 c. alfalfa sprouts
2 c. salsa (see recipe)

Preparation time: 25 minutes
Bean soak: 1 hour to overnight
Cooking time: 1 hour
Servings 10 to 12

Baked Beans

6 c. cooked navy beans

1/4 c. water

2 onions, chopped

2 Tbsp. molasses

1 c. tomato sauce

1 1/2 tsp. chili powder

3/4 tsp. dry mustard

1 Tbsp. Worcestershire
    sauce

Combine all ingredients in a 2-quart casserole.

Bake, uncovered, in a 325 degree oven for 1 1/2 hours.

Preparation time: 15 minutes
Cooking time: 1 1/2 hours
Servings: 6 to 8

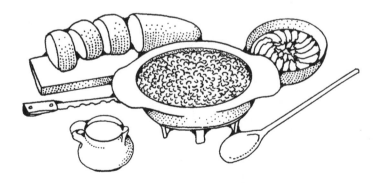

BAR-B-Q Beans

1 onion, chopped
1 green pepper, chopped
1 garlic clove, crushed
1/4 c. water
1 1/2 tsp. dry mustard
1 1/2 tsp. chili powder
1/2 tsp. ground cumin
1/2 tsp. tumeric
1 c. tomato sauce
1 1/2 Tbsp. unsulphured
    molasses or malt syrup
1/2 Tbsp. apple cider
    vinegar
Dash Tabasco sauce
4 c. cooked beans

In medium saucepan, saute onion, green pepper, and garlic in water for 5 minutes.

Add mustard, chili powder, cumin and tumeric. Stir to mix well.

Add remaining ingredients; mix well.

Cook, covered, over low heat 30 minutes to blend flavors.

Serve on whole wheat buns, like Sloppy Joe mix, with catsup and mustard, if desired.

Preparation time: 15 minutes
Cooking time: 30 minutes
Servings: 6

Refried Beans

6 c. cooked pinto beans (see recipe)
1/2 c. stock from cooking beans, or water
1 tsp. onion powder
1/2 tsp. chili powder
1/2 tsp. garlic powder
1/2 c. picante sauce or salsa (see recipe)

In medium saucepan, mash cooked beans with stock or water until desired consistency is reached.

Add onion, chili and garlic powders; mix well. Stir in picante sauce or salsa.

Cook over low heat about 15 minutes, or until heated through.

Serve in bean enchiladas, on tostados, in pita bread, no fat commercial corn chips, or with home-baked corn chips.

Preparation time: 5 minutes
Cooking time: 15 minutes
Servings: 8

Three Bean Casserole

2 large onions, sliced and
    separated in rings
1 1/2 tsp. garlic powder
1 tsp. dry mustard
1/2 c. brown sugar
1/4 c. apple cider vinegar
1 can (16 oz.) dark red
    kidney beans, drained
1 can (16 oz.) garbanzo
    beans, drained
1 can (16 oz.) green lima
    beans, drained

Place onion rings, garlic powder, mustard, brown sugar and vinegar in a large skillet.

Cover; cook 20 minutes over medium heat.

Combine beans in a 3-quart casserole. Stir in onion mixture.

Bake, covered, at 350 degrees for 45 minutes.

Preparation time: 15 minutes
Cooking time: 20 minutes
Baking time: 45 minutes
Servings: 10

Blackeyed Peas

1 pkg. (16 oz.) dry blackeyed peas
5 c. water
1 onion, chopped, or 1 Tbsp. onion powder
1/4 tsp. garlic powder
2 tsp. salt (optional)
1/4 tsp. black pepper

In a large saucepan, sort and wash peas.

Add water; cover and bring to a boil for 2 minutes.

Remove from heat and let stand overnight (or at least 1 hour).

Drain most of liquid.

Add all other ingredients; return to boil, lower heat, cover and simmer 30 minutes.

Preparation time: 10 minutes
Soaking time: 1 hour
Cooking time: 30 minutes
Servings: 6 to 8

Cornbread Salad

Keeps several days in refrigerator.

1 pan baked cornbread (see recipe)
3 stalks celery, chopped
2 large bell peppers, chopped
1 small jar chopped pimientos
1 c. green onions with stems, chopped
1/2 c. sweet onions, chopped fine
2 large tomatoes, diced
1 1/2 c. fat free mayonnaise

Crumble cornbread in a 2-quart covered casserole.

Mix in vegetables and mayonnaise.

Chill.

A little purple onion and/or coarsely ground pepper can be added for color and extra flavor.

Preparation time: 20 minutes
Servings: 6

Cornbread Dressing

Use plain cornbread baked
    without corn or chilies
6 slices whole wheat bread
3 or 4 medium onions,
    chopped fine
1 1/2 c. celery, chopped fine
1/2 c. water
2 1/2 tsp. sage (optional)
Salt and pepper to taste
2 cans (14 oz.) defatted
    chicken broth, more if
    needed

In a large bowl, crumble cornbread and whole wheat bread.

In a small saucepan, saute onions and celery in water until onions are transparent, 5 to 10 minutes.

Add to bread mixture along with remaining ingredients; mix well.

Pour into a 9 x 13-inch baking dish.

Bake uncovered in 350 degree oven for 30 minutes.

Preparation time: 20 minutes
Cooking time: 5 to 10 minutes
Baking time: 30 minutes
Servings: 8 to 10

Baked Brown Rice

1 c. brown rice
3 tsp. onion, minced
1 tsp. Mrs. Dash
2 1/2 c. beef bouillon, low sodium
1 tsp. dehydrated parsley

Brown the rice in a nonstick skillet over medium high heat, stirring or shaking constantly.

When golden brown, place in 1-quart covered casserole.

Mix onion and Mrs. Dash with rice.

Pour hot beef bouillon (mix as per directions on can) over the rice mixture.

Bake in 350 degree oven for one hour.

Garnish with dehydrated parsley.

Note: More water may be needed before it is done.

Preparation time: 15 minutes
Baking time: 1 hour
Servings: 4 to 6

Sweet and Sour Sauce
(over Rice)

6 Tbsp. vinegar
3/4 c. water
All of juice from 15 1/4 oz.
   can pineapple tidbits
1 Tbsp. soy sauce, low
   sodium
1/4 tsp. salt (optional)
2 1/2 Tbsp. cornstarch
1/4 c. cold water
1/4 c. onions, chopped
2 Tbsp. water
1/4 c. green pepper,
   chopped
2 stalks celery, chopped
1/2 c. pineapple tidbits,
   drained
1 can (8 oz.) sliced, peeled
   and drained water
   chestnuts (optional)
3 Tbsp. brown sugar
4 c. cooked brown rice

Combine first five ingredients in a 1-quart glass measuring cup and microwave on high 4 minutes or until it begins to boil.

Mix cornstarch and water well.

Slowly add cornstarch mixture to vinegar mixture and stir briskly.

Cook until thickened and clear, approximately 30 seconds.

Mix 2 tablespoons water and onion in bowl and microwave 2 minutes. Stir in green pepper, celery, water chestnuts and pineapple tidbits; microwave 30 seconds.

Add to vinegar mixture and stir in sugar. Serve hot over cooked rice.

Preparation time: 10 minutes
Cooking time: 7 to 8 minutes
Servings: 4 to 6 (about 3 1/2 cups sauce)

Rice Casserole

1 c. uncooked brown rice
2 1/2 c. water, boiling
1 c. mushrooms, sliced
2 c. canned tomatoes, diced
1 green pepper, chopped
1/2 c. onion, chopped
1/2 c. fat-free soy milk
Dash of paprika
1/2 tsp. Mrs. Dash
1/4 tsp. black pepper
1 c. whole wheat bread crumbs

In medium saucepan, add brown rice to boiling water.

Cover, turn to low and steam for 45 minutes or until water evaporates.

Mix together all the vegetables, skim soy milk, and seasonings.

Using a fork, lightly mix with rice and put in a sprayed, covered 2-quart casserole.

Cover with whole wheat bread crumbs.

Bake in 350 degree oven about 30 minutes.

Preparation time: 15 minutes
Cooking time: 45 minutes
Baking time: 30 minutes
Servings: 6

Mushroom Curry

1/2 c. water
1/2 lb. fresh mushrooms;
　chop stems, leave caps
　whole
1 onion, minced
1 Tbsp. curry powder
2 cooking apples, chopped
　fine (chop one of apples
　just before serving; toss
　with 1 Tbsp. lemon
　juice)
Seasonings to taste: Mrs.
　Dash, salt, etc.
Paprika, sprinkle
2 2/3 c. fat-free milk
4 1/2 c. cooked brown rice,
　hot (2 c. raw) or 4 1/2 c.
　cooked bulgur wheat,
　hot 1 1/2 c. raw)

In medium saucepan, saute mushroom caps in water 2 to 3 minutes; remove from liquid and set aside.

In same liquid, place onion, curry powder, 1 chopped apple and mushroom stems and saute 3 to 5 minutes, making sure apple does not get mushy.

Remove from heat, add seasoning to taste, sprinkle of paprika, and milk.

Place grain in 2 1/2 qt. casserole.

Spread mushroom sauce evenly on top. Arrange mushroom caps on top. Sprinkle with more paprika.

Bake casserole at 350 degrees until sauce is firm, about 30 minutes.

Sprinkle freshly chopped apple over top just before serving.

Preparation time: 15 to 20 minutes
Cooking time: 10 minutes
Baking time: 30 minutes
Servings: 8 to 10

Spanish Rice

2 c. uncooked brown rice
3 1/2 c. water
1 can (29 oz.) tomato sauce
1/2 c. onions, chopped
1/2 c. celery, chopped
1/2 c. green pepper,
    chopped
1 tsp. parsley flakes
1/8 tsp. ground pepper
1/4 tsp. Mrs. Dash
1/4 tsp. garlic powder
1/8 tsp. red pepper
1/2 tsp. salt (optional)
1/2 tsp. chili powder
1/4 tsp. cumin
1/2 tsp. oregano leaves

In a large nonstick saucepan, stir the rice over medium heat to toast the rice evenly.

Add all ingredients and mix well.

Bring to a boil; reduce heat and simmer, covered, for about 1 hour or until all liquid is absorbed.

Preparation time: 15 minutes
Cooking time: 1 1/4 hours
Servings: 8 to 10

Rice Sublime

1 c. uncooked brown rice
2 1/2 c. water
1 onion, chopped
2 c. fresh mushrooms,
    sliced
1/4 c. low sodium tamari
    (soy sauce)
1/4 tsp. garlic powder
1/2 tsp. Mrs. Dash
1/8 tsp. black pepper
1 1/2 c. frozen green peas
1 jar (4 oz.) chopped
    pimientos

In medium saucepan, mix rice, water, onion, mushrooms and seasonings together.

Bring to a boil; cover, lower heat and cook 45 minutes.

Add green peas and pimientos, stirring lightly with a fork to mix, and cook another 15 minutes.

Preparation time: 15 minutes
Cooking time: 1 hour
Servings: 4

Rice Curry
Serve hot or cold.

1 onion, chopped
1 bell pepper, chopped
3 stalks celery, chopped
1 large green apple,
   chopped
1 c. water
1/2 c. raisins
4 c. cooked brown rice
1 tsp. curry powder
1 Tbsp. low sodium tamari
   (soy sauce)
Salt to taste on your plate

In large saucepan, cook onion, bell peppers, celery and apple in 1/2 c. water for 10 minutes.

Add raisins and remaining water; cook 10 minutes longer.

Add rice, curry powder, and tamari. Stir to mix well.

Continue to cook until heated through, about 10 minutes. Stir occasionally.

Salt to taste.

Preparation time: 15 minutes
Cooking time: 35 minutes
Servings: 6 to 8

Toasted Rice Pilaf

3 c. cooked brown rice (made from toasted rice)

2 c. mushrooms, sliced

2 1/2 c. beef bouillon, low sodium

4 tsp. dehydrated onion flakes

4 tsp. parsley, minced

To toast rice, spread two cups of brown rice on a shallow baking sheet, one layer deep.

Bake at 325 to 425 degrees for 10 to 25 minutes, stirring occasionally.

Let rice cool, store in canister or jar and cook just as you would plain rice.

Combine ingredients in 2-quart casserole, mix well, and bake uncovered at 375 degrees for 25 to 35 minutes, until piping hot.

Preparation time: 20 minutes
Baking time: 25 to 35 minutes
Servings: 4

Rice Bake

1/2 c. water
1/2 c. onion, chopped
1 c. uncooked brown rice
1 1/2 c. tomatoes, chopped
1/2 tsp. brown sugar
3 c. defatted chicken broth
1 bay leaf (optional)
1 garlic clove or 1/4 tsp.
　　garlic powder
1 tsp. basil leaves
1 tsp. parsley flakes
(Fat-free chicken broth is
　　available)

Combine all ingredients in a 2-quart casserole dish.

Cover and bake in 350 degree oven 1 hour or until liquid is absorbed and rice is tender.

Remove bay leaf before serving.

Preparation time: 10 minutes
Baking time: 1 hour
Servings: 6

Plantarian Rice

4 radishes, trimmed and
　sliced
1 tsp. rice vinegar
3 garlic cloves, minced
1 Tbsp. water
4 scallions, thinly sliced
1/2 c. mushrooms, thinly
　sliced
3 c. cooked brown rice
1 c. frozen peas, defrosted
1/4 c. water chestnuts,
　sliced
1 Tbsp. low sodium soy
　sauce

Combine radishes with vinegar
in a small bowl and set aside.

Place garlic and water in a large
saucepan over medium heat.

Add scallions and mushrooms;
saute 5 minutes.

Add and mix rice, radishes and
remaining ingredients.

Heat through. Serve hot.

Preparation time: 20 minutes
Cooking time: 20 minutes
Servings: 6

Corn and Rice Casserole

3 c. cooked brown rice
1 pkg (10 oz.) frozen whole
   kernel corn, thawed
1/2 c. onion, minced
1 1/2 c. fat-free soy milk
1 1/2 tsp. salt (or to taste)
1/4 tsp. pepper
1/2 tsp. paprika

In a large bowl, combine all ingredients except paprika.

Pour into a shallow 2-quart casserole dish. Sprinkle with paprika.

Cover and bake at 350 degrees for 30 to 35 minutes.

Preparation time: 10 minutes
Baking time: 30 to 35 minutes
Servings: 4 to 6

Chicken-Flavored Rice Mix

For gift-giving, package in a pretty container and decorate with colorful ribbons or bows. Be sure to attach preparation instructions.

1 c. uncooked long-grain rice

1 Tbsp. chicken bouillon, instant, low sodium

1 Tbsp. parsley flakes

1 tsp. celery flakes

1 tsp. dried minced onion

1 tsp. sugar or equivalent substitute

1/2 tsp. salt (optional)

Combine all ingredients.

Store in small plastic bag or container.

To prepare: In medium saucepan, combine rice mix with 2 cups water.

Cover and bring to a boil, reduce heat and simmer 15 minutes or until rice is tender.

Preparation time: 5 minutes
Cooking time: 15 minutes
Servings: 3 to 5

Spaghetti with Fantastic Spaghetti Sauce

You can make the sauce early in the day and reheat just before serving.

2 cans (28 oz.) tomatoes, slightly chopped

2 cans (29 oz.) tomato sauce

3 c. onion, chopped

2 c. bell pepper, chopped

5 or 6 c. mushrooms, sliced

1 Tbsp. garlic, minced

2 Tbsp. wine vinegar

2 tsp. Mrs. Dash

2 Tbsp. basil

1 lb. egg-free whole wheat or spinach spaghetti

4 quarts water, boiling

Combine all ingredients except basil, spaghetti, and water in a large saucepan or skillet.

Bring to boil; reduce heat and simmer about 1 hour; add the basil and simmer 30 minutes longer.

About 15 minutes before serving, drop egg-free whole wheat or spinach spaghetti into boiling water and cook until tender, or about 10 minutes.

Serve with sauce. (Freeze leftover sauce for future use.)

Preparation time: 15 minutes
Cooking time: 1 1/2 hours
Servings: 10 to 12

Tamale Pie Casserole

2 onions, chopped
1/2 c. water
2 tsp. chili powder
1/2 c. tomato sauce
1 1/2 c. frozen corn
1-8 oz. can chopped green
   chilies
4 c. cooked pinto beans,
   mashed (see recipe)
2 c. cornmeal
3 c. water
Paprika, sprinkle
1/4 c. parsley, snipped with
   scissors

In large saucepan, cook onions in 1/2 cup water for 5 minutes.

Add 1 teaspoon of chili powder, tomato sauce, corn and chilies. Cook 5 minutes.

Add beans and cook another 10 minutes over low heat.

Remove from heat.

Combine cornmeal with 3 cups water and rest of chili powder in medium saucepan and cook over medium heat until mixture thickens, stirring constantly to keep cornmeal from lumping.

Using a 9 x 13-inch nonstick pan, spread half of the cornmeal mixture over bottom.

Pour bean mixture over this and spread. Then spread remaining cornmeal mixture over top and sprinkle with paprika.

Bake at 350 degrees for 45 minutes or until it bubbles.

Sprinkle with parsley and serve.

Preparation time: 15 minutes
Cooking time: 35 minutes
Baking time: 45 minutes
Servings: 8

Barley Pilaf with Peas

3 c. water
3 low sodium chicken
   bouillon cubes
1 c. barley
1 pkg. (10 oz.) frozen peas
1/2 c. onion, chopped
1 garlic clove, minced
1/4 c. water
2 Tbsp. low sodium soy
   sauce (optional)

In a medium saucepan, bring 3 cups water and bouillon cubes to a boil; stir in barley.

Reduce heat, cover and simmer 10 to 12 minutes, stirring occasionally. Drain and set aside.

In a large skillet, saute peas, onion and garlic in 1/4 cup water for 5 minutes; reduce heat.

Stir in barley and soy sauce.

Cover and continue cooking until heated through, stirring occasionally.

Preparation time: 10 minutes
Cooking time: 25 to 30 minutes

Broccoli and Stuffing Casserole

1 pkg. (16 oz.) frozen broccoli
Your favorite nonfat
stuffing mix

Cook broccoli by directions until just tender.

Prepare stuffing mix according to directions.

Layer stuffing and broccoli in a 2-quart casserole dish.

Cover and bake at 350 degrees for 20 minutes or until heated through.

Preparation time: 12 minutes
Cooking time: 15 minutes
Baking time: 20 minutes
Servings: 4 to 6

Broccoli Surprise

1 bag (16 oz.) frozen broccoli cuts
Salt and pepper to taste
1 can (17 oz.) cream style corn
1 c. fat-free soy milk
1 Tbsp. cornstarch
Butter Buds to taste
1 c. whole wheat bread crumbs

Thaw broccoli, but do not cook. Place in 2-quart casserole and sprinkle with salt and pepper.

Combine corn, milk, cornstarch and Butter Buds. Stir well.

Pour over broccoli, sprinkle with bread crumbs.

Bake at 350 degrees for 25 to 30 minutes or until firm and broccoli is tender.

Preparation time: 20 minutes
Baking time: 25 to 30 minutes
Servings: 4

Corn Okra Creole

1 c. green pepper, chopped
1/2 c. onion, chopped
1/4 c. water
2 c. fresh or frozen corn or
   1 can (16 oz.) whole kernel
   corn
1 1/2 c. fresh okra, sliced, or
   1 pkg. (16 oz.) frozen okra
1 1/2 c. tomatoes, peeled and
   chopped
1 Tbsp. tomato paste
1/4 tsp. thyme
1/4 tsp. black pepper, coarsely
   ground
Salt to taste (optional)
1/2 tsp. Tabasco sauce
   (optional)

In a large saucepan, saute pepper and onion 5 minutes.

Add corn and okra; cook over medium heat 10 minutes, stirring occasionally.

Add tomatoes, tomato paste and seasonings; mix thoroughly.

Cover and simmer 5 minutes more, stirring occasionally.

Preparation time: 15 to 25 minutes
Cooking time: 20 minutes
Servings: 4 to 6

Hearty Eggplant Barley Bake

1/2 c. onion, chopped

1/2 c. mushrooms, chopped

1/4 c. green pepper, chopped

1 Tbsp. garlic, minced

1/4 c. water

1 c. eggplant, cubed

2 Tbsp. water

1 can (16 oz.) tomatoes, chopped

1 1/2 c. water

3/4 c. quick-cooking barley

1/2 c. chili sauce

1/4 c. fresh parsley, chopped

1 tsp. honey

1 tsp. Worcestershire sauce

1/2 tsp. dried marjoram

1/4 tsp. black pepper

In a large nonstick frying pan, saute onions, mushrooms, green pepper and garlic in 1/4 cup water over medium heat for 5 minutes.

Add eggplant and 2 tablespoons water, saute about 10 minutes.

Add tomatoes with their juice and all remaining ingredients.

Bring to a boil, cover, reduce heat and simmer 20 minutes or until barley is tender.

Preparation time: 20 minutes
Cooking time: 35 minutes

Ratatouille with Noodles, Pasta or Rice

Good dish for picnics.

1/4 c. water
1 garlic clove, minced
1 large onion, sliced
3 zucchini, sliced
1 eggplant, diced
1 green pepper, diced
1/2 c. water or tomato juice
2 tsp. oregano leaves
1 tsp. sugar (optional)
Salt to taste (optional)
Pepper to taste
2 large tomatoes, cut into
   wedges
4 to 6 cups cooked noodles,
   pasta or brown rice, cold

In a large, deep kettle, heat water and saute garlic and onion until golden in color.

Add zucchini, eggplant and green pepper.

Cook over medium heat, stirring occasionally, until vegetables are crisp tender, about 15 minutes.

Add water or tomato juice and seasonings.

Lower heat, cover and simmer about 15 minutes until sauce is thickened slightly.

Add tomato wedges and heat through.

Remove from heat and cool. Refrigerate and then serve cold with cold noodles, pasta or rice.

Preparation time: 15 minutes
Cooking time: 40 to 45 minutes
Cooling time: overnight
Servings: 6 to 8

Oven Fried Potatoes

Wash and dry, but do not peel, 4 potatoes.

Drop into a pot of boiling water, lower heat to simmer, and cook until barely tender.

Remove from the pot and refrigerate.

Alternate method: Microwave 4 potatoes for 15 minutes; don't overcook.

Refrigerate.

When potatoes are cool, peel them carefully and slice lengthwise as for French fries.

Spread the potatoes on a nonstick baking sheet and season with onion powder, garlic powder, paprika, black pepper, and/or chili powder.

Brown in a 400 degree oven.

Turn with a spatula to brown the other side.

Potatoes will be crispy.

Yummy! Even better than greasy french fries.

Preparation time: 10 minutes
Baking time: 20 to 25 minutes in oven 7 to 8 minutes in microwave
Cooling time: 1 hour or more
Servings: 4

Green Bean and Potato Casserole

1 1/2 c. cooked green beans, or
    canned, drained
2 c. boiled potatoes, chopped
1/2 c. celery, diced
2 Tbsp. onion, finely chopped
2 Tbsp. water
1 1/2 Tbsp. flour
1 1/2 c. fat-free soy milk
1/2 tsp. Mrs. Dash
1/4 tsp. dill weed
1/8 tsp. pepper
1/2 tsp. salt or salt to taste
1 c. soft whole wheat bread
    crumbs
Paprika, sprinkle

Combine green beans, potatoes and celery in 1 1/2-quart casserole.

Saute onion in water. Stir in flour.

Add skim soy milk slowly, stirring constantly until slightly thickened.

Add seasonings.

Pour over vegetables in casserole.

Sprinkle bread crumbs over top, then paprika.

Bake covered at 350 degrees for 30 minutes; uncover and bake 5 minutes more.

Preparation time: 20 minutes
Baking time: 35 minutes
Servings: 4 to 6

Savory Green Beans and Potatoes

3 medium red potatoes, cut
  into chunks
1 medium onion, chopped
2 Tbsp. water
1 can (16 oz.) cut green beans,
  drained
1/4 c. cider vinegar
1 tsp. sugar
1/2 tsp. dry mustard
2 Tbsp. water
Pepper to taste
2 Tbsp. parsley, minced

In a large skillet, cook potatoes and onion in 2 tablespoons water over medium-high heat until golden; add beans.

Combine vinegar, sugar and mustard with 2 tablespoons water in a small bowl.

Pour over bean mixture.

Cook until moisture is almost gone, stirring occasionally.

Season with pepper.

Garnish with minced parsley.

Preparation time: 15 minutes
Cooking time: 20 minutes
Servings: 4 to 6

Tabouli

2 c. bulgur wheat
Water to cover wheat
1 c. carrots, sliced
1 c. broccoli, chopped
Boiling water
2 firm ripe tomatoes, chopped
1 cucumber, chopped
4 green onions, sliced
2 garlic cloves, minced
1/2 c. fresh mint, chopped, or
  2 Tbsp. dry mint flakes
  and/or parsley
1 tsp. basil
Juice of 2 lemons

In a medium bowl, place bulgur; cover with water and soak overnight.

Or, place bulgur in a large microwave dish; cover with water and cook in microwave 8 to 10 minutes or until water is absorbed, turning dish once after 5 minutes.

Blanch carrots and broccoli for 2 minutes by placing vegetables in boiling water in a medium saucepan; return to boil and time 2 minutes.

Plunge immediately into cold water. When cool, drain and place in large bowl.

Add other ingredients and mix lightly.

Cover and chill before serving.

Preparation time: 20 minutes
Bulgur soaking: overnight, or cooking in microwave 10 minutes
Blanching time: 5 minutes
Cooling time: 5 minutes
Chilling time: several hours
Servings: 4 to 6

Southern Okra Chowder

3 c. okra, sliced (fresh or
    frozen)
2 c. canned tomatoes, chopped
1 medium green pepper, sliced
2 1/2 c. cooked lima beans
1 c. canned corn
1/2 c. onion, minced
1 tsp. salt (optional)
1/2 tsp. parsley, minced, or
    1/4 tsp. dry
1 c. water

Place all ingredients in large saucepan.

Bring to boil; reduce heat and simmer over medium heat 20 minutes.

Preparation time: 20 minutes
Cooking time: 20 minutes
Servings: 8 to 10

Stuffed Peppers

8 lg. green peppers, cored
1 onion, diced
1/2 c. celery, chopped
1 c. mushrooms, chopped
1/4 c. water
2 c. tomato sauce (1 c. for topping)
3 c. cooked brown rice
1 tsp. thyme
1 tsp. basil
1/2 to 1 tsp. garlic powder

Blanch peppers by dropping into boiling water in a large uncovered kettle. Bring to a boil; hold at boiling 2 to 3 minutes.

Drain and immediately plunge into cold water to stop cooking process. When cold, drain and set aside.

In a large saucepan, saute onion, celery and mushrooms in water over medium heat, stirring constantly, until onion is transparent and other vegetables are crisp-tender.

Add 1 cup tomato sauce, rice and seasonings; mix well.

Remove from heat and stuff mixture into blanched peppers; place in large baking dish.

Pour the remaining tomato sauce over the peppers, a little on each.

Cover and bake at 400 degrees for 15 minutes, or until heated completely.

Preparation time: 20 minutes
Cooking time: 30 minutes
Servings: 8

Baked Acorn Squash

2 medium acorn squash, sliced crosswise in 1-inch circles, seeds removed

1/2 c. apple cider or apple juice

1/2 tsp. salt (optional)

1/8 tsp. ground cinnamon

1/8 tsp. ground mace

Place squash in a 15 x 10 x 1-inch baking pan. Pour cider or juice over squash.

Combine remaining ingredients and sprinkle on top.

Cover with foil. Bake at 325 degrees for 45 minutes or until squash is tender.

Preparation time: 15 minutes
Baking time: 45 minutes
Servings: 6

Acorn Squash and Apple Bake

2 medium acorn squash

2 cooking apples, cored and sliced

1/2 c. liquid Butter Buds (mix 1 packet Butter Buds in 1/2 c. hot tap water)

1 Tbsp. all-purpose flour

1 tsp. salt (optional)

1/2 tsp. ground mace

Cut squash in half lengthwise; remove seeds. Cut into 1/2 inch slices and peel squash.

Arrange in a sprayed 12 x 8-inch baking dish and top with apples.

Combine remaining ingredients in a small bowl; spoon over apple slices.

Cover tightly with foil.

Bake at 350 degrees for 1 1/4 hours or until squash is tender.

Preparation time: 20 minutes
Baking time: 1 1/4 hours
Servings: 8

Microwave-Baked Winter Squashes

Acorn, butternut, banana squashes, etc. Incredibly delicious, nutritious and low-calorie.

Unsweetened applesauce

Cinnamon, sprinkle

Cut and remove seeds.

Microwave squash upside down with a little water, covered, on High for 12 minutes.

Turn right side up and put applesauce in the center.

Sprinkle with cinnamon.

Microwave another minute.

Preparation time: varies, according to amount of squash
Baking time: about 13 minutes
Servings: varies

Sweet Potato Gratin

8 medium sweet potatoes
2 c. fat free soy milk
1 Tbsp. cornstarch
1 garlic clove, minced
1/4 tsp. ground pepper
1 Tbsp. fresh parsley, snipped

In a 4-quart saucepan, cook the potatoes in water to cover for 45 minutes, or until easily pierced with a fork.

Drain and plunge into cold water to cool. Peel and slice cross-wise into 1/8-inch rounds.

Spray a 10-inch pie plate with nonstick spray.

Arrange sweet potatoes in pie plate, overlapping as necessary to fit. (May be prepared up to 2 days ahead. Wrap well and refrigerate.)

In a medium bowl, combine the milk, cornstarch, garlic and pepper.

Pour over the potatoes. Bake at 300 degrees for 35 minutes.

Sprinkle with snipped parsley just before serving.

Preparation time: 10 minutes
Cooking time: 45 minutes
Baking time: 35 minutes
Servings: 10 to 12

Split pea Dressing for Baked Potatoes

1/3 c. canned split pea soup
1/3 tsp. parsley
1/4 tsp. chives
1/8 tsp. dill weed
Salt to taste (optional)
Pepper to taste

Beat all ingredients together in a small bowl; spoon over potatoes.

Preparation time: 10 minutes
Servings: 2

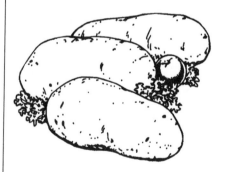

Pureed Carrot Dressing for Baked Potatoes

1/3 c. pureed carrots
2 tsp. dry minced onion
2 tsp. parsley
4 tsp. white wine vinegar
Dash of paprika

Combine all ingredients in a small bowl.

Dollop on baked potatoes.

Preparation time: 10 minutes
Servings: 2

Bean Dip Dressing for Baked Potatoes

Any fat free bean dip.

Slice each baked potato lengthwise from top to about 1/4 inch of bottom; insert bean dip.

Place on cookie sheet; put back in a 425 degree oven for a couple of minutes or until reheated. Yummy!

Preparation time: 2 to 5 minutes
Servings: variable

Sweet Potato Pineapple Casserole

8 medium sweet potatoes

1/2 c. brown sugar or less to taste

1/2 c. granulated sugar or less to taste

1 c. orange juice

1 can (8 1/2 oz.) crushed pineapple

1/2 c. liquid Butter Buds (mix 1 packet Butter Buds in 1/2 c. hot tap water)

Bake potatoes.

Peel and cut potatoes into chunks into a 12 x 8 1/2-inch baking pan.

Mix remaining ingredients in a small saucepan; bring to a boil and pour over potatoes.

Bake in a 350 degree oven for 25 minutes.

Preparation time: 10 minutes
Potato baking time: 1 hour in oven—6 to 8 minutes in microwave
Casserole baking time: 25 minutes
Servings: 8 to 10

Baked Sweet Potatoes

Select unblemished potatoes.

Scrub and bake at 400 degrees for 1 hour for medium sized potatoes. (If preparing one or two, bake in microwave oven 6 to 8 minutes.)

Use seasonings of choice: Butter Buds, Pepper, Mrs. Dash (any flavor), lemon and herb and lemon pepper especially good. Raisins, or peel, mash and season to taste.

A baked potato makes a wonderful entree.

A sprinkle of nutmeg, ginger or cinnamon with fruit and/or a little fruit juice are good.

Reheat in oven or microwave oven. Store unused potatoes in refrigerator.

Preparation time: varies according to number of potatoes baked
Baking time: 1 hour in oven (6 to 8 minutes in microwave)
Servings: varies

Low Calorie Dressings for Baked Potatoes

Vegetable stew, or
Vegetable soup, or
Split pea soup, or any kind of
  bean soup, or diced
  tomatoes and chives
Finely sliced broccoli and, or
  cauliflower
Add a dash of Mrs. Dash
  seasoning
Cooked Chili (see recipe)

Slice each baked potato lengthwise from top to about 1/4 inch of bottom; insert your favorite dressing.

There are endless choices, use your imagination. Just a little pepper and/or a little dash of salt makes a baked potato great.

Try a dash of cayenne pepper.

Preparation time: 2 to 5 minutes
Servings: variable

Dilled Potatoes

6 medium potatoes, peeled
    and quartered
1/2 c. water
2 small onions, diced
1/2 tsp. salt
3/4 tsp. dill weed
1/4 tsp. Mrs. Dash
Dash of black pepper
Dash of cayenne pepper

Place the potatoes in a saucepan with water and all other ingredients.

Bring to boil, reduce heat and simmer, covered, over low heat for 20 minutes or until potatoes are tender.

Preparation time: 10 minutes
Cooking time: 20 minutes
Servings: 4

Scalloped Potatoes

2 very large baking potatoes,
    boiled in their jackets until
    tender
1/4 c. flour
1/2 tsp. salt (optional) or to
    taste
1/4 c. water
1 medium onion, chopped
1/8 tsp. pepper
2 c. fat-free soy milk
2 tsp. parsley flakes
Paprika, sprinkle

Peel potatoes and slice thin.

Combine salt and flour and
dredge potato slices. Place in a
9 x 13-inch dish.

Saute onion in water. Add
pepper, skim soy milk, and
parsley to onions and warm.
Pour over potatoes.

Sprinkle with paprika.

Cover and bake at 350 degrees
for 45 minutes.

Remove cover and bake for 15
minutes more.

Preparation time: 15 minutes
Cooking time: 10 minutes
Baking time: 1 hour
Servings: 6

Tomato Scalloped Potatoes

5 c. potatoes, peeled and sliced (about 8)
1 onion, chopped
1 c. corn or carrots, sliced
1 c. tomato sauce
1 c. water
2 Tbsp. whole wheat flour
2 Tbsp. low sodium tamari (soy sauce)
1/4 tsp. dill weed

Layer potatoes, onion, and chosen vegetables in a large casserole dish.

Combine the remaining ingredients, stirring well to mix flour.

Pour over potatoes and vegetables.

Cover and bake at 375 degrees for 1 1/4 hrs. Uncover and bake 30 minutes longer to form a crust on top if desired.

Helpful hints: This also may be made in a microwave oven. It will take about 20 minutes on high power.

Preparation time: 20 minutes
Cooking time: 1 3/4 hours
Servings: 6

Potato Casserole Dinner

6 potatoes, sliced
2 carrots, sliced
1 green pepper, sliced
1 c. fresh or frozen green peas
1 zucchini, sliced
1 c. green beans (optional)
2 onions, sliced
1 c. fresh or frozen corn
1 c. broccoli florets

Sauce:
3 c. tomato sauce
2 Tbsp. low sodium soy sauce
2 tsp. parsley flakes
1 tsp. dry mustard
1 tsp. ground thyme
1/8 tsp. oregano
1 tsp. chili powder

Layer the vegetables in a large casserole dish in order listed.

In a medium bowl, mix sauce ingredients and pour over vegetables.

Bake, covered, in a 350 degree oven about 1 1/2 hours. Can be prepared ahead for company dinner.

Serve with whole-grain bread and a tossed green salad.

Preparation time: 30 minutes
Baking time: 1 1/2 hours
Servings: 8

Mashed Potato Pie

5 medium potatoes, peeled and chopped
1 c. water
1/4 c. fat-free soy milk
Salt to taste (optional)
1/8 tsp. pepper
3 large carrots, cut into
**   1 1/2" julienne strips**
1 (10 oz.) pkg. frozen green
**   peas, thawed and drained**
Green pepper rings (optional)
Fresh parsley sprigs (optional)

In medium saucepan, cook potatoes in 1/2 cup boiling water over low heat until tender.

Drain well; mash until smooth. Add skim soy milk, salt and pepper; stir until smooth.

In a large saucepan, cook carrots in 1/2 cup boiling water over low heat until crisp-tender, about 5 minutes.

Stand carrots upright around inside edge of a round 1 1/2-quart casserole dish. Cover bottom of dish with peas.

Spoon potatoes on top of peas, spreading to carrots.

Bake at 350 degrees for 20 minutes.

Garnish with green peppers and parsley.

Preparation time: 30 minutes
Cooking time: 20 minutes
Baking time: 20 minutes
Servings: 6

Mock Beef Stew

6 c. water
1/2 c. whole wheat flour
1/2 c. low sodium soy sauce
4 large potatoes, chopped
6 carrots, sliced
2 onions, diced
3 stalks celery, chopped
2 c. mushrooms, sliced
2 c. frozen peas
1 tsp. Mrs. Dash
Salt and pepper to taste

In a large kettle, bring 4 cups water to a boil.

Meanwhile mix in a jar 1/2 c. flour and 2 c. water. Shake and mix well; add to boiling water, stirring until smooth.

Add soy sauce and all of the vegetables except peas. Cook until barely tender, about 30 to 45 minutes.

Add peas just before stew is done, as they need very little cooking.

Season when done with Mrs. Dash and salt and pepper as desired.

One cup cooked barley may be added; cook as per directions on box. Also, other favorite vegetables may be added.

Preparation time: 15 minutes
Cooking time: 1 hour
Servings: 8

Taco Pizza Pie

Use Pizza Crust recipe on pages 251-252.

1 clove garlic, crushed or
   minced
1/4 tsp. salt
1/2 tsp. cumin
1 tsp. chili powder
1 4-oz. can chopped green
   chilies, drained
1 16-oz. can vegetarian refried
   beans
2 medium tomatoes, chopped
3 green onions, chopped
1/3 c. coarsely chopped green
   peppers
2 c. Zero-fat Rella Mozzarella
   substitute from Sharen's
   finest (available in health
   food stores or Fred Meyer's
   supermarket) grated

Prepare pizza dough. Roll into 13" circle. Place on ungreased pizza pan.

In medium bowl, combine garlic, salt, cumin, chili powder, green chilies and refried beans.

Spread over pizza dough. Sprinkle vegetables on top. Sprinkle cheese over pizza.

Bake 12-20 minutes or until crust is golden brown on edges.

Preparation time: 30 minutes
Baking time: 12-20 minutes
Servings: 8

Tomato Corn Chowder

12 oz. pkg. frozen corn
1 medium onion, chopped
1 clove garlic, minced or
    crushed
1 stalk celery, thinly sliced
1 large carrot, thinly sliced
2 medium potatoes, peeled and
    diced (or leave skins on but
    scrub well)
1 16 oz. can chopped tomatoes
    (don't drain)
1 tsp. salt (optional)
1/4 tsp. pepper
1/2 tsp. basil
3 cups vegetable stock
1 can (16 oz.) cream-style corn
1 cup rice or soy milk (fat-free)

In a 5-qt. pan add all ingredients but cream-style corn and milk.

Bring to a boil over medium/high heat, stirring often.

Reduce heat; cover and simmer until potatoes are fork-tender (about 30 minutes).

Add cream-style corn and milk and heat through without boiling.

Preparation time: 20 minutes
Cooking time: 30 minutes
Servings: 6

Glorified Zucchini

4 to 6 c. zucchini, thinly sliced
1/2 lb. fresh mushrooms, sliced
2 stalks celery, sliced
1 onion, sliced
1/2 c. water
1/2 tsp. dried thyme
1/8 tsp. ground pepper
1 tsp. Mrs. Dash

Place zucchini, mushrooms, celery, onion, water, and Mrs. Dash in large saucepan.

Add the thyme and pepper.

Simmer, covered, 15 to 20 minutes or until tender.

Preparation time: 15 minutes
Cooking time: 20 minutes
Servings: 4 to 6

Zucchini Casserole

4 c. zucchini, sliced about 1/4 inch thick

1 onion, thinly sliced

1 jar (4 oz.) chopped pimientos

1/2 tsp. oregano leaves

1 tsp. basil

1 can (16 oz.) tomato sauce

Salt and pepper to taste

Place zucchini in the bottom of a medium baking dish.

Separate onion into rings and lay over zucchini.

Spoon the pimientos over the top of the onions and zucchini.

Sprinkle herbs over this; pour the tomato sauce over all and salt and pepper to taste.

Cover and bake at 375 degrees for 30 minutes.

Preparation time: 15 minutes
Baking time: 30 minutes
Servings: 6

Vegetable Stir Fry

Several Tbsp. water
1 onion, layers separated and
   cut in 1-inch squares
1 c. broccoli florets
1/2 c. cauliflower florets
1 carrot, cut in 1/8-inch thick
   slices, parboiled
1 c. snow peas, washed and
   trimmed
1/2 c. fresh mushrooms, sliced
1/2 c. celery, sliced diagonally
1 small can water chestnuts,
   drained
2 or 3 garlic cloves, minced
1-inch fresh ginger, peeled and
   minced
2 Tbsp. cornstarch
1/2 c. water
1/2 c. low sodium soy sauce
Several green onions cut in
   1-inch pieces and sliced
   lengthwise, for topping

Place water and onion in heated
wok or skillet and cook until
onion is transparent.

Add broccoli and cauliflower,
cover and steam for 2 minutes.

Add remaining vegetables; stir
constantly for few minutes. Do
not overcook.

Mix cornstarch, water and soy
sauce and add to vegetables,
stirring constantly.

Add more soy sauce if needed
to make sauce desired
consistency.

Sprinkle green onions on top
and serve immediately over hot,
cooked brown rice.

Preparation time; 30 minutes
Cooking time: 10 minutes
Servings: 6

Vegetable Stew

A super healthy combination of plant foods.

5 potatoes, peeled and chopped
4 onions, chopped
4 or 5 carrots, sliced
4 or 5 stalks celery, chopped
1 large can (46 oz.) tomato
juice
1 large can (28 oz.) tomatoes,
cut up
1/2 bag frozen okra
1 c. barley
1 1/2 c. frozen corn
1 c. frozen peas

In a large kettle, combine first seven ingredients. Bring to boil; lower heat and simmer about 30 minutes.

In the meantime, cook the barley according to instructions on box.

Add barley, corn and peas to soup mixture and simmer 15 minutes more. Don't overcook.

Can be stored in refrigerator 1 week, or frozen, as desired.

Preparation time: 25 minutes
Cooking time: 50 minutes
Servings: 6 quarts

Vegetable Chop Suey

1/4 c. water
2 garlic cloves, crushed
2 medium onions, chopped
2 stalks celery, sliced
   diagonally
1/4 lb. broccoli, chopped
1/4 lb. mushrooms, sliced
3 c. water
1 c. snow peas
1/2 c. green onions, sliced in
   one inch pieces
1 c. bean sprouts
3 Tbsp. low sodium tamari
   (soy sauce)
5 or 6 Tbsp. cornstarch
1/2 c. water
5 c. cooked brown rice

Put 1/4 c. water in a large pot, add crushed garlic, onions, celery, broccoli, and mushrooms; saute about 5 minutes.

Add 3 cups water, snow peas, green onions, bean sprouts, and tamari. Bring to a boil and cook about 10 minutes.

Dissolve cornstarch in 1/2 cup cold water. Remove pot from heat.

Gradually add cornstarch mixture, stirring well. Return to heat and stir until thickened.

Serve immediately over brown rice.

Preparation time: 20 minutes
Cooking time: 30 minutes
Servings: 6

Stir Fry with TVP

TVP Preparation
1 cup water
2 teaspoons beef bouillon
1 cup TVP beef-style strips

Remaining Ingredients
1 tablespoon cornstarch
3 tablespoons rice vinegar
1/4 cup lite soy sauce
1/4 cup water
1/2 tablespoon sugar
1/4 teaspoon red pepper
1/2 teaspoon ground ginger
1 clove garlic, minced
1 pound fresh broccoli, sliced
1 cup fresh cauliflower, sliced
1 white onion, sliced
2 stalks celery, sliced
1/2 red beel pepper, julienned
1/2 green bell pepper, julienned

Optional Ingredients
1 can (5 oz.) water chestnuts,
    drained
1 can mushrooms (4 oz.)
2 cups bean sprouts (fresh)

In a small sauce pan, bring 1 cup water to a boil. Add TVP and beef bullion. Remove from heat and let stand 10 minutes.

Prepare vegetables before starting to cook. Combine rice vinegar, soy sauce, 1/4 cup water, sugar, red pepper and cornstarch, mix well and set aside.

In a wok or large skillet pour 1/4 cup water. Stir in ginger and garlic and saute for one minute. Add TVP, broccoli and cauliflower and continue cooking for 3 minutes. Add onion, celery and bell pepper. Cook 3 more minutes. Add cornstarch mixture, continue cooking for 3 minutes. Add any or all optional ingredients and cook one more minute. Serve immediately. Serve with rice for a complete meal.

Preparation time: 30 minutes
Cooking time: 10 minutes
Servings: 4-6

Note: TVP - Soy bean product, 4% fat.
Replaces meat, high in protein, 52%
Available from: Harvest Direct, P.O. Box 4514,
Decatur, IL 62525, 1(800) 835-2867

For a complete explanation of the cause of degenerative diseases and how to change your lifestyle to prevent or reverse disease — read Earl Updike's companion book (with the bright yellow cover).

**"THE MIRACLE DIET —
14 DAYS TO NEW VIGOR AND HEALTH."**

SIDE DISHES

The Miracle Diet

The Miracle Diet is a plant-centered diet program that allows your body to seek its ideal weight with natural, high energy. It is based upon plants, not vegetables. The five basic starches are the basis of the diet.

- **Grain**   (wheat, oats, and barley)
- **Rice**   (a basic grain)
- **Corn**   (a basic grain)
- **Legumes** (beans, peas, and lentils)
- **Potatoes** (the only vegetable)

Beets with Orange Sauce

1/3 c. sugar
1 Tbsp. cornstarch
1/2 c. orange juice
2 tsp. orange peel, grated
2 cans (16 oz.) sliced beets,
   drained

In a medium saucepan, mix sugar and cornstarch; add orange juice and orange peel.

Cook over medium heat, stirring constantly, until mixture thickens and begins to boil.

Add beets and return to boil.

Remove from heat and let stand at least 30 minutes.

Just before serving, reheat thoroughly.

Preparation time: 10 minutes
Cooking time: 15 minutes
Marinating time: 30 minutes
Servings: 8 to 10

Pickled Beets
(Chinese Style)

1 can (16 oz.) sliced beets, drained, reserve liquid
1/3 c. sugar
1/3 c. cider vinegar
2 tsp. cornstarch
8 whole cloves
1 Tbsp. catsup
1/3 tsp. vanilla
1/2 c. beet juice
Dash of salt (optional)

Mix all ingredients in a small saucepan and cook 3 minutes over medium heat, or until the mixture thickens.

Cool and store in refrigerator. Recipe can easily be increased. Simple, yet delicious.

Use as a side dish, add to salads.

Preparation time: 10 minutes
Cooking time: 10 minutes
Servings: 2

Beets
(Harvard Style)

1/2 c. sugar
1 Tbsp. cornstarch
1/3 c. beet juice
1/4 c. apple cider vinegar
2 cans (16 oz.) beets, sliced or
cubed

Mix sugar and cornstarch in a medium saucepan.

Add beet juice and vinegar and cook over medium heat, stirring constantly. Boil 5 minutes.

Add beets to hot sauce and let stand 30 minutes.

Return to boiling just before serving.

Preparation time: 10 minutes
Cooking time: 15 minutes
Marinating time: 30 minutes
Servings: 8 to 10

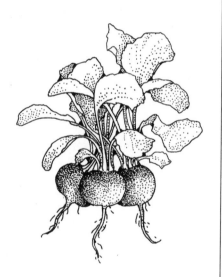

Beets
(Norwegian Sweet and Sour Style)
Serve hot or cold.

2 lbs. (about 10) medium-size
    fresh beets or 2 cans
    (16 oz.) canned sliced beets
    and liquid
2 to 3 qts. water
2 to 3 tsp. salt (optional)
2 c. reserved beet liquid
1/4 c. vinegar
1/4 c. sugar
1 tsp. salt (optional)
1/2 tsp. caraway seeds
10 whole cloves
8 drops red food coloring
    (optional)
1 Tbsp. cornstarch
1/4 c. water

Cut leaves off beets, leave short stem. Scrub thoroughly.

In a large kettle, add water, about 2 inches deep (2 to 3 quarts) and salt (1/4 teaspoon per cup of water); bring to boil and add beets. Water should cover beets roots; if more is needed, add boiling water. Bring water back to boiling as quickly as possible; reduce heat, cover and boil at a moderate rate until beets are tender, 30 to 45 min.

Drain and reserve liquid in measuring cup. Plunge beets into running cold water. Peel off and discard skin, stem and root end from beets. Cut beets into thin slices and set aside.

In a large saucepan, mix beet liquid, vinegar, sugar, salt, caraway seeds, cloves, and food coloring. Blend the cornstarch and water together in a cup to form a smooth past. Mix into mixture in saucepan. Bring rapidly to boiling. Reduce heat and cook 3 to 5 minutes, or until thickened, stirring constantly. Add beets and cook until heated thoroughly.

Preparation time: fresh beets—
25 minutes canned beets—
10 minutes.
Cooking time: fresh beets—
1 1/4 hours canned beets—
25 minutes
Servings: 6

Cabbage Special

1/3 c. apple juice
1 Tbsp. lemon juice
2 Tbsp. honey or corn syrup
4 c. cabbage, shredded
3 medium onions, diced
2 cooking apples, diced
1/4 c. raisins
1/4 tsp. Mrs. Dash

In a large saucepan, heat first 3 ingredients to boiling.

Add all other ingredients.

Return to boil, lower heat and simmer 10 to 12 minutes until barely tender.

Preparation time: 15 minutes
Cooking time: 15 minutes
Servings: 4 to 6

Cabbage Stir Fry

4 c. cabbage, shredded
1 green pepper, thinly sliced
2 large onions, thinly sliced
2 large tomatoes, cut into thin
　wedges
Salt and pepper to taste

Combine vegetables and toss lightly into 2 Tbsp water.

Saute with salt and pepper over medium heat, about 10 minutes, stirring twice during cooking period.

Preparation time: 15 minutes
Cooking time: 10 minutes
Servings: 6 to 8

Cabbage Sautéed

1 small head green cabbage, chopped
1/4 c. water
3 Tbsp. fresh lemon juice
Salt to taste (optional)
Freshly ground pepper to taste

In a large skillet, heat water; add cabbage.

Saute, stirring frequently, about 10 minutes, or until cabbage is crisp-tender.

Sprinkle with lemon juice; add salt and pepper to taste, or seasonings of your choice.

Toss to mix and serve immediately.

Preparation time: 10 minutes
Cooking time: 10 to 12 minutes
Servings: 4

Red Cabbage
(Spiced Style)

4 c. red cabbage, shredded

2 onions, thinly sliced

1 medium apple, sliced

1 small potato, thinly sliced

1/2 c. water

1/2 tsp. salt (optional)

2 Tbsp. apple cider vinegar

1/4 c. sugar

1/4 tsp. cloves

1/8 tsp. pepper

In a large saucepan, combine cabbage, onions, apple and potato in boiling salted water; cover, reduce heat and simmer until tender, 12 to 15 minutes.

Drain and combine with remaining ingredients. Serve immediately.

Preparation time: 15 minutes
Cooking time: 15 minutes
Servings: 4

Note: Green cabbage may be substituted. Either kind of cabbage makes an appropriate Christmas dish.

Cabbage
(St. Patrick's Style)

1 small head (1 1/4 lb.) green cabbage
1 bay leaf
1 small onion, thinly sliced
1 tsp. dry dill weed
1 carrot, coarsely grated
2/3 c. defatted chicken stock

Cut cabbage into 8 wedges. Arrange in 2 concentric circles in a 9-inch pie dish. (Dish will be quite full.)

Tuck bay leaf under the cabbage.

Sprinkle on the onion, dill and carrot; pour stock over all.

Cover plate with vented plastic wrap.

Microwave on High 4 minutes. Rotate dish 1/2 turn. Microwave 4 minutes more.

Let stand, covered, about 5 minutes. Serve warm.

Preparation time: 10 minutes
Microwave time: 8 minutes
Servings: 4

Carrots
(California Orange Style)

1 lb. carrots, peeled and sliced 1/4 inch thick
1/2 tsp. salt (optional)
3/4 c. water
1 tsp. orange peel, grated
1 orange, peeled, sectioned and cut in bite-size pieces
1 Tbsp. green onion, minced (optional)
Butter Buds, sprinkle

In a large saucepan, cook carrots, covered in salted water until crisp-tender, about 20 minutes.

Drain.

Add orange peel, orange sections and onion.

Sprinkle with Butter Buds.

Heat through.

Serve immediately.

Preparation time: 20 minutes
Cooking time: 25 minutes
Servings: 6

Carrots
(Glazed Style)

8 large carrots, thinly sliced
1/4 c. undiluted frozen apple juice, thawed
1 Tbsp. orange rind, grated
1 tsp. cornstarch
1/8 tsp. ground cloves

Steam carrots over boiling water for 15 minutes or until tender.

Combine apple juice, orange rind, cornstarch and cloves in a large saucepan.

Mix until smooth, then cook and stir constantly until mixture has thickened and cleared.

Add the cooked carrots to the sauce.

Serve hot.

Preparation time: 20 minutes
Cooking time: 30 minutes
Servings: 6 to 8

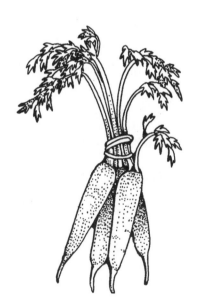

Carrots
(Herbed Style)

4 c. carrots, sliced
1/2 c. onion, minced
2 Tbsp. rice vinegar
1 tsp. basil
2 or more garlic cloves, minced
Salt to taste (optional)

In a medium saucepan, blanch carrots in boiling water for 2 minutes.

To blanch, place carrots in boiling water; return to boil and time 2 minutes.

Plunge immediately into cold water to stop cooking.

Drain and add onion, vinegar and herbs.

Use any other herbs of your choice. Experiment!

Preparation time: 10 minutes
Blanching time: 5 minutes
Cooking time: 5 minutes
Servings: 4 to 6

Carrots
(Sweet and Sour Style)

1 lb. carrots, peeled and diagonally sliced
1 medium green pepper, chopped
1/3 c. sugar or brown sugar
1 tsp. cornstarch
1/2 tsp. salt (optional)
1 can (8-oz.) pineapple chunks
2 tsp. apple cider vinegar
2 tsp. soy sauce, low sodium

In large saucepan, cook carrots, covered, in a small amount of boiling water until tender.

Add green pepper; cook 3 minutes.

Drain; set aside.

Combine sugar, cornstarch, and salt in a medium-sized saucepan.

Drain pineapple and reserve juice.

Add water to juice to make 1/3 c. liquid; stir into sugar mixture.

Stir in vinegar and soy sauce; cook over low heat until bubbly, stirring constantly.

Stir into vegetables and add pineapple; cook until heated throughout.

Preparation time: 20 minutes
Cooking time: 30 minutes

Corn
(Seasoned Style)

3 c. frozen corn, thawed
1 jar (2 oz.) pimientos
1 can (4 oz.) chopped green
   chilies

Cook together in medium
saucepan for about 5 minutes.

Preparation time: 5 minutes
Cooking time: 5 minutes
Servings: 4

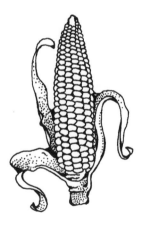

Corn Salad
(Fiesta Style)

1 can whole-kernel corn, drained

1 c. fresh tomato, chopped

1 c. cucumber, peeled and
  chopped

1/2 c. celery, chopped

1/2 c. green or sweet red
  pepper, diced

2 green onions, sliced

1/2 c. bottled fat free Italian
  salad dressing

Combine all ingredients.

Chill several hours before serving.

Preparation time: 20 minutes
Chilling time: several hours
Servings: 4 to 6

Breaded Mushrooms Deluxe

1 lb. fresh mushrooms, sliced
5 slices whole wheat bread, crumbled
4 egg whites, beaten
2 tsp. Mrs. Dash

Wash mushrooms.

Dip the sliced mushrooms into the beaten egg whites and place on a lightly sprayed nonstick cookie sheet.

Combine Mrs. Dash seasoning with the bread crumbs; sprinkle over the mushrooms.

Bake in 350 degree oven for 20 minutes or until tender and crisp.

Preparation time: 15 minutes
Baking time: 20 minutes
Servings: 6 to 8

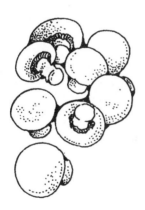

Okra Tomato Bake

3 c. fresh okra, sliced,
  or 2 c. frozen cut okra
1 c. tomato juice or tomatoes,
  chopped
1 medium onion, chopped
1/4 tsp. oregano
1/4 tsp. garlic powder
1/4 tsp. Mrs. Dash
Dash of pepper
1 c. whole wheat bread crumbs

In a medium bowl, combine all ingredients except bread crumbs.

Place in 1 1/2-quart nonstick baking dish and sprinkle with bread crumbs.

Bake in a 350 degree oven for 45 minutes.

Preparation time: 5 minutes with frozen okra,
 15 minutes with fresh okra
Baking time: 45 minutes
Servings: 4

Garden Medley

1/4 c. liquid Butter Buds (mix
  1/2 packet Butter Buds in
1/4 c. hot tap water)
2 medium zucchini squash, cut
  in julienne strips
1 sweet red pepper,
  cut in julienne strips
1 green pepper,
  cut in julienne strips
1 yellow pepper,
  cut in julienne strips
1/2 tsp. seasoned salt (optional)
Dash pepper

In a large skillet, heat liquid Butter Buds.

Saute vegetables until crisp-tender.

Season with salt and pepper, or seasonings of choice.

Preparation time: 20 minutes
Cooking time: 10 minutes
Servings: 4 to 6

For a complete explanation of the cause of degenerative diseases and how to change your lifestyle to prevent or reverse disease — read Earl Updike's companion book (with the bright yellow cover).

"THE MIRACLE DIET — 14 DAYS TO NEW VIGOR AND HEALTH."

SOUPS

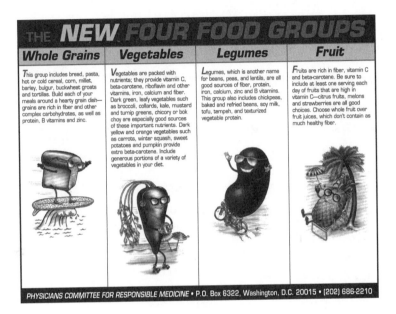

THE NEW FOUR FOOD GROUPS

Whole Grains	Vegetables	Legumes	Fruit
This group includes bread, pasta, hot or cold cereal, corn, millet, barley, bulgur, buckwheat groats and tortillas. Build each of your meals around a hearty grain dish—grains are rich in fiber and other complex carbohydrates, as well as protein, B vitamins and zinc.	Vegetables are packed with nutrients; they provide vitamin C, beta-carotene, riboflavin and other vitamins, iron, calcium and fiber. Dark green, leafy vegetables such as broccoli, collards, kale, mustard and turnip greens, chicory or bok choy are especially good sources of these important nutrients. Dark yellow and orange vegetables such as carrots, winter squash, sweet potatoes and pumpkin provide extra beta-carotene. Include generous portions of a variety of vegetables in your diet.	Legumes, which is another name for beans, peas, and lentils, are all good sources of fiber, protein, iron, calcium, zinc and B vitamins. This group also includes chickpeas, baked and refried beans, soy milk, tofu, tempeh, and texturized vegetable protein.	Fruits are rich in fiber, vitamin C and beta-carotene. Be sure to include at least one serving each day of fruits that are high in vitamin C—citrus fruits, melons and strawberries are all good choices. Choose whole fruit over fruit juices, which don't contain as much healthy fiber.

PHYSICIANS COMMITTEE FOR RESPONSIBLE MEDICINE • P.O. Box 6322, Washington, D.C. 20015 • (202) 686-2210

It's truly a miracle!

- Prevent heart-artery disease
- Reverse heart disease
- Reverse adult diabetes
- Prevent adult diabetes
- Lower blood pressure
- Lose weight permanently
- Prevent many cancers
- Prevent Osteoporosis

Barley Mushroom Soup

6 c. mushrooms, sliced
1 c. celery, diced
1 c. carrots, finely diced
2 large onions, diced
4 c. cooked barley
4 c. defatted beef broth
4 c. water
1/2 tsp. garlic powder
1/2 tsp. thyme
1 tsp. basil leaves
1 tsp. parsley flakes
1 tsp. dill weed
1/4 tsp. chili powder
1 tsp. salt (optional)
1 tsp. Mrs. Dash
1 tsp. oregano
4 tsp. Worcestershire sauce

In large kettle, saute vegetables in 1 cup water until crisp tender.

Add all remaining ingredients and simmer at least 1 hour.

Preparation time: 20 minutes
Cooking time: 1 1/4 hours
Servings: 10 to 12

Bean with Vegetables Soup

1 c. great northern beans
or any dried white beans of
   choice
6 c. water
2 tsp. low sodium instant
chicken bouillon
2 carrots, sliced
1 medium onion, chopped
1 stalk celery, diced
2 ripe tomatoes, diced
1/2 small head cabbage,
chopped (about 4 cups)
1 Tbsp. basil or parsley leaves
Salt to taste (optional)
Pepper to taste

Sort and wash beans.

In a large kettle, boil beans in water 2 minutes.

Remove from heat, cover and soak 1 hour.

Return to boil; reduce heat, cover and simmer 1 hour or until beans are tender.

Add vegetables and simmer 12 to 15 minutes longer.

Stir in basil or parsley, salt and pepper.

Preparation time: 20 minutes
Bean cook and soak: 1 hour and 5 minutes
Cooking time: 1 1/4 hours
Servings: 6 to 8

Black Bean Soup

2 c. black beans
6 to 8 c. water
2 Tbsp. red wine vinegar
1/2 tsp. dried thyme
1/2 tsp. dried oregano
2 Tbsp. low sodium soy sauce
2 onions, chopped
1 garlic clove, minced
2 c. tomatoes, chopped
1 c. celery, chopped
1 Tbsp. jalapeno pepper,
   minced
1/2 c. green onion, chopped
2 Tbsp. salsa (see recipes)

Sort and wash beans.

Combine beans and water in a large pot; bring to a boil, cover and boil 2 minutes.

Remove from heat and soak for 1 hour.

Return to boil, reduce heat and simmer 1 hour.

Add all seasonings and vegetables except green onions and salsa.

Simmer 1 hour longer or until beans are tender.

Serve hot with garnish of green onions and salsa.

Preparation time: 20 minutes
Soaking time: 1 hour
Cooking time: 2 hours
Servings: 10 cups

Shaker Bean Soup

This soup tastes especially good in cold weather.

1 lb. dry great northern beans
3 qts. water
2 tsp. low sodium beef bouillon
  granules
1 large onion, chopped
3 celery stalks, diced
2 carrots, shredded
Salt to taste (optional)
1/2 tsp. pepper
1/2 tsp. dried thyme
1 can (28 oz.) tomatoes,
blended to puree
2 Tbsp. brown sugar
1 1/2 c. fresh spinach leaves,
  finely shredded

Sort and rinse beans. Place in a Dutch oven or soup kettle; cover with water and bring to a boil.

Boil 2 minutes; remove from heat, cover and let stand 1 hour.

Drain beans and discard liquid. Add 3 quarts water.

Bring to a boil; reduce heat and simmer, covered, 1 hour or until tender.

Add bouillon, onion, celery, carrots, salt, pepper and thyme. Simmer, covered, 30 minutes or until beans are tender.

Add tomatoes and brown sugar.

Cook for 10 minutes.

Before serving, add spinach and cook for another 5 minutes.

Preparation time: 15 minutes
Bean soak: 1 hour
Cooking time: 1 hour and 45 minutes
Servings: 15 to 20

Speedy Bean Soup

(Use only beans with no added fat)

2 cans (16 oz.) fat-free lima beans
3 cans (15 oz.) great northern or navy beans, undrained
2 cans (15 oz.) pinto beans, undrained
1 can (4 oz.) chopped green chilies
1 medium onion, finely chopped
1/2 to 3/4 tsp. Tabasco sauce
1/2 tsp. garlic powder
1/4 tsp. pepper
1 can (15 oz.) tomato sauce

In a large Dutch oven or soup kettle, combine all ingredients. Simmer about 20 minutes.

Preparation time: 15 minutes
Cooking time: 20 minutes
Servings: 12 to 15

Wintry Day Bean Soup

2 c. mixed dry beans (great
   northern, navy, black,
   garbanzo, green split peas,
   pinto and red beans)
2 qts. water
1 large onion, chopped
1 garlic clove, minced
1 tsp. chili powder
1 can (28 oz.) tomatoes,
   chopped
1 to 2 Tbsp. lemon juice
Salt to taste (optional)
Pepper to taste

Sort and rinse beans; place in
large kettle with water and boil
2 minutes.

Cover, remove from heat and let
stand 1 hour.

Add onion, garlic, chili powder
and tomatoes and simmer 45
minutes or until tender.

Add lemon juice, salt and
pepper and simmer about 30
minutes longer.

Preparation time: 15 minutes
Bean soak: 1 hour
Cooking time: 1 1/4 hours
Servings: 8

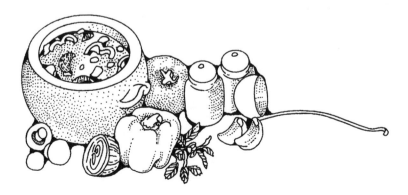

Red Bean Stew
(Mexican Style)

1 c. water
3/4 c. celery, chopped
3/4 c. green pepper, chopped
1 c. onion, chopped
2 garlic cloves, minced
1 can (28 oz.) tomatoes,
    chopped
2 cans (15 oz.) red kidney
    beans, drained
1/4 c. raisins
1 Tbsp. red wine vinegar
1 1/2 tsp. chili powder
1 1/2 tsp. parsley
3/4 tsp. basil
3/4 tsp. oregano
3/4 tsp. ground cumin
1/2 tsp. ground allspice
1/8 tsp. pepper
1/8 tsp. bottled hot pepper
    sauce
1 bay leaf

Heat water in a Dutch oven; add celery, green pepper, onion and garlic; saute 5 minutes.

Stir in the remaining ingredients.

Bring to a boil; then reduce the heat and simmer covered for 1 hour.

Uncover and simmer an additional 30 minutes or until the stew is the desired consistency.

Remove bay leaf before serving.

Preparation time: 15 minutes
Cooking time: 1 hour and 35
 minutes
Servings: 6

Chili

2 1/2 c. dried pinto, navy or
   great northern beans
1 c. brown rice
7 1/2 c. water
2 green peppers, chopped
3 onions, chopped
1 Tbsp. low-sodium soy sauce
1 can (28 oz.) tomatoes,
   chopped, or 2 c. fresh
   tomatoes, chopped
6 garlic cloves, crushed
3 tsp. chili powder
1 tsp. cumin (optional)
1 c. corn kernels

Note: Soaking beans overnight cuts
down on cooking time. Or, you may
wish to bring beans and water to a boil,
cover and boil 2 minutes; remove from
heat and let stand 1 hour. Then add
remaining ingredients except corn and
simmer 1 hour, then continue as above.

Place beans, rice, and water in a
large pot.

Cover and cook over fairly low
heat, about 1 1/2 hours.

The vegetables, spices, and
tomatoes can be prepared while
the beans and rice are beginning
to cook.

After 90 minutes, add
remaining ingredients to the
pot, except corn kernels.

Cook 2 more hours; uncover
during the last 30 minutes of
cooking and add the corn
kernals.

Can be cooked longer than 3
1/2 hours if desired.

Makes excellent leftovers;
spoon into pita bread or over
corn chips.

Preparation time: 30 minutes
Cooking time: 3 1/2 hours
Servings: 8

Yummy Bean Soup

2 c. 10-bean soup mix*
6 c. water
1 can (28 oz.) tomatoes,
   chopped
2 onions, chopped
1 garlic clove, minced,
   or 1/2 tsp. garlic powder
1/2 tsp. pepper
2 tsp. salt (optional)
   or 1 1/2 tsp. Mrs. Dash

*You can also make your own
10-bean mix.*

Suggested varieties are 2 cups
each:

Pinto beans	Lima beans
Navy beans	Garbanzo beans
Kidney beans	Great northern beans
Blackeyed peas	Green split peas
Black beans	Yellow split peas

Sort and wash beans. Mix in a large
container and store unused beans in
refrigerator or freezer.

Place beans and water in a large
kettle.

Bring to a boil; cover and boil 2
minutes.

Remove from heat and let stand
1 hour.

Add all other ingredients.

Return to boil; reduce heat and
simmer 1 1/2 hours.

Preparation time: 15 minutes
Bean soak: 1 hour
Cooking time: 1 1/2 hours
Servings: 8

Palouse Chili Verde
(Soup)

1 lb. green split peas	Sort and rinse peas; place in a Dutch oven with water, bouillon, pepper flakes, garlic, onions, cumin and oregano.
6 c. water	
4 tsp. low sodium instant chicken bouillon	
1/2 tsp. pepper flakes	Heat to boiling.
4 garlic cloves, minced	
2 large onions, chopped	Reduce heat to simmer, cover and simmer until peas are tender, about 30 minutes.
1 Tbsp. ground cumin	
1 Tbsp. ground oregano	
2 to 3 medium green peppers, chopped	Add green peppers and green chilies and simmer 10 minutes more.
2 cans (4 oz.) chopped green chilies	
Salt to taste (optional)	Add salt and pepper to taste.
Pepper to taste	
1/2 c. fresh parsley, chopped	Top each serving with chopped parsley.

Preparation time: 20 minutes
Cooking time: 40 minutes
Servings: 6

Taco Soup

1/4 c. water

1 small onion, chopped

3 cans (4 oz.) chopped green
    chilies

1 tsp. salt (optional)

1 tsp. pepper

1 can (15 oz.) pinto beans,
    rinsed and drained

1 can (16 oz.) lima beans,
    rinsed and drained

1 can (14 1/2 oz.) hominy,
    drained

3 cans (14 1/2 oz.) stewed
    tomatoes

1 can (15 oz.) red kidney
    beans, rinsed and drained

1 pkg. (1 1/4 oz.) taco
    seasoning

1 1/2 c. water

Tortilla chips (optional, see
recipes. No fat chips are
available in health food stores
and supermarkets.

Try Tostitos baked with no
added fat.)

In a large soup kettle, saute
onion in water until tender.

Add all ingredients except
chips; bring to a boil.

Reduce heat and simmer 30
minutes.

Serve with tortilla chips, if
desired.

Preparation time: 15 minutes
Cooking time: 40 minutes
Servings: 10 to 15

Blackeyed Pea Chowder

1 c. water
1 c. celery, chopped
1 c. onion, chopped
1 c. green pepper, chopped
2 cans (16 oz.) blackeyed peas,
    rinsed and drained
1 can (10 1/2 oz.) defatted beef
    consommé
2 cans (14 1/2 oz.) stewed
    tomatoes

In a large saucepan, saute celery, onion and green pepper in water 5 minutes.

Add all remaining ingredients; heat thoroughly.

Preparation time: 10 minutes
Cooking time: 20 minutes
Servings: 8 to 9

Broccoli Soup

1 lb. broccoli, coarsely
  chopped
3 cans (10 1/2 oz.) low sodium
  chicken broth, defatted
1 small onion, quartered
1/4 tsp. black pepper
1/2 c. fat-free soy milk

In a large saucepan, over medium heat, bring broccoli, broth, onion and pepper to a boil.

Reduce heat; cover. Simmer 30 minutes or until vegetables are tender.

Pour half the broccoli mixture into electric blender container; blend until smooth.

Repeat with remaining broccoli mixture.

Return to saucepan; stir in milk.

Cook and stir over medium-high heat until hot.

Preparation time: 10 minutes
Cooking time: 45 to 50 minutes
Servings: 5

Cream of Broccoli Soup

4 medium potatoes, peeled and diced

10 c. water

2 medium onions, diced

1/4 tsp. garlic powder

1/2 tsp. parsley flakes

1 tsp. salt (optional)

1/4 tsp. black pepper

2 tsp. Butter Buds

**1/2 tsp. celery flakes or
 1 Tbsp. celery leaves, minced**

1/4 to 1/2 tsp. curry powder

1/2 c. flour

1 c. water

**1 bag (16 oz.) frozen chopped
 broccoli**

Combine first 10 ingredients in large kettle.

Bring to a boil and cook on medium heat until potatoes are very soft, about 30 minutes.

Mash well. In a pint jar, add flour and water; cover and shake vigorously until smooth.

Stir into broth and simmer until thickened.

Add broccoli; cover and simmer over medium heat 12 to 15 minutes.

Preparation time: 20 minutes
Cooking time: 45 minutes
Servings: 10 to 12

Cabbage Soup

8 c. water
1 c. onion, chopped
3 carrots, chopped
2 garlic cloves, minced
1 bay leaf
1 tsp. dried leaf thyme
1/2 tsp. paprika
8 c. cabbage, coarsely chopped
   (1 head)
2 cans (16 oz.) tomatoes,
   chopped
2 tsp. salt (optional)
1/2 to 3/4 tsp. Tabasco sauce
1/4 c. parsley, chopped
3 Tbsp. lemon juice
3 Tbsp. sugar
1 can (16 oz.) sauerkraut

In a large soup kettle, add 2 cups water, onion, carrots, garlic, bay leaf, thyme and paprika.

Bring to boil, reduce heat and simmer 20 minutes.

Add remaining 6 cups water, cabbage, tomatoes, salt and Tabasco.

Bring to boil. Cover; simmer 1 hour.

Add parsley, lemon juice, sugar and sauerkraut.

Cook uncovered for 30 minutes longer.

Preparation time: 20 minutes
Cooking time: 1 hour and 50 minutes
Servings: 12

Carrot Soup
(Creamy Style)

1/4 c. water
3 medium leeks, thoroughly
   rinsed and thinly sliced
   (white part only)
1 lb. carrots, thinly sliced
1/2 lb. small long white
   potatoes, quartered
1 large stalk celery, thinly
   sliced
5 c. chicken broth, defatted
1 1/2 tsp. dried tarragon
   leaves, crushed
Salt to taste (optional)
1/4 tsp. white pepper, or to
   taste
1/4 c. watercress, finely
   chopped, or a few
   additional flecks dried
   tarragon to garnish

In heavy soup kettle saute leeks in water 2 minutes.

Add carrots, potatoes, celery, stock, tarragon, salt and pepper.

Bring to a boil, cover and cook over medium heat until carrots are very soft (about 20 minutes).

In blender or food processor, puree soup in batches.

Return soup to kettle to reheat before serving.

Garnish with watercress or tarragon.

Preparation time: 15 minutes
Cooking time: 30 minutes
Servings: 6

Corn Soup

1 medium onion, chopped
1 bell pepper, chopped
1/2 c. water
1/2 tsp. ground cumin
1/2 tsp. garlic powder
1/4 tsp. dried minced garlic
1 can (2 oz.) green chilies,
    diced
1 jar (2 oz.) chopped pimientos
1 can (16 oz.) tomatoes,
    drained and chopped
1/2 tsp. salt (optional)
4 c. defatted chicken broth
2 Tbsp. cornstarch in
    1/4 c. water
4 c. frozen corn, thawed

In a large saucepan, saute onion
and pepper in water about 5
minutes.

Add spices, vegetables and salt;
bring to a boil.

Cover, reduce heat and simmer
15 minutes.

Add broth and thicken with
cornstarch mixture.

Add corn and simmer 10
minutes.

Preparation time: 15 minutes
Cooking time: 30 minutes
Servings: 10 to 12

Corn Soup
(Creamy Style)

4 c. frozen corn, thawed
4 c. fat-free soy milk
4 Tbsp. cornstarch or 4 Tbsp.
  flour
1/2 tsp. dill weed
1/4 tsp. black pepper
1 tsp. Mrs. Dash

Put the corn in a food processor and process it until slightly chopped.

Empty the corn into a large saucepan.

In a pint jar, place 1 cup of milk and cornstarch or flour.

Cover tightly; shake vigorously to mix thoroughly.

Add to corn along with the remaining milk and seasonings.

Over medium heat, cook 7 to 10 minutes until thickened.

Preparation time: 15 minutes
Cooking time: 15 minutes
Servings: 4 to 6

Four Grain Soup

2/3 c. lentils
1/4 c. barley
1/2 c. whole wheat berries
1/2 c. brown rice
10 c. water
1 Tbsp. onion powder
1 tsp. basil leaves
1/4 c. parsley flakes
1 1/2 tsp. garlic powder
1/2 tsp. cumin
1 1/2 c. onion, chopped
1/2 c. carrots, sliced
1/2 c. celery, sliced
1/2 c. potatoes, cubed
1 c. frozen peas
1 c. frozen corn kernels
3 Tbsp. low sodium soy sauce

In a large soup kettle, place the grains, water, herbs and spices.

Bring to a boil and cook over medium heat for 1 hour.

Add the fresh vegetables and cook an additional 30 minutes.

Add the frozen vegetables and cook 10 minutes longer.

Stir in soy sauce.

Preparation time: 30 minutes
Cooking time: 1 1/2 hours
Servings: 8 to 10

Lentil Vegetable Stew

2 c. dry lentils
3/4 c. uncooked brown rice
1 can (28 oz.) tomatoes,
    chopped
1 can (48 oz.) tomato or
    vegetable juice
4 c. water
3 garlic cloves, minced
1 large onion, chopped
2 celery stalks, chopped
3 carrots, sliced
1 bay leaf
1 tsp. dried basil
1 tsp. dried oregano
1 tsp. dried thyme
1/2 tsp. pepper
3 Tbsp. fresh parsley, minced
1 zucchini, sliced
2 medium potatoes, peeled and
    diced
2 Tbsp. lemon juice
1 tsp. dry mustard
Salt to taste (optional)

In a 6-quart Dutch oven or soup kettle, combine first 15 ingredients.

Bring to a boil. Reduce heat and simmer, covered, until rice and lentils are tender, 45 to 60 minutes.

Add additional water or tomato juice if necessary.

Stir in all the remaining ingredients.

Cover and continue to cook until vegetables are tender, about 30 minutes.

Remove bay leaf and serve.

Preparation time: 20 minutes
Cooking time: 1 1/2 hours
Servings 15 to 20

Lentil Soup

Even better the next day.

2-1/2 c. lentils (1 lb.)
2 onions, chopped
2 cloves garlic, crushed
2 stalks celery, chopped
1 tsp. dry parsley
1 - 16 oz. can tomatoes, pureed

Cook lentils in 2 quarts of boiling, salted water for 1 hour.

Chop onion, garlic, and celery, put into saucepan with parsley, and tomatoes.

Cook for 10 minutes. Pour into pot with lentils, cover.

Simmer 15 more minutes.

Preparation time: 20 minutes
Cooking time: 1hour 25 minutes
Servings: 6 to 8

Mushroom Barley Soup

Especially good when spirits are sagging, this wholesome soup is the perfect pick-me-up. It develops a fuller flavor when made a day or two in advance.

1 1/2 c. yellow onions, chopped
1 c. carrots, peeled and sliced
1/2 lb. mushrooms, wiped
    clean, thinly sliced
4 c. low sodium beef broth,
    defatted
1/4 c. parsley, chopped
1/2 c. barley, rinsed and
    drained
1/4 tsp. black pepper

Place all ingredients in a large heavy saucepan; bring to a boil over moderately high heat.

Lower heat so mixture bubbles gently; simmer partly covered for 40 minutes or until barley is tender.

Serve hot.

Preparation time: 20 minutes
Cooking time: 40 minutes
Servings: 4

Onion Soup

4 medium onions, chopped
1/4 c. water
2 cans (10 1/2 oz.) defatted beef
  broth (mixed with water
  as per directions; total =
  4 c.)
2 Tbsp. soy sauce, low sodium
1/2 tsp. dry mustard (optional)
Dash of thyme
1/4 tsp. garlic powder

In a medium saucepan, saute onions in water, about 5 minutes.

Add broth and seasonings.

Bring to a boil; reduce heat, and simmer, covered, for at least 30 minutes before serving to enhance the flavor.

Preparation time: 10 minutes
Cooking time: 35 minutes
Servings: 4

Onion Barley Soup

4 onions, sliced
1/2 c. water
6 c. defatted beef broth
1 c. cooked barley
2 Tbsp. soy sauce, low sodium
1/2 tsp. dry mustard
1/2 tsp. thyme leaves
1/4 tsp. garlic powder

In large saucepan, saute onions in water about 5 minutes.

Add beef broth and barley; bring to a boil.

Add seasonings; reduce heat.

Simmer, covered, about 30 minutes before serving.

Preparation time: 10 minutes
Cooking time: 35 minutes
Servings: 6

Split Pea Soup

2 c. dry split peas
2 quarts water
1 onion, finely diced
2 carrots, finely diced
1 tsp. parsley flakes
2 celery stalks, finely diced
1/4 tsp. pepper
1 bay leaf
1/4 tsp. Mrs. Dash
1/8 tsp. garlic powder

Sort and wash peas. Place peas and water in a large saucepan; cover and bring to boil for 2 minutes.

Remove from heat and let stand 1 hour.

Add remaining ingredients and simmer for 1 hour.

Discard bay leaf.

If desired, put soup through sieve or blend until smooth.

Return to saucepan and heat before serving.

Preparation time: 15 minutes
Soaking time: 1 hour
Cooking time: 1 hour
Servings: 5 to 6

Potato Chowder

4 c. potatoes, peeled and diced
1/2 c. onion, finely chopped
1 c. carrot, grated
1 tsp. salt (optional)
1/4 tsp. pepper
1 Tbsp. dried parsley flakes
4 tsp. low sodium instant chicken bouillon
6 c. fat-free soy milk
1/2 c. flour
Paprika, sprinkle

In large Dutch oven or kettle, combine potatoes, onion, carrot, salt, pepper, parsley flakes and bouillon.

Add enough water to just cover vegetables; cook until vegetables are tender, about 15 to 20 minutes.

Do not drain.

Measure 1 1/2 cups milk and add flour to milk, stirring with wire whisk.

Add remaining milk to undrained vegetables, then stir in milk mixture.

Stir until blended.

Simmer for 15 minutes on low heat and thicken.

Garnish with paprika.

Preparation time: 15 minutes
Cooking time: 45 minutes
Servings: 8 to 10

Potato Soup

6 to 8 medium potatoes, peeled
   and cubed
6 c. water
1 Tbsp. onion powder or 1
   med. onion, chopped
1/8 tsp. garlic powder
1 bay leaf
1 stalk celery, diced or 1 Tbsp.
   celery flakes
   or 1/8 tsp. celery seed
1 tsp. salt (optional)
1/8 tsp. pepper
1/8 tsp. dill weed
1/16 tsp. or dash paprika
1 tsp. parsley flakes
2 Tbsp. flour
1/2 c. water

Place potatoes and 6 cups water in large saucepan.

Add all seasonings.

Cook until very tender.

Remove 1/3 to 1/2 potatoes to a bowl and mash well.

Remove bay leaf and discard.

Return mashed potatoes to saucepan.

Heat and thicken with flour that has been mixed with 1/2 cup water in a covered jar, stirring constantly, until soup is desired consistency.

Preparation time: 15 minutes
Cooking time: 45 minutes
Servings: 6 to 8

Potato Soup
(Cream Style)

4 large potatoes, peeled diced

1 onion, diced

3 stalks celery, diced

2 c. water or defatted chicken broth

1/2 tsp. dill weed

1/2 tsp. Mrs. Dash

2 Tbsp. chives, chopped

1 c. fat-free soy milk

3 Tbsp. flour

Variations: Add 1/4 teaspoon freshly ground pepper, 1 teaspoon basil leaves, and/or 1/2 teaspoon garlic powder in addition to or instead of other herbs. Blend part of soup mixture in blender if desired.

Place potatoes, onion, celery and water in a large saucepan.

Add dill weed, Mrs. Dash and chives; simmer until potatoes are tender, about 30 minutes.

Place milk and flour in a pint jar.

Shake vigorously to mix thoroughly.

Add to potato mixture; simmer 5 to 10 minutes, or until thickened.

Preparation time: 20 minutes
Cooking time: 40 minutes
Servings: 4 to 6

Pumpkin Soup

1/4 c. green pepper, chopped
2 Tbsp. onion, chopped
1 tsp. parsley flakes or fresh
   parsley, minced
1/8 tsp. thyme leaves
1 bay leaf
1/4 c. water
1 (9 oz.) can tomatoes, diced
2 c. pumpkin or winter squash,
   cooked and mashed
2 c. water
2 low sodium chicken bouillon
   cubes
1 Tbsp. flour
2 c. fat-free soy milk
1 tsp. salt (optional)
1/8 tsp. pepper

In a Dutch oven, saute pepper, onion, parsley, thyme and bay leaf in water 5 minutes; do not brown.

Add tomatoes, pumpkin or squash, water, bouillon cubes and bring to a boil.

Reduce heat, simmer 30 minutes, stirring occasionally.

In small bowl, combine flour and milk, blend well.

Stir into soup mixture; add salt and pepper.

Cook over medium heat, stirring frequently until mixture boils.

Remove bay leaf and serve.

Preparation time: 15 minutes
Cooking time: 45 minutes
Servings: 6 to 8

Tomato Soup
(Creamy, Chilled Style)

1/2 c. water
1 medium yellow onion, chopped
1 medium carrot, peeled and grated
4 large ripe tomatoes (about 1 1/2 lbs.), peeled, cored, seeded and chopped
1 c. low sodium defatted chicken broth
2 Tbsp. basil leaves, crushed
1 c. fat-free soy milk
1 tsp. lemon juice
1/4 tsp. black pepper
Fresh parsley for garnish

In a large, heavy saucepan, saute the onion and carrot in water until the vegetables are soft, 5 to 8 minutes.

Add the tomatoes, chicken broth and basil; bring to a boil over moderate heat.

Adjust the heat so that the mixture bubbles gently.

Cook, uncovered, stirring occasionally for 10 minutes.

In an electric blender or food processor, puree the soup in 3 batches, whirling each batch 30 seconds.

Stir in the milk.

Cover the soup and refrigerate at least 2 hours before serving.

Serve in chilled bowls with a sprig of parsley as garnish.

Preparation time: 10 minutes
Cooking time: 20 minutes
Chilling time: 2 hours
Servings: 4 to 6

Minestrone in Minutes

1/2 c. water
1 c. onion, chopped
1 can (16 oz.) tomatoes,
  chopped
2 small zucchini, cubed
3 low sodium beef bouillon
  cubes, skim off any fat
3 c. water
2 c. cabbage, finely chopped
1 can (15 oz.) great northern
  beans, undrained
1 tsp. dried basil
2 Tbsp. fresh parsley, chopped

In a Dutch oven or soup kettle,
saute onion in 1/2 cup water for
5 minutes.

Add all remaining ingredients.

Simmer 1 hour.

Preparation time: 20 minutes
Cooking time: 1 hour and 5
  minutes
Servings: 8 to 10

Tomato Soup

1 can (29 oz.) tomatoes,
   crushed
1 Tbsp. sugar
2 c. skim soy milk
1 Tbsp. cornstarch
1/4 c. water
1 c. cooked brown rice
   (optional)
1/2 tsp. salt (optional)
1/8 tsp. black pepper
1/4 tsp. garlic powder
3/4 tsp. onion powder
Pinch of thyme leaves
1 tsp. parsley flakes

Place tomatoes and sugar in a medium saucepan; simmer, covered, while preparing sauce.

In a large saucepan, heat milk almost to a boil; add cornstarch that has been mixed with water in a jar, stirring constantly, until thickened.

Add rice and seasonings.

Stir tomatoes gradually into sauce, stirring constantly.

Serve immediately.

Preparation time: 10 minutes
Cooking time: 20 minutes
Servings: 6

Tomato and Rice Soup

1/2 c. water
1 c. onion, chopped
1 c. celery, chopped
2 c. brown rice, cooked
1 can (46 oz.) tomato juice or
  2 cans (28 oz.) tomatoes,
  chopped
4 tsp. low sodium instant
  chicken bouillon
1 tsp. basil
1/2 tsp. dill weed

In a Dutch oven or soup kettle, saute onion and celery in water over medium heat 5 minutes.

Add all other ingredients, bring to a boil and simmer 15 minutes.

Preparation time: 15 minutes
Cooking time: 20 minutes
Servings: 10 to 12

Gazpacho

Soup Base:
2 1/2 c. tomato juice
3 Tbsp. wine vinegar
1 tsp. low sodium soy sauce
1 tsp. garlic, minced
2 tsp. parsley, snipped
1/8 tsp. Tabasco sauce or to
taste
1/2 tsp. salt (optional)
1/8 tsp. pepper
1 Tbsp. lemon juice

Vegetable Garnishes:
1 c. tomatoes, finely chopped
1/2 c. celery, finely chopped
1/2 c. green pepper, finely
chopped
1/2 c. onion, finely chopped
1 small cucumber, peeled,
seeded, and finely chopped
Fresh parsley for garnish

In large bowl, combine soup base ingredients; mix well.

Stir in vegetable garnishes except parsley and refrigerate, covered, at least 4 hours or overnight.

Garnish with parsley.

Serve cold.

Preparation time: 30 minutes
Cooling time: 4 hours or
overnight
Servings: 5

Vegetable Soup
(Made Easy)

1 can (46 oz.) tomato juice
2 pkg. (10 oz.) frozen mixed
**   vegetables**
1 can (10 1/2 oz.) defatted beef
**   broth**
1 bay leaf
1 c. water
1/2 c. quick-cooking pearled
**   barley**
1 Tbsp. instant minced onion
1 Tbsp. sugar
1/2 tsp. thyme leaves, crushed

In a 4-quart saucepan or Dutch oven combine all ingredients.

Cover, bring to a boil.

Reduce heat and simmer 10 to 12 minutes or until barley is tender.

Remove bay leaf and serve.

Preparation time: 10 minutes
Cooking time: 12 minutes
Servings: 10

Vegetable Soup
(Italian Style)

1 c. onion, diced
1 c. celery, sliced
1 c. carrots, sliced
2 garlic cloves, minced
1 can (16 oz.) tomatoes
1 can (15 oz.) tomato sauce
1 can (15 oz.) red kidney beans, undrained
2 c. water
5 tsp. low sodium beef bouillon granules
1 Tbsp. parsley flakes
1 tsp. salt (optional)
1/2 tsp. oregano
1/2 tsp. basil
1/4 tsp. black pepper
2 c. cabbage, shredded
1 c. fresh or frozen cut green beans
1/2 c. small elbow macaroni
Fresh parsley for garnish

In a large heavy kettle, add all ingredients except cabbage, green beans and macaroni.

Bring to a boil. Lower heat; cover and simmer 20 minutes.

Add cabbage, green beans and macaroni; bring to a boil and simmer until vegetables are tender, 12 to 15 minutes.

Add water or broth if a thinner soup is desired.

Garnish with parsley.

Preparation time: 20 minutes
Cooking time: 35 minutes
Servings: 12

Vegetable Noodle Soup

4 carrots, sliced

3 stalks celery, diced

1 large onion, diced

1/2 c. water

2 cans (16 oz.) defatted
   chicken broth

1 c. mini noodles

1 small can sliced mushrooms

1 tsp. basil leaves

1/2 tsp. garlic powder

1/2 tsp. thyme leaves

1/8 tsp. black pepper

1 tsp. parsley flakes

1 tsp. salt (optional)

1/8 tsp. paprika

1/4 tsp. chili powder

3/4 tsp. dill weed

In a large saucepan, saute carrots, celery, and onion in water.

Add chicken broth and all other ingredients.

Simmer for at least 1 hour.

Preparation time: 15 minutes
Cooking time: 1 1/4 hours
Servings: 4 to 6

SALADS

In this Miracle Cookbook you will find a whole new world of exciting tastes and aromas. Recipes using the herbs, spices, and flavors will delight your senses. Experience the joy of the best possible health! Eliminate the harmful fat and salt from your food. Use instead the ravishing reds of tomatoes and peppers; the garnishing greens of spinach and salads; the yummy yellows and oranges of citrus and carrots; all combined to make dining a rich, colorful delight.

For a complete explanation of the cause of degenerative diseases and how to change your lifestyle to prevent or reverse disease — read Earl Updike's companion book (with the bright yellow cover).

"THE MIRACLE DIET — 14 DAYS TO NEW VIGOR AND HEALTH."

"For the Best Possible Health"

The Miracle Diet

Easy

Permanent Weight Loss

Fat Free | Cholesterol Free | High Fiber

• Look better . . . Feel Better
• Save Money on Food
• Save on Medical / Dental Bills
• Lose Weight Permanently
• Increase Your Energy

• Eat all you want
• Never be hungry
• Lose up to 10 lbs per month
• Learn how Fat makes *you* Fat
• Avoid the killers Cholesterol and Fat!
• Become a Plantarian

14 days to New Vigor and Health

Earl F. Updike

Forward by Neal D. Barnard, M.D. President of the National Physicians Committee for Responsible Medicine

VEGETABLE SALADS

- **Eat to live ... Don't live to eat**
- **Think of food as fuel**
- **Treat yourself with preventive medicine**

Then God said, "Behold, I have given you every plant yielding seed that is on the surface of all the earth, and every tree which has fruit yielding seed; it shall be food for you ... " —Genesis 1:29

Black Bean Chili Salad

1 pkg. (12 oz.) black beans
2 c. onion, chopped, divided
12 garlic cloves, chopped,
   divided
2 cans (20 oz.) whole tomatoes,
   chopped, undrained
1 green pepper, chopped
1 tsp. salt (optional)
1 tsp. black pepper
2 Tbsp. chili powder
1 1/2 Tbsp. ground cumin
1/8 tsp. crushed red pepper

Accompaniments:
Corn Strips or Cornmeal Oat
Pones or Corn Tortilla Chips
(see recipes) 1 c. lettuce, thinly
sliced

In large heavy pot, cover the beans with water and bring to a boil for 2 minutes.

Turn off heat; let soak 1 hour.

Turn on heat; add 1 1/2 cups onions and 8 garlic cloves; simmer until beans are tender, about 1 hour.

Drain liquid from beans. (Beans can be cooked in advance and frozen until needed.)

Add tomatoes and remaining onion, green pepper, 4 garlic cloves, salt, pepper, chili powder, cumin and red pepper; simmer until last added raw vegetables are crisp tender, 10 to 15 minutes.

Serve on individual plates garnished with accompaniments, as desired.

Preparation time: 20 minutes
Cooking time: 2 1/4 hours
Servings: 8

Four Bean ✓ Salad

1 can (17 oz.) large lima beans, drained

1 can (16 oz.) cut green beans, drained

1 can (16 oz.) wax beans, drained

1 can (15 oz.) red kidney beans, drained

1/2 c. celery, chopped

1/2 c. onion, chopped

1/2 c. green pepper, chopped

3/4 c. white vinegar

1/2 c. sugar

1/4 tsp. salt (optional)

1/8 tsp. pepper

Combine vegetables in a large bowl.

Combine vinegar and next 3 ingredients in a jar.

Cover tightly and shake vigorously until sugar dissolves; pour over vegetables.

Cover and chill at least 2 hours, stirring occasionally.

Preparation time: 25 minutes
Chilling time: 2 hours
Servings: 8 to 10

Sliced Beet Salad

Vinaigrette Dressing:
1/2 tsp. salt (optional)
Freshly ground pepper
1/2 tsp. Dijon mustard
1/2 tsp. sugar
2 Tbsp. vinegar (wine, herb or
cider vinegar)

Vegetables:
1 lb. beets, cooked and peeled
or 1 can (16 oz.) whole
beets, sliced
1/2 red onion, peeled, trimmed
and sliced, separated into
rings
Lettuce leaves

In a medium bowl, combine vinaigrette ingredients and whisk together until dissolved.

Place sliced beets and onion into bowl with dressing; toss.

Cover and chill for 2 hours.

Arrange lettuce leaves on serving plates; spoon beet and onion mixture over lettuce.

Serve immediately.

Preparation time: 20 minutes
Chilling time: 2 hours
Servings: 4 to 6

Norwegian Salad

2 cans French style green
beans, drained and chopped
1 can (16 oz.) English peas,
    drained
1 jar (4 oz.) diced pimiento
1 green pepper, chopped
4 ribs celery, cut thin
    diagonally
1 medium onion, chopped
1 c. red wine vinegar
1 1/2 c. sugar
1 tsp. salt (optional)

In a large saucepan, heat vinegar, sugar and salt together, stirring until dissolved.

Add pepper, celery and onion to vinegar mixture.

Stir beans, peas and pimiento into vinegar mixture.

Place in covered serving bowl and let stand in refrigerator 24 hours.

Keeps several days under refrigeration.

Preparation time: 20 minutes
Chilling time: 24 hours
Servings: 10 to 12

Southwest Salad

1 1/2 c. iceberg or romaine lettuce, torn

1 1/2 c. carrots, shredded

2 Tbsp. cilantro, chopped

2/3 c. cooked garbanzo beans

1/2 c. red onion, diced

1 c. fresh corn kernels, cooked or canned

1 c. cherry tomatoes, halved

2 c. alfalfa sprouts, loosely packed

Prepared nonfat dressing of choice

In a large mixing bowl, toss lettuce, carrots and cilantro.

Distribute the mixture evenly between two large serving bowls.

Top each mixture with an equal portion of garbanzo beans, onion, corn, tomatoes, and sprouts.

Toss gently with dressing or serve dressing on the side.

Serve with Tortilla Chips or Cornmeal Oat Pones (see recipes).

Preparation time: 20 minutes
Servings: 2

Broccoli Salad

1 large head fresh broccoli,
    chopped in bite-size pieces
1/2 c. raisins
1/2 c. onion, chopped
1/2 c. fat free mayonnaise
1/2 c. sugar
1 Tbsp. cider vinegar

Combine broccoli, raisins and onions in a large bowl.

Mix remaining ingredients and toss with broccoli mixture.

Cover and chill several hours until serving time.

Preparation time: 25 minutes
Chilling time: 2 to 3 hours
Servings: 6 to 8

Carrot ✓ Raisin Salad

6 medium carrots, shredded
1 c. raisins, or less
1/4 c. fat free mayonnaise or
** salad dressing**
Lemon juice, if desired

In a medium bowl, mix all ingredients well. One cup drained, crushed pineapple can also be added, if desired.

Cover and refrigerate until time to serve.

Preparation time: 15 minutes
Servings: 6 to 8 half-cup servings

Note: Can be made with no dressing and instead use juice from pineapple, if desired.

Cauli-flower and Broccoli Salad

3 c. cauliflower, cut in bitesize pieces

3 c. broccoli, cut in bite-size pieces

1/2 c. red onion, sliced

1/3 c. raisins

3/4 c. fat free mayonnaise or salad dressing, or use half of each

1/4 c. sugar

2 Tbsp. cider vinegar

Combine first 4 ingredients in large bowl; toss.

In a small bowl, mix dressing, sugar and vinegar.

Pour over vegetable mixture.

Toss well.

Cover and refrigerate for at least 2 hours before serving.

Preparation time: 25 minutes
Chilling time: 2 hours
Servings: 6 to 8

Three Coleslaws

4 c. cabbage, shredded
1 medium carrot, shredded
1 onion, finely chopped
1/2 c. fat free mayonnaise
1 tsp. mustard (optional)
1/4 c. sugar or sugar substitute
Dash of salt (optional)
Dash of paprika

Combine all ingredients except paprika in medium serving bowl.

Sprinkle paprika over top.

Cover and refrigerate until serving time.

Preparation time: 15 minutes
Servings: 4 to 6

Variation #1:

1 small green cabbage, shredded
1 large carrot, shredded
2 c. cauliflower florets, cut in
   bite size pieces
1/2 green bell pepper, chopped
4 radishes, thinly sliced
4 scallions, thinly sliced

Dressing:
2 tsp. fresh ginger root, grated,
   or 1/2 tsp. ground ginger
2 garlic cloves
1/4 to 1/2 tsp. hot red pepper
   flakes
1/2 c. white wine vinegar
2 Tbsp. low sodium soy sauce

Prepare vegetables in large serving bowl.

Place dressing ingredients in blender; process until smooth and add to vegetables. Salt to taste.

Cover and chill 2 to 3 hours.

Preparation time: 25 minutes
Chilling time: 2 to 3 hours
Servings: 4 to 6

Variation #2:

6 c. cabbage, finely shredded
2 c. carrots, thinly sliced
1/2 c. green onion, sliced
1/2 c. red bell pepper, chopped
1 c. celery, sliced small
1 c. fat free Miracle Whip™
1 Tbsp. Dijon mustard
1/2 tsp. salt (optional)
1/4 tsp. pepper

In a large bowl, combine first 5 ingredients.

In a small bowl, whisk together the Miracle Whip, mustard, salt and pepper.

Pour the dressing over the cabbage mixture and toss to coat.

Chill, covered, 2 to 3 hours to allow flavors to blend.

Preparation time: 25 minutes
Chilling time: 2 to 3 hours
Servings: 18 (1/2 cup each)

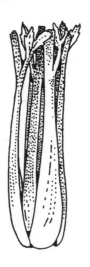

Coleslaw
(Holiday Style)

2 c. green cabbage, shredded
2 c. red cabbage, shredded
1 green bell pepper, finely
   chopped
1 red bell pepper, finely
   chopped
1 unpeeled red apple, cored
   and finely chopped
2 Tbsp. fresh dill leaves,
   minced; or 2 tsp. dill weed
6 Tbsp. nonfat mayonnaise
1 tsp. prepared mustard
1/4 c. apple cider or juice
Salt and pepper to taste

Combine ingredients in large
plastic bag; close tightly and
shake well to blend.

Refrigerate several hours before
serving in large serving dish.

Preparation time: 25 minutes
Chilling time: several hours
Servings: 8

Coleslaw
(Chinese Style)

5 c. Chinese cabbage, coarsely chopped

1 c. carrots, shredded

1 c. green onions with tops (cut several times lengthwise, then into 1inch pieces)

1 c. mushrooms, chopped

Dressing:

2 Tbsp. sugar

1 Tbsp. fresh cilantro or parsley, minced

1/2 tsp. salt (optional)

1/4 tsp. black pepper

1/2 tsp. ground ginger

1/4 c. wine vinegar

1 Tbsp. low sodium soy sauce

In a large serving bowl, toss all vegetables to mix.

In a small bowl, combine dressing ingredients; whisk until well-blended.

Pour dressing over slaw; toss and cover.

Refrigerate 2 hours before serving; toss again just before serving.

Note: Chinese cabbage is also sold as Napa cabbage and is not the same as Bok Choy.

Preparation time: 20 minutes
Chilling time: 2 hours
Servings: 12

Nine Day Coleslaw

Dressing:
1 3/4 c. apple cider vinegar
1/4 c. water
1 Tbsp. celery seed
1 Tbsp. sugar
3/4 tsp. salt (optional)

Coleslaw:
3 lb. cabbage, shredded
2 c. onions, finely chopped
2 c. carrots, shredded
1 c. green pepper, finely
    chopped
1 c. sweet red pepper, finely
    chopped
1 c. celery, finely chopped
1 1/2 c. sugar (optional)

Combine dressing ingredients in a small saucepan; bring to a boil.

Cool; set aside.

Combine coleslaw vegetables in large bowl.

Stir in sugar; let stand until sugar dissolves.

Stir occasionally.

After sugar dissolves, drain off any excess liquid.

Pour cooled dressing over cabbage mixture, stirring well.

Cover and refrigerate.

This coleslaw keeps well under refrigeration; it also freezes well. Try it for a big get-together.

Preparation time: 45 minutes
Chilling time: several hours
Servings: 3 quarts coleslaw

Cucumbers and Onions

2 large cucumbers, sliced
1 large Vidalia onion or any
 mild onion, sliced
1/2 c. sugar
1/2 c. cider vinegar
2 Tbsp. dried parsley
Salt and pepper (optional)
Fat free mayonnaise (optional)

Combine cucumbers and onion in large bowl.

Whisk together sugar, vinegar and parsley and pour over vegetables.

Cover and marinate in refrigerator for 2 to 3 hours or overnight.

To serve, drain marinade from vegetables and top with 2 tablespoons of mayonnaise, salt and pepper if desired.

Preparation time: 20 minutes
Chilling time: 2 to 3 hours or
 overnight
Servings: 8 to 10

Frozen Cucumber Salad

**2 qts. unpeeled small
    cucumbers, sliced
2 medium onions, sliced
1 Tbsp. salt (NOT optional)
1 c. cider vinegar
1 c. sugar, or less according to
    taste (optional)**

In a large bowl, combine
cucumbers, onions and salt.

Let mixture soak for 3 hours.

In a small saucepan, warm the
vinegar and sugar; stir to
dissolve sugar.

Drain cucumbers and add
vinegar mixture.

Ladle into plastic freezer
containers or bags and freeze.

When ready to use, defrost and
serve chilled.

Preparation time: 25 minutes
Servings: 1 1/2 quarts salad

Potato Salad

6 c. diced cooked potatoes
1 medium onion, chopped
1/2 c. celery, diced
3/4 c. sweet relish
2 Tbsp. mustard
2 c. fat free mayonnaise
Salt and pepper to taste

Lightly toss all ingredients together in large bowl.

Cover and refrigerate until serving time:

Preparation time: 15 minutes
Servings: 6

Potato Salad Vinaigrette

2 lb. new potatoes, about 6
  medium
1/4 c. green bell pepper,
  chopped
1/4 c. radishes, thinly sliced
1/4 c. green onions, finely
  chopped
1/2 c. celery, chopped
2 Tbsp. fresh parsley, minced
1/4 c. plus 2 Tbsp. apple cider
  vinegar
2 Tbsp. water
2 tsp. Dijon mustard
1/2 tsp. salt (optional)
1/4 tsp. pepper
1/4 tsp. celery seed

In a medium saucepan, cook unpeeled potatoes until just tender; cool.

Cut potatoes into 1/2-inch cubes (peel, or leave unpeeled as desired).

In medium bowl, combine potatoes, bell pepper, radishes, onions, celery and parsley.

For dressing, combine vinegar and remaining ingredients in a jar.

Cover and shake vigorously.

Pour dressing over potato mixture; toss gently.

Cover and chill before serving.

Preparation time: 35 minutes
Chilling time: several hours
Servings: 6

Marinated Tomatoes

3 large fresh tomatoes, sliced
   thick
1/4 c. red wine vinegar
1 tsp. salt or less (optional)
1/4 tsp. pepper
1/2 garlic clove, minced
2 Tbsp. onion, chopped
1 Tbsp. parsley, chopped
1 Tbsp. fresh basil, chopped,
   or 1 tsp. dried basil

Arrange tomatoes in a large shallow dish.

Combine remaining ingredients in a jar; cover tightly and shake well.

Pour evenly over tomato slices. Cover and refrigerate for several hours.

Preparation time: 20 minutes
Chilling time: 3 hours
Servings: 8

Sliced Tomato Salad

2 large tomatoes
1 small mild onion
Fat free Italian dressing
Basil leaves
Pepper

Slice tomatoes onto individual salad plates.

Top with sliced onions, separated into rings.

Sprinkle lightly with dressing, basil leaves and pepper.

Preparation time: 10 minutes
Servings: 4

Tomato Cucumber Salad

1/2 c. fat free mayonnaise
1 tsp. vinegar
1 tsp. sugar
1/2 tsp. lemon juice
1 tsp. sweet basil leaves
1/4 tsp. salt (optional)
1/8 tsp. black pepper
3 c. tomatoes, cored and
    chopped
2 c. cucumbers, chopped

In a small bowl, mix first 7 ingredients.

Place tomatoes and cucumbers in a medium bowl; add dressing and toss lightly.

Preparation time: 20 minutes
Servings: 10 to 12

Tomato and Cucumber Raita

1 medium ripe tomato, diced
1 medium cucumber, peeled,
**   seeded and diced**
1/4 c. onion, minced
1 tsp. salt (optional)
1 tsp. ground cumin
1 c. nonfat mayonnaise

In a medium bowl, combine diced tomato and cucumber and minced onion with salt. Set aside.

Place cumin in a small pan and toast it over medium heat, shaking the pan so it does not burn.

Toast just until the cumin changes color slightly and becomes very aromatic.

Sprinkle the cumin over the vegetable mixture.

Add mayonnaise and mix well.

Refrigerate for one hour before serving to blend flavors.

Serve on individual plates as salad on lettuce leaves, or in small individual bowls with pita bread to scoop up the salad.

Preparation time: 20 minutes
Chilling time: 1 hour
Servings: 4

Six-Layer Salad

1 small head iceberg lettuce, torn into bite-size pieces
1 small head cauliflower, broken into florets
1 small red onion, sliced
1 small green pepper, diced
1 c. fat free mayonnaise or salad dressing
2 Tbsp. sugar (optional)
1/2 c. seasoned croutons as garnish (see recipe in appetizers)

Layer lettuce, cauliflower, onion and green pepper in a 3-quart serving bowl.

Combine mayonnaise or salad dressing and sugar; spread over top of salad, sealing to edge of bowl.

Cover tightly; chill at least 8 hours.

Toss gently before serving and sprinkle seasoned croutons over top.

Preparation time: 20 minutes
Chilling time: 8 hours
Servings: 8 to 10

Icebox Vegetable Salad

1/2 c. sugar (optional)
1 Tbsp. flour
1/2 c. cider vinegar
1/4 c. water
1 tsp. prepared mustard
1 bag (20 oz.) frozen mixed
　　vegetables cooked and
　　drained
1 1/2 c. macaroni twists,
　　cooked
4 ribs celery, chopped
1 medium onion, diced
1 green pepper, diced
1 can (15 oz.) red kidney beans,
　　drained

In a small saucepan, blend sugar and flour; add vinegar, water and mustard.

Heat and cook until thickened, stirring constantly.

Cool slightly. In a large serving bowl, combine remaining ingredients and toss with cooled dressing.

Cover and chill well.

Preparation time: 30 minutes
Chilling time: 3 hours
Servings: 12

Zucchini Harvest Salad

4 c. zucchini, thinly sliced
1 c. celery, sliced
1 c. fresh mushrooms, sliced
1/4 c. green pepper, chopped
1/4 c. red pepper, chopped
1 c. mild or medium picante
sauce or salsa (see recipes)
1/2 c. vinegar
3 Tbsp. sugar (optional)
1/2 tsp. oregano
1 garlic clove, minced
Lettuce leaves

In a large mixing bowl, combine first 5 ingredients; toss to mix.

In a small bowl or jar, combine all remaining ingredients except lettuce and mix or shake well.

Pour over vegetables.

Cover and chill several hours or overnight.

Serve in a large bowl lined with lettuce leaves or in individual lettuce cups.

Preparation time: 25 minutes
Chilling time: 3 hours or
 overnight
Servings: 8

Vegetable Salad
(Christmas Style)

Dressing:
3 Tbsp. fresh lemon juice
3 Tbsp. white wine vinegar
1 tsp. salt (optional)
1/2 tsp. sugar (optional)
Freshly ground black pepper,
  sprinkle

Vegetables:
2 c. cauliflower, thinly sliced
1/2 c. green pepper, chopped
1/2 c. red pepper, chopped
Cut circles of green and red
  pepper (optional)

Put all dressing ingredients in a jar; shake well.

Combine cauliflower and peppers except pepper circles in a medium bowl; pour dressing over all and toss lightly.

Place in pretty glass bowl; cover and marinate in refrigerator for several hours or overnight.

This festive salad travels well and holds up beautifully on the buffet table, so it's ideal for making ahead. It can easily be doubled.

Garnish with cut circles of green and red peppers, if desired.

Preparation time: 20 minutes
Chilling time: several hours or
  overnight
Servings: 6 to 8

Salad Dressing
(SouthWest Style)

2/3 c. Fat Free Miracle Whip™
2 tsp. salsa
Pinch of Mexican seasoning or
**   pinch each of cumin, chili**
powder and oregano

In a small bowl, whisk Miracle Whip until thin and smooth.

Add remaining ingredients; whisk again until thoroughly blended.

Preparation time: 5 minutes
Servings: 2/3 cup dressing

Spinach Salad

1 large bunch spinach, washed, stemmed and dried
6 cauliflower florets, chopped
4 oz. mushrooms, wiped and sliced
1 onion, thinly sliced and separated into rings
Fat free Italian or herb dressing

In a large bowl, tear spinach leaves into bite size pieces.

Toss with remaining vegetables, cover and chill.

Add dressing and toss lightly at serving time.

Preparation time: 30 minutes
Chilling time: 1 hour or more
Servings: 4

Spinach Green Salad

Dressing:
1/4 c. lemon or lime juice
1/4 c. honey
2 Tbsp. parsley, snipped
1/4 tsp. black pepper
1/8 tsp. nutmeg

Salad:
8 to 10 c. (10 to 12 oz.) spinach
  leaves, washed, dried,
  stems removed and
 torn into bite-size pieces
1 c. celery, thinly sliced
  diagonally
4 medium radishes, trimmed
  and thinly sliced
2 green onions, including tops,
  chopped
1 can (11 oz.) mandarin
  oranges, drained

Combine dressing ingredients in a jar; cover and shake well.

Refrigerate until ready to toss with salad.

Place spinach in a large salad bowl. Add celery, radishes, onions and oranges.

Cover and chill.

At serving time, add dressing and toss lightly.

Preparation time: 30 minutes
Chilling time: several hours
Servings: 8 to 10

PASTA AND RICE SALADS

"Let food be thy medicine."
—Hippocrates, about 431 B.C.

This Food Guide Pyramid is a step in the right direction but falls far short of the Best Possible Health diet based mainly on plant foods.

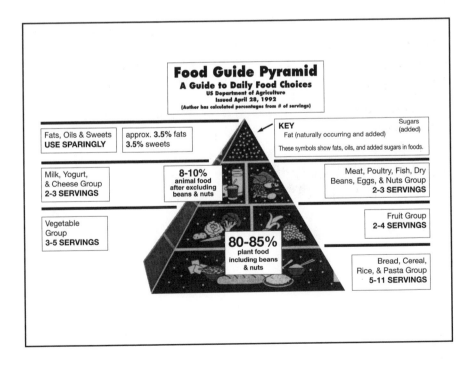

Food Guide Pyramid
A Guide to Daily Food Choices
US Department of Agriculture
Issued April 28, 1992
(Author has calculated percentages from # of servings)

Fats, Oils & Sweets
USE SPARINGLY

approx. **3.5%** fats
3.5% sweets

KEY
Fat (naturally occurring and added)
Sugars (added)
These symbols show fats, oils, and added sugars in foods.

Milk, Yogurt, & Cheese Group
2-3 SERVINGS

8-10%
animal food after excluding beans & nuts

Meat, Poultry, Fish, Dry Beans, Eggs, & Nuts Group
2-3 SERVINGS

Vegetable Group
3-5 SERVINGS

80-85%
plant food including beans & nuts

Fruit Group
2-4 SERVINGS

Bread, Cereal, Rice, & Pasta Group
5-11 SERVINGS

Macaroni Garden Salad

1/2 c. fat free mayonnaise or
   salad dressing
2 tsp. dill weed
3 tsp. Mrs. Dash
1/4 tsp. dry mustard
1/4 tsp. pepper
4 c. cooked egg-free macaroni
6 green onions, chopped fine
1 large bell pepper, chopped
2 stalks celery, chopped
1 large tomato, chopped
1 c. cooked green peas
1/4 c. parsley, chopped
1 cucumber, chopped
4 or 5 Tbsp. diced pimiento
1/2 c. fat free Italian dressing

Mix mayonnaise or salad dressing with dill weed, Mrs. Dash, mustard and pepper.

Pour over cooled, cooked macaroni that has been placed in a large bowl.

Mix well; add remaining ingredients and toss gently.

Cover and refrigerate at least 2 hours before serving.

Preparation time: 30 minutes
Chilling time: 2 hours or more
Servings: 6

Pasta Salad

4 c. cooked Rainbow Pasta
1 small bunch green onions,
chopped
12 cherry tomatoes, sliced
1/4 c. fat free Italian Dressing
1/4 tsp. garlic powder
1/2 tsp. oregano
1/2 tsp. basil
1/8 tsp. pepper
1/2 tsp. salt (optional)
Paprika, sprinkle

Toss ingredients together in medium bowl; sprinkle with paprika.

Cover and refrigerate until serving time.

May also add, using large bowl:

Diced celery and/or
Broccoli
Radishes
Cucumbers
Green peppers
Cauliflower
More seasonings to taste

Preparation time: 15 to 25 minutes
Servings: 6 to 10 depending on amount of ingredients used

Rice Salad
(Country Style)

Dressing:
1/2 c. fat free mayonnaise
1/4 c. prepared mustard
2 Tbsp. sugar (optional)
1 tsp. vinegar
1/4 tsp. salt (optional)
1/8 tsp. pepper
1 to 2 Tbsp. fat-free soy milk, if
   needed

Salad:
3 c. brown rice, cooked, chilled
1/4 c. sweet pickle relish
1 jar (2 oz.) chopped pimiento,
   drained
1/3 c. green onions with tops,
   finely chopped
1/4 c. green pepper, finely
   chopped
1/4 c. celery, finely chopped
1 c. fresh mushrooms, finely
   chopped

Garnish:
Fresh parsley and cherry
   tomatoes

In a small bowl, combine all dressing ingredients except milk; set aside.

In a large bowl, combine all salad ingredients.

Pour dressing over rice mixture; stir gently.

Add milk if mixture is dry.

Cover and chill several hours before serving.

Garnish with parsley and cherry tomatoes.

Preparation time: 25 minutes
Chilling time: several hours
Servings: 10

Rice and Bean Salad

This salad can serve as a light main dish or a side dish.

3 1/2 c. iceberg lettuce, shredded
1 small red onion, thinly sliced
2 c. cooked brown rice, cooled (cook ahead)
1 pkg. (10 oz.) frozen peas, thawed
1 can (15 oz.) red kidney beans, drained
1 c. fat free Italian salad dressing

In a large straight-sided glass bowl, layer the salad: 1 1/2 cups lettuce, half of onion, 1 cup of cold brown rice and half of package of peas.

Repeat. Top with red kidney beans and final layer of 1/2 cup lettuce.

Cover and chill.

About 1 hour before serving time, pour the dressing evenly over the salad and return to the refrigerator until serving time.

Preparation time: 25 minutes
Chilling time: undressed salad, 2 to 3 hours dressed salad, 1 hour
Servings: 4 to 6 as main dish 8 as side dish

Rice Salad
(Hawaiian Style)

with Sweet Dressing

1 1/2 c. cooked brown rice
1 c. tiny broccoli florets,
    blanched
1 c. fresh pineapple chunks,
    well drained
(reserve juice for dressing)
2 Tbsp. scallions, finely
    chopped, white part only
1 large carrot, finely chopped
1/3 c. raisins or dried
    cranberries
1/3 c. water chestnuts, chopped
Sweet Dressing (recipe follows)

In a large mixing bowl, toss together all ingredients except dressing.

Add dressing; toss again until thoroughly coated.

Preparation time: 20 minutes
Servings: 4 to 6

Variation: Try substituting other dried fruits for raisins and grated apples for the pineapple.

Sweet Dressing

2/3 c. fresh pineapple juice, reserved from previous salad recipe
1 tsp. ginger root, grated
1 tsp. garlic, minced
1 tsp. brown sugar (optional)
Splash low sodium soy sauce
Splash brown rice vinegar or apple cider vinegar

In a small saucepan, combine all ingredients.

Bring to a simmer and cook over low heat, stirring occasionally, until liquid has thickened and reduced, about 7 minutes.

Remove from heat; cool to room temperature.

Preparation time: 5 minutes
Cooking time: 10 minutes
Servings: 1/2 cup

Wild Rice and Cranberry Salad

Salad:
1 qt. water
1 lb. wild rice, rinsed
2 bay leaves
2 whole oranges
2 c. cranberries
2 c. seedless grapes, halved

Mustard Vinaigrette:
3/4 c. vinegar
3 tsp. shallots, minced
1 tsp. Dijon mustard
1/8 tsp. ground pepper

In a 3-quart saucepan over high heat, bring the water to a boil.

Add the rice and bay leaves.

Cover; reduce heat to medium and cook for 40 to 50 minutes, or until the rice is tender and the water is absorbed.

Discard bay leaves.

Fluff the rice with a fork and chill. (May be prepared 1 day ahead.)

While the rice is cooking, remove the rind from the oranges with a potato peeler and cut into fine slivers; set aside.

Reserve flesh for later use.

Blanch the cranberries in a pot of boiling water for 3 minutes; drain and set aside.

Just before serving, in a large bowl, add the rind, cranberries and grapes to the rice.

In a small bowl, whisk together the vinaigrette ingredients. (May be prepared ahead. Store in tightly covered jar in refrigerator.)

Shake before pouring over the rice mixture and mixing well.

Preparation time: 1 hour
Chilling time: several hours, at least
Servings: 12

FRUIT SALADS

"If we eat wrongly, no doctor can cure us;
if we eat rightly, no doctor is needed."
—Dr. Victor G. Rocine, about 1930

Dr. Oliver Alabaster M.D.

Dr. Oliver Alabaster, M.D., director of the Institute for Disease Prevention at George Washington University Medical Center says, "At least 70 percent of cancer is thought to be preventable. Changing dietary habits requires people to be willing to take steps now to reduce their risk of something years ahead."

"Our modern diet is really an anathema to our whole historical evolution," Alabaster said. "Why should we expect our bodies to react well to it? In the evolutionary time scale meat is a relatively new phenomenon. It used to be fruit, nuts, cereal, and vegetation were really the basis of the human diet over the millennia. The good news is that we now realize that we can, to a great degree, control our risks of cancer and other diseases through decisions we make ourselves. I hope we will take advantage of it."

Banana Salad

1/2 c. sugar
3 Tbsp. white vinegar
2 egg whites, beaten stiffly
Pinch of salt (optional)
5 medium bananas, quartered
    lengthwise
    and cut into 1/2-inch pieces
2 c. seedless green grapes,
    halved

Combine first 4 ingredients in a small saucepan, stirring well.

Cook over medium heat, stirring constantly, until mixture boils; boil 1 minute.

Remove from heat; cover and chill. In a large serving dish, combine bananas, grapes.

Pour dressing over fruit, stirring gently.

Serve immediately.

Preparation time: 20 minutes
Servings: 6 to 8

Frozen Banana Salad

4 bananas, mashed
1 can (8 1/2 oz.) crushed
  pineapple, drained
1 Tbsp. lemon juice
1 jar (6 oz.) maraschino
  cherries, drained and
  cut in quarters
1/2 c. sugar (optional)
8 oz. nonfat mayonnaise
Lettuce leaves

In a medium bowl, combine all ingredients except lettuce, stir well, and pour into a 9" square pan.

Freeze until firm; cut into 3-inch squares and serve on lettuce leaves.

Preparation time: 20 minutes
Servings: 9

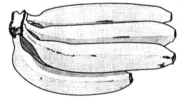

Fruit Salad

#1.

Apple chunks
Banana chunks
Pineapple chunks
Strawberry chunks
Orange juice

#2.

Peach slices
Pear slices
Orange sections
Banana slices
Orange juice

#3.

Watermelon chunks
Honeydew chunks
Cantaloupe chunks
Grapes

Prepare one of the above
combinations, toss lightly,
cover and chill.

Serve cold.

Garnish each dish with a sprig
of mint, if desired.

Preparation time: varies
Chilling time: 1 hour or more
Servings: varies

Fruit Salad
(Holiday Style)

1 can (15 1/2 oz.) pineapple chunks, reserve juice

1/2 c. sugar (optional)

3 Tbsp. cornstarch

3 bananas, sliced

2 cans (11 oz.) mandarin oranges, drained

3 medium unpeeled apples, chopped

1/2 lb. red seedless grapes, halved

Drain pineapple; place juice in small saucepan.

Add to the juice sugar and cornstarch that have been mixed in a small bowl; cook over low heat, stirring constantly until thickened and smooth.

Cool. In a large bowl, combine fruit; add dressing, stirring well.

Cover and chill before serving.

Preparation time: 30 minutes
Chilling time: 2 hours
Servings: 10 to 12

Orange and Red Onion Salad

Grapefruit sections can be substituted for orange sections.

2 Tbsp. fresh lemon juice
1 tsp. Dijon mustard
1/2 tsp. sugar (optional)
1/2 tsp. salt (optional)
1/4 tsp. white pepper
1/2 c. liquid Butter Buds™
  (mix 1 packet Butter Buds
  in 1/2 c. hot tap water)
1 bunch romaine lettuce, torn
  into bite-size pieces
2 medium oranges, peeled and
  sectioned
1 small red onion, thinly sliced

In a small bowl, combine first 5 ingredients.

Beat in liquid Butter Buds.

In a large serving bowl, combine lettuce, orange sections and onion slices.

Toss with dressing.

Serve immediately.

Preparation time: 20 minutes
Servings: 6

Honey Orange Salad

Lettuce leaves for 6 salad
  plates
4 to 5 oranges, peeled and
  sectioned
1/2 c. honey
3 Tbsp. lemon juice
1/8 tsp. salt (optional)
4 Tbsp. crushed pineapple,
  drained

Arrange orange sections on
lettuce leaves. Combine
remaining ingredients in a small
bowl; stir well and pour over
orange sections.

Preparation time: 20 minutes
Servings: 6

Honey Fruit Salad

1 (15 1/4 oz.) can pineapple
  chunks, undrained
1 large apple, cored and diced
2 medium oranges, sectioned
  and chopped, or
 1 can mandarin oranges
1 banana, sliced
1/2 c. orange juice
1/4 c. honey
1 Tbsp. lemon juice

Combine first four ingredients
in a large bowl; set aside.

Combine remaining ingredients
for dressing; pour over fruit
mixture, stirring gently.

Cover and chill.

Preparation time: 15 minutes
Servings: 6

Fresh Fruit Salad
(Layered)

Citrus Sauce:
2/3 c. fresh orange juice
1/3 c. fresh lemon juice
1/3 c. brown sugar
1 cinnamon stick
1/2 tsp. grated orange peel
1/2 tsp. grated lemon peel

Fruit Salad:
2 c. fresh pineapple, cubed
1 pt. fresh strawberries, hulled
   and sliced
2 kiwi fruit, peeled and sliced
2 oranges, peeled and sectioned
1 pink grapefruit, peeled and
   sectioned
1 c. seedless red grapes

In a small saucepan, bring all sauce ingredients to a boil; simmer 5 minutes.

Cool. Meanwhile, in a large clear glass salad bowl, arrange fruit in layers in order listed.

Remove cinnamon stick from sauce and pour sauce evenly over fruit.

Cover and refrigerate several hours.

Preparation time: 30 minutes
Chilling time: 3 hours
Servings: 10 to 12

CONGEALED SALADS

"Nature cures when given the opportunity."
—Dr. Bernard Jensen

THE **NEW FOUR FOOD GROUPS**

Whole Grains	Vegetables	Legumes	Fruit
This group includes bread, pasta, hot or cold cereal, corn, millet, barley, bulgur, buckwheat groats and tortillas. Build each of your meals around a hearty grain dish—grains are rich in fiber and other complex carbohydrates, as well as protein, B vitamins and zinc.	Vegetables are packed with nutrients; they provide vitamin C, beta-carotene, riboflavin and other vitamins, iron, calcium and fiber. Dark green, leafy vegetables such as broccoli, collards, kale, mustard and turnip greens, chicory or bok choy are especially good sources of these important nutrients. Dark yellow and orange vegetables such as carrots, winter squash, sweet potatoes and pumpkin provide extra beta-carotene. Include generous portions of a variety of vegetables in your diet.	Legumes, which is another name for beans, peas, and lentils, are all good sources of fiber, protein, iron, calcium, zinc and B vitamins. This group also includes chickpeas, baked and refried beans, soy milk, tofu, tempeh, and texturized vegetable protein.	Fruits are rich in fiber, vitamin C and beta-carotene. Be sure to include at least one serving each day of fruits that are high in vitamin C—citrus fruits, melons and strawberries are all good choices. Choose whole fruit over fruit juices, which don't contain as much healthy fiber.

PHYSICIANS COMMITTEE FOR RESPONSIBLE MEDICINE • P.O. Box 6322, Washington, D.C. 20015 • (202) 686-2210

The Physicians Committee for Responsible Medicine says whole grains, legumes (beans, peas, lentils), vegetables and fruits are essential for good health; milk and meat are non-essential to good health.

Cranberry Christmas Salad

1/2 Tbsp. orange rind, grated
1 medium orange, peeled and
    ground
2 c. fresh cranberries, ground
2 tart apples, unpeeled, seeded
    and ground
1/2 c. sugar (optional)
1/3 c. crushed pineapple,
    undrained
1/2 c. seedless red grapes,
    halved
1 pkg. (3 oz.) raspberry
    flavored gelatin
3/4 c. nonfat mayonnaise

Combine first 8 ingredients in a
large bowl; chill 1 hour.

Prepare gelatin according to
package directions; chill until
partially set.

Fold mayonnaise into gelatin;
add fruit mixture, stirring
gently.

Spoon into 7-cup compote.

Chill thoroughly.

Garnish, if desired.

Preparation time: 30 minutes
Chilling time: fruit mixture—1
hour gelatin—1 hour
    finished salad—several hours
Servings: 8 to 10

Cranberry Orange Salad

1 pkg. (3 oz.) lemon gelatin
1 c. boiling water
1 c. orange juice, cold
1 jar (16 oz.) cranberryorange relish
1 apple, unpeeled, chopped

In a medium bowl, dissolve gelatin in boiling water.

Add orange juice and let stand in refrigerator until almost jelled.

Combine cranberry-orange relish, chopped apple; fold into almost jelled mixture.

Pour into 1-quart mold.

Chill until firm.

Preparation time: 15 minutes
Chilling time: first jellingabout 1 hour, second jelling-several hours
Servings: 6

Fruit Gelatin Ring Mold

Serve with nonfat dressing of your choice as a salad or dessert.

2 pkgs. (3 oz.) lemon-flavored gelatin
1 1/2 c. boiling water
2 c. fruit syrup, drained from peaches and pineapple
1 can (16 oz.) unsweetened peach halves drained
1 can (8 1/4 oz.) unsweetened pineapple slices, drained
1 can (16 oz.) unsweetened dark sweet pitted cherries, drained
Salad greens

Dissolve gelatin in boiling water in medium pan.

Add fruit syrup and chill until slightly thickened.

Pour 1/2 cup gelatin into the bottom of an 8-inch ring mold (1 1/2 quarts) and chill until almost firm.

Set pineapple slices, evenly spaced, in gelatin and put a dark sweet cherry in the center of each slice.

Pour in more gelatin to just cover. Chill until firm. Stand peach halves upright against sides of mold between pineapple slices and place cherries above pineapple slices.

Pour in gelatin to cover peaches about 1/2 and chill until firm.

Add remaining gelatin and chill thoroughly.

Unmold onto a large serving plate and garnish with salad greens.

Preparation time: 30 minutes
Chilling time: several hours
Servings: 6 to 8

Raspberry Salad

Colorful and easy to prepare

3 pkg. (3 oz. each) raspberry gelatin
2 1/4 c. boiling water
1 jar (25 oz.) applesauce
1 c. cranberry juice cocktail
3 Tbsp. lemon juice
Lettuce cups

In a large bowl, dissolve gelatin in boiling water. Stir in remaining ingredients, except lettuce.

Pour into 9 x 13-inch dish.

Refrigerate until congealed. Serve in lettuce cups.

Preparation time: 15 minutes
Refrigeration time: several hours
Servings: 10 to 12

Tomato Aspic with Cabbage Slaw

3 envelopes unflavored gelatin
3/4 c. cold tomato juice
5 1/4 c. tomato juice
1 Tbsp. onion, grated
1 Tbsp. salt (optional)

Soften gelatin in cold tomato juice in a small bowl. In a medium saucepan, add remaining tomato juice; bring to a boil.

Add onion, salt and softened gelatin, stirring until the gelatin is dissolved.

Pour into an 8-inch ring mold (1 1/2-quarts). Chill until completely set, at least 3 or 4 hours.

Unmold ring on a serving plate. Fill the center with your favorite cabbage slaw (see recipes).

Garnish outside also with slaw.

Preparation time: 20 minutes
Chilling time: 4 hours
Servings: 12 to 15

This is a "plantarian," not vegetarian program.
plan•tar´•i•an (plan tar´ ian) n. [plant + arian] a person whose basic diet revolves around plants (starches), supplemented with vegetables and fruit.

It's truly a miracle!

- Prevent heart-artery disease
- Reverse adult diabetes
- Lower blood pressure
- Prevent many cancers

- Reverse heart disease
- Prevent adult diabetes
- Lose weight permanently
- Prevent Osteoporosis

Let food be thy medicine.
—Hippocrates, about 431 B.C.

BREADS

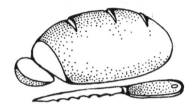

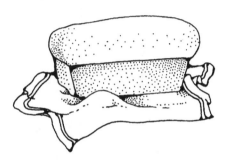

The Miracle Diet

The Miracle Diet is a plant-centered diet program that allows your body to seek its ideal weight with natural, high energy. It is based upon plants, not vegetables. The five basic starches are the basis of the diet.

- **Grain**   (wheat, oats, and barley)
- **Rice**   (a basic grain)
- **Corn**   (a basic grain)
- **Legumes**   (beans, peas, and lentils)
- **Potatoes** (the only vegetable)

BREADMAKER BREADS

Note: Breadmaker directions vary. Adapt the order of ingredients and general method for your specific breadmaker. Times required for baking in the breadmaker will vary depending on the model and the type yeast used. If you live in a high altitude location, you may need to experiment with adjustments such as using less yeast than the recipe calls for, or using rapid rise yeast instead of regular yeast. When using rapid rise yeast, be sure to use hot water (125 to 130 degrees).

Bread is the Staff of Life.

Bread
(100% Whole Wheat)

2 1/2 tsp. or 1 pkg. yeast
3 c. whole wheat flour
1/4 c. gluten
1/8 c. cracked wheat
1 tsp. salt (optional)
1 1/4 c. hot water (125 to 130 degrees)
2 Tbsp. molasses or honey
2 egg whites or 1 1/2 tsp. egg replacer mixed in 3 Tbsp. water

In order listed, put all ingredients in pan, select white bread and push start.

Preparation time: 15 minutes
Time in breadmaker: 2 1/2 to 4 1/4 hours
Servings: 1 large loaf or 18 dinner rolls

Variations: For cinnamon raisin bread: At the sound of the "beep" in the second mixing, add 1 1/2 tablespoons cinnamon and 3/4 cup raisins. For 100% whole wheat dinner rolls, follow directions for dinner rolls with Basic White Bread recipe.

Bread
(Whole Wheat)

(for the smaller bread maker)

1 1/2 tsp. yeast
2 1/2 c. whole wheat flour
1/4 c. gluten
1 tsp. salt (optional)
2 Tbsp. honey
1/4 c. egg whites
1 c. hot water
2 Tbsp. cracked wheat

In order listed, put all ingredients in pan, select white bread and push start.

Preparation time: 10 minutes
Time in breadmaker: 2 1/2 to 4 1/4 hours
Servings: 1 small loaf

Wheat and Honey Bread

1 pkg. rapid rise yeast
2 1/2 c. whole wheat flour
1 c. bread flour
1 tsp. salt (optional)
2 Tbsp. honey
1 Tbsp. corn syrup
2 egg whites or 1 1/2 tsp. egg
    replacer mixed in 3 Tbsp.
    water
1 c. + 2 Tbsp. hot water
    (120 to 130 degrees)

In the order listed, put all ingredients in pan, select white bread, and push start.

Preparation time: 15 minutes
Time in breadmaker: 2 1/2 to 4 1/4 hours
Servings: 1 large loaf

White Bread

(Basic)

1 pkg. yeast
3 c. bread flour
1 Tbsp. sugar
1 tsp. salt (optional)
2 Tbsp. fat-free soy milk
1 Tbsp. corn syrup
1 1/4 c. hot water (115 to 120
    degrees)

Pour yeast to one side of inner pan

Add rest of ingredients in the order given.

Select white bread and push "Start."

Preparation time: 15 minutes
Time in breadmaker: 2 1/2 to 4 1/4 hours
Servings: 1 large loaf or 18 dinner rolls

For dinner rolls: Turn breadmaker off after "beep." Make dough into 18 equal balls, place in nonstick muffin tins.

Let rise in warm place until doubled in size.

Bake at 400 degrees for 12 to 15 minutes

Balls of dough can be frozen for future use. Let rise 3 to 4 hours before baking.

Molasses Brown Bread

Weizenkeimbrot

2 1/2 c. whole wheat flour
1 1/2 c. wheat bran
1/3 c. brown sugar
1/2 tsp. salt (optional)
1 c. raisins (light and dark)
2 tsp. baking soda
1 7/8 c. fat-free soy milk with
    1 Tbsp. vinegar
1/3 c. molasses

Preheat oven to 325 degrees. Spray a 9 x 5 x 3-inch loaf pan with nonstick spray.

Combine the flour, wheat bran, brown sugar, salt and raisins in a medium mixing bowl; mix well.

In a small mixing bowl, mix baking soda, skim soy milk and molasses, using a wooden spoon.

This mixture will start to bubble. Immediately stir in into the dry ingredients.

Spoon the batter into sprayed pan and bake at once.

The bread will be done when a toothpick comes out clean, about 1 hour.

Turn out of the pan and cool on a wire rack.

Preparation time: 20 minutes
Baking time: 1 hour
Servings: 1 loaf—about 12 slices

Banana Wheat Bread

2 1/2 tsp. or 1 pkg. yeast
1 3/4 c. all-purpose flour or
   bread flour
1/4 c. gluten
1 1/2 c. whole wheat flour
2 medium size ripe bananas,
   sliced into pan
1/4 c. honey
1/4 c. warm water (115 to 120
   degrees)
2 Tbsp. applesauce
2 Tbsp. corn syrup
1/2 tsp. vanilla
2 egg whites or 1 1/2 tsp. egg
   replacer mixed with
 3 Tbsp. water
1 tsp. baking soda

Place ingredients in pan in the order listed.

Select white bread and press "start".

Turn baking control most of way toward "light".

At the sound of "beep" in second kneading, add 1/2 to 2/3 cup raisins, if desired.

Preparation time: 20 minutes
Time in breadmaker: 2 1/2 to 4 1/4 hours
Servings: 1 large loaf

Cinnamon Raisin Bread

1 pkg. yeast
2 1/2 c. bread flour
1 c. whole wheat flour
2 Tbsp. sugar
1 tsp. salt (optional)
2 tsp. cinnamon
1 Tbsp. corn syrup
1/4 c. fat-free soy milk
1 1/4 c. warm water
2/3 c. raisins

In the order listed, put all ingredients into the pan, select white bread and push "Start". Or, wait and add the raisins at the "beep" in the second mixing. Set temperature gauge part way toward "light".

Preparation time: 15 minutes
Time in breadmaker: 2 1/2 to 4 1/4 hours
Servings: 1 large loaf

Herb Bread

1 pkg. yeast

1 1/2 c. whole wheat flour

2 c. bread flour

1 1/2 Tbsp. sugar

1 1/2 tsp. salt (optional)

1/2 tsp. dried sage

1/4 tsp. dried thyme

1/4 tsp. dried marjoram

1/2 c. onion, minced

1 1/2 Tbsp. corn syrup or
   applesauce

1 c. + 2 Tbsp. warm water
(115 to 120 degrees)

In order listed, place all ingredients in pan; select white bread and press "start".

Preparation time: 15 minutes
Baking time: 2 1/2 to 4 1/4 hours
Servings: 1 large loaf

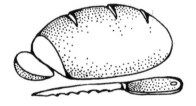

Oat Bran Bread

1 pkg. yeast
1 c. quick-cooking oatmeal
1 1/2 c. bread flour
2 1/4 c. oat bran
1 3/4 c. whole wheat flour
1/4 c. gluten
1 tsp. salt (optional)
2 Tbsp. light or dark corn
  syrup
2 Tbsp. honey
2 egg whites or 1 1/2 tsp. egg
  replacer mixed in 3 Tbsp.
  water
2 c. + 2 Tbsp. very warm water

Place ingredients in pan in the order listed, select white bread and push "Start".

This recipe is very large and may kick up some flour over the edge or on the glass dome at the beginning. The pan will be very full and the bread may not rise very much. If it does rise too much, cut down on the liquid; if it seems too dry, increase the liquid.

Preparation time: 20 minutes
Time in breadmaker: 2 1/2 to 4 1/4 hours
Servings: 1 large loaf

Oat Bran Bread Variations

For Oat Bran Fresh Apple Bread:
Use same ingredients listed in previous recipe, but after egg whites or egg replacer, add 2 cups freshly grated apple (peeled) and 1 1/2 cups very warm apple juice instead of water.

For Oat Bran Prune Bread:

Use same ingredients listed in previous recipe and add 1 cup pitted prunes cut in small pieces plus 1/8 teaspoon nutmeg (optional) before adding water.

For Oat Bran Raisin Bread:

Use same ingredients listed in previous recipe and add 1 cup raisins plus 1 to 2 teaspoons cinnamon before adding water.

Oatmeal Bread

1 pkg. yeast
1 c. rolled oats, whirred in blender
2 c. bread flour
1 c. whole wheat flour
1 Tbsp. sugar
1 tsp. salt (optional)
1 Tbsp. corn syrup
1 1/4 to 1 3/4 c. warm water

Whirl oats in blender until fine.

Add all ingredients to pan in order listed.

Select white bread and push "Start".

Preparation time: 15 minutes
Time in breadmaker: 2 1/2 to 4 1/4 hours
Servings: 1 large loaf

Sweet Potato and Raisin Bread

1 pkg. dry yeast
2 c. bread flour
1 c. whole wheat flour
1/4 c. light brown sugar
1 tsp. salt (optional)
3 egg whites or 2 1/4 tsp. egg
   replacer mixed in 1/4 c.
   water
1 1/2 Tbsp. corn syrup
1 c. mashed sweet potatoes
1/2 c. warm water (115 to 120
   degrees)
2/3 c. raisins

Place first 9 ingredients in breadmaker pan in order listed, select white bread and push "start".

At the sound of the "beep" in second mixing, add 2/3 cup raisins.

Preparation time: 15 minutes
Time in breadmaker: 2 1/2 to 4 1/4 hours
Servings: 1 large loaf

Lemon Date Bread

1 pkg. yeast
2 1/2 c. bread flour
1 c. whole wheat flour
1 Tbsp. gluten
1 tsp. salt (optional)
2 Tbsp. corn syrup
3 Tbsp. honey
1 small lemon, chopped and
  seeded
Hot water
1 c. date bits or pitted dates,
  cut in raisin-size pieces

Turn baking control most of way toward "light".

Place first 7 ingredients in the breadmaker pan in the order listed.

Whirl the lemon with 1/2 cup hot water in an electric blender to puree the lemon; then add hot water to make 1 1/4 cup plus 2 tablespoons liquid (115 to 120 degrees). Pour into the pan.

Select white bread and push "start".

Add the dates when breadmaker "beeps" during second kneading.

Preparation time: 20 minutes
Time in breadmaker: 2 1/2 to 4 1/4 hours
Servings: 1 large loaf

Pumper-nickel Bread

(for automatic breadmaker)

1 1/2 pkgs. yeast
2 c. rye flour
1/2 c. unprocessed wheat bran
   or oat bran cereal
1 3/4 c. bread flour
2 tsp. caraway seed
1 1/2 tsp. salt (optional)
1 Tbsp. carob powder
3 Tbsp. molasses
1 Tbsp. corn syrup or
   applesauce
1 1/4 c. warm water (115 to 120
   degrees)

Add all ingredients in the order listed.

Select white bread and press "start".

Preparation time: 15 minutes
Baking time: 2 1/2 to 4 1/4 hours
Servings: 1 large loaf

Russian Black Bread

(for automatic breadmaker)

1 pkg. yeast
1 Tbsp. white sugar
1 1/2 c. bread flour
1 1/2 c. rye flour
1/4 c. whole wheat flour
1/2 c. unprocessed bran flakes
1 Tbsp. caraway seeds
1 tsp. salt (optional)
1 tsp. instant Postum™
1 1/2 tsp. dill seeds
2 Tbsp. carob powder

Mix and heat the following
   over low heat to 115
   degrees:
1 c. + 2 Tbsp. water
2 Tbsp. molasses
2 Tbsp. cider vinegar
2 Tbsp. dark corn syrup

Add all ingredients in order
listed to the pan, select white
bread and push "Start".

A perfect companion for stews
or thick soups.

Preparation time: 20 minutes
Time in breadmaker: 2 1/2 to 4
1/4 hours
Servings: 1 short large loaf

Rye Bread

(for automatic breadmaker)

1 pkg. yeast
2 c. rye flour
2 c. bread flour
1 Tbsp. sugar
1 tsp. salt (optional)
1 Tbsp. honey
1 Tbsp. corn syrup
1 tsp. allspice (optional)
1 Tbsp. caraway seeds
   (optional)
1 1/2 c. warm water

Place above ingredients in pan in order listed.

Select white bread and press "Start".

Preparation time: 15 minutes
Time in breadmaker: 2 1/2 to 4 1/4 hours
Servings: 1 short large loaf

Pizza Crust

1 pkg. rapid rise yeast
1 c. bread flour
1 1/4 c. whole wheat flour
1/4 c. gluten
1 tsp. sugar
1 tsp. salt (optional)
2 Tbsp. corn syrup
1 1/4 c. hot water

Put all ingredients in breadmaker and push "start".

Stop breadmaker after first kneading. Let dough rest 15 minutes, then spread out in pizza pan.

Add sauce and toppings.

Bake at 450 degrees for 15 to 20 minutes.

Preparation time: 25 minutes
Time in breadmaker: 15 minutes
Baking time: 20 minutes
Servings: 1 pizza crust

Whole Wheat Pizza Crust

1 pkg. rapid rise yeast
2 1/4 c. whole wheat flour
1/4 c. gluten
1 tsp. sugar
1 tsp. salt (optional)
1 1/4 c. hot water

Put all ingredients in breadmaker.

Stop breadmaker after first kneading; let dough rest 15 minutes then spread out in pizza pan.

Add sauce and toppings.

Bake at 450 degrees for 15 to 20 minutes.

Preparation time: 25 minutes
Time in breadmaker: 15 minutes
Baking time: 20 minutes
Servings: 1 pizza crust

Julekake
(Christmas Cake)

1 pkg. dry yeast or rapid rise
    yeast
3 1/2 c. bread flour
1/4 c. sugar
1/2 tsp. salt (optional)
2 egg whites (or 1 1/2 tsp. egg
    replacer mixed in 3 Tbsp.
    water)
1 tsp. ground cardamom
2 Tbsp. corn syrup
1 c. + 2 Tbsp. hot water (125 to
    130 degrees)

Turn baking control most of way toward "light." Place above ingredients in pan in order listed. Select white bread and push "start". At the sound of the "beep" in the second mixing, add the following:

1/3 c. golden raisins
1/4 c. finely chopped candied pineapple
1/4 c. finely chopped candied cherries

Preparation time: 20 minutes
Time in breadmaker: 2 1/2 to 4 1/4 hours
Servings: 1 large loaf

HANDMADE YEAST BREADS

"Nature cures when given the opportunity."

—Dr. Bernard Jensen

- **Eat to live . . . Don't live to eat**
- **Think of food as fuel**
- **Treat yourself with preventive medicine**

"Something Lovin' from the Oven"

Herb Bread

3 c. whole wheat flour
5 to 5 1/2 c. all-purpose flour,
    divided
2 pkg. yeast
3 Tbsp. sugar
1 Tbsp. salt (optional)
1 tsp. dried sage
1/2 tsp. dried thyme
1/2 tsp. dried marjoram
1 medium onion, minced,
    about 1 c.
3 Tbsp. corn syrup or
    applesauce
3 c. warm water (120 to 130
    degrees)

In a large mixing bowl, combine whole wheat flour, 1 cup all-purpose flour, yeast, sugar, salt, herbs, onion, corn syrup (or substitute) and water.

Beat with an electric mixer on low until moistened; then beat on medium for 3 minutes.

By hand, stir in enough of the remaining flour to form a stiff dough.

Turn out on lightly floured surface and knead until smooth and elastic, about 8 to 10 minutes.

Place in a lightly greased bowl, turning once to grease top. Cover and let rise in a warm place until doubled, about 1 hour.

Punch dough down. Shape into 2 balls and place in 2 sprayed 2-quart casseroles.

Cover and let rise until almost doubled, about 45 minutes.

Brush tops with skim soy milk.

Bake at 350 degrees for 40 to 45 minutes.

Remove from casseroles to cool on wire racks.

Preparation time: 30 minutes
Rising time: 1 3/4 hours
Baking time: 45 minutes
Servings: 2 large loaves

Whole Wheat Batter Bread

2 1/2 c. whole wheat flour
(about)

1 pkg. yeast

1/4 c. gluten

1 Tbsp. sugar

3/4 tsp. salt (optional)

1/8 tsp. baking soda

1/3 c. fat-free soy milk

1 1/4 c. water (120 to 130
degrees)

2 Tbsp. applesauce or corn
syrup

For a white loaf: use about 3 cups bread flour and omit gluten. In mixing, use 1 1/2 cups flour in dry mixture and follow above remaining instructions.

Combine 1 cup flour, yeast, gluten, sugar, salt, baking soda and dry milk in medium sized mixing bowl.

Add warm water and applesauce (or substitutes) to dry mixture and beat well 3 minutes.

Add 1/2 cup flour and beat 2 more minutes. (If using electric mixer, mix liquid into dry ingredients on low speed just until blended. Increase speed to medium, beat 2 minutes.

Add 1/2 cup flour to make a thick batter and beat 2 more minutes.) With spoon, stir in enough remaining flour to make a stiff batter.

Spoon into a 9 x 5-inch nonstick loaf pan lightly sprayed with nonstick spray.

Cover and let rise in a warm place until doubled, about 1 hour.

Bake at 375 degrees for 35 to 40 minutes. Remove from pan and cool.

Preparation time: 20 minutes
Rising time: 1 hour
Cooking time: 40 minutes
Servings: 1 loaf

Savory Casserole Batter Bread

4 3/4 c. bread flour (about)
2 Tbsp. sugar
1 tsp. salt (optional)
1 tsp. basil leaves
1 tsp. oregano leaves
1/2 tsp. garlic powder
1 pkg. yeast
1 c. fat-free soy milk
1 c. water
2 Tbsp. applesauce or corn syrup
1 egg white beaten with 1 Tbsp. water or 3/4 tsp. egg replacer mixed in 1 Tbsp. water and beaten

In a large bowl, combine 2 cups flour, sugar, salt, basil, oregano, garlic powder and yeast.

Heat milk, water and applesauce (or substitutes) to 120 to 130 degrees.

Add to dry mixture; beat 2 minutes at medium speed of mixer. Add 1/2 cup flour. Beat at high speed 2 minutes. Stir in enough remaining flour to make a stiff batter. Cover; let rise in warm draft-free place until doubled in size, about 1 hour.

Stir batter down. Beat vigorously, about 1/2 minute. Turn into a 2-quart casserole dish that has been sprayed with nonstick spray. Cover; let rise until double in size, about 30 minutes.

Beat egg white and water or egg replacer and water; brush loaf.

Bake at 375 degrees for 45 to 50 minutes or until done. Remove from casserole; cool on wire rack.

Preparation time: 20 minutes
Rising time: 1 hour and 30 minutes
Baking time: 50 minutes
Servings: 1 loaf

Oatmeal Batter Bread

2 tsp. salt (optional)
2 pkg. yeast
5 c. bread flour (about)
1 c. quick cooking oats
1/2 c. light molasses
2 Tbsp. applesauce or corn
    syrup
2 1/4 c. water

In a large bowl, combine salt, yeast and 2 cups flour. In a 2-quart saucepan, mix oats, molasses, applesauce (or substitute) and water.

Over low heat, heat until very warm (120 to 130 degrees).

With mixer at low speed, gradually beat liquid into dry ingredients just until blended. Increase speed to medium; beat 2 minutes.

Beat in 1/2 cup flour to make a thick batter; continue beating 2 minutes, scraping bowl often. With spoon, stir in about 2 1/2 cups flour to make a stiff dough that leaves side of bowl.

Cover bowl; let rise in warm place until doubled, about 1 hour. Spray well two 2-quart round, shallow casseroles with nonstick spray.

Stir dough down; divide in 2 and turn into casseroles. With nonstick spray on fingers, turn each dough over to coat with spray; shape into ball.

Cover; let rise in warm place until doubled, about 45 minutes. Heat oven to 350 degrees and bake 40 minutes or until done.

Remove from casseroles and cool on wire racks.

Preparation time: 20 minutes
Rising time: 1 hour and 45 minutes
Baking time: 45 minutes
Servings: 2 loaves (about 12 slices each)

Whole Wheat Pita Bread

1 pkg. yeast
1 c. warm water (105 to 115 degrees)
1 Tbsp. sugar
1 1/2 c. all-purpose flour
1/2 tsp. salt (optional)
1 1/2 c. whole wheat flour

Dissolve yeast in warm water in a medium mixing bowl; add sugar and let stand 5 minutes.

Add all-purpose flour and salt; beat at low speed of an electric mixer until smooth.

Gradually stir in whole wheat flour.

Turn dough out onto a floured surface; knead 3 minutes until smooth and elastic.

Cover dough and let rest 10 minutes.

Divide dough into 6 equal portions; shape each portion into a smooth ball.

Pat each ball into a 5-inch circle.

Place circles on lightly sprayed baking sheets. Bake at 375 degrees for 8 to 10 minutes.

Cut in half with scissors to make bread rounds or pockets.

Preparation time: 35 minutes
Baking time: 10 minutes
Servings: 12 pita rounds or 6 bread pockets

Onion-Dill Whole Wheat Pita Bread

1 pkg. dry yeast
1 1/4 c. warm water (105 to
   115 degrees)
2 Tbsp. sugar
1/4 c. chopped dehydrated
   onion
2 Tbsp. dill seed
1 Tbsp. corn syrup
1/2 tsp. salt (optional)
1 1/2 c. bread flour
1 1/2 c. whole wheat flour

Dissolve yeast in warm water in a large mixing bowl.

Add sugar and let stand 5 minutes.

Add onion, dill seed, corn syrup, salt and bread flour and beat until smooth.

Gradually stir in whole wheat flour.

Turn dough onto a floured surface and knead 3 minutes until smooth and elastic.

Cover dough and let rest 10 minutes.

Divide dough into 6 equal portions and shape each into a smooth ball.

Pat each ball into a 5-inch circle.

Place circles on nonstick baking sheets; bake at 375 degrees for 10 minutes.

Cut in half with scissors to make bread rounds or pockets.

Preparation time: 35 minutes
Baking time: 10 minutes
Servings: 12 pita rounds or 6 bread pockets

CORNMEAL BREADS

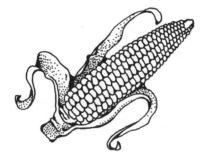

Corn is a Basic Grain and has fed many civilizations
for thousands of years.

Cornbread
(Plain)

1 c. cornmeal
1 c. flour
4 tsp. baking powder
1/2 tsp. salt (optional)
2 egg whites or 1 1/2 tsp. egg
replacer mixed in 3 Tbsp.
   water
1 c. fat-free soy milk

In a medium mixing bowl, combine dry ingredients.

In a small bowl, mix all remaining ingredients; add to dry ingredients and mix well.

Pour into a sprayed 8-inch square baking pan or 8-inch heavy skillet.

Bake in 425 degree oven for 25 to 30 minutes.

Preparation time: 15 minutes
Baking time: 30 minutes
Servings: 4 to 6

Cornbread
(Mexican Style)

1 c. cornmeal

1 c. flour

4 tsp. baking powder

1/2 tsp. salt (optional)

2 egg whites or 1 1/2 tsp. egg
  replacer mixed in 3 Tbsp.
  water

1 c. fat-free soy milk

1/2 c. frozen corn

4 oz. chopped green chilies or

 4 oz. chopped jalapeno

  peppers

In a medium mixing bowl,
combine dry ingredients.

In a small bowl, mix all
remaining ingredients ; add to
dry ingredients and mix well.

Pour into a sprayed 8-inch
square baking pan or 8-inch
heavy skillet.

Bake in 425 degree oven for 25
to 30 minutes.

Preparation time: 15 minutes
Baking time: 30 minutes
Servings: 4 to 6

Cornbread
(Georgia Style)

2 1/2 c. cornmeal, medium ground
1 tsp. salt (optional)
2 tsp. baking powder
2 c. fat-free soy milk
4 egg whites or 1 Tbsp. egg replacer mixed in 1/4 c. + 2 Tbsp. water

In a medium bowl, combine cornmeal, salt and baking powder.

In a small bowl, mix skim soy milk and egg whites or egg replacer; add to cornmeal mixture and mix quickly. (It should be a medium pour batter. If too thick, add a little water; if too thin, add a bit of cornmeal.)

Pour into a sprayed, heavy, 8-inch skillet and bake at 450 degrees for 25 to 30 minutes.

Preparation time: 15 minutes
Baking time: 30 minutes
Servings: 8 to 10

Hearty Oat and Cornbread

1 c. oats, quick or old
   fashioned
1 c. cornmeal
1/2 c. all-purpose flour
1 Tbsp. baking powder
1/4 tsp. salt (optional)
1 c. fat-free soy milk
1/2 c. frozen kernel corn,
   thawed
2 Tbsp. applesauce
2 egg whites or 1 1/2 tsp. egg
   replacer mixed in 3 Tbsp.
   water
2 Tbsp. onion, finely chopped

Heat oven to 425 degrees.
Spray 8 or 9-inch square baking
pan with nonstick spray.

In a medium bowl, combine dry
ingredients.

Add remaining ingredients that
have been combined in a small
bowl; mix well.

Spread evenly into prepared
pan.

Bake 20 to 25 minutes or until
edges are lightly browned.
Serve warm.

Preparation time: 15 minutes
Baking time: 25 minutes
Servings: 9

Cornmeal Strips

6 Tbsp. flour
6 Tbsp. cornmeal
2 egg whites or 1 1/2 tsp. egg replacer mixed in 3 Tbsp. water
1/4 tsp. salt (optional)

In a small bowl, combine all ingredients. (If all dry ingredients are not moistened, add a bit of water.)

Knead just enough to make a smooth dough.

Roll thin to about 1/8-inch thick.

Cut in 1/2-inch strips.

Place on ungreased cookie sheet and bake at 350 degrees for 30 minutes.

Recipe may be doubled. Store in airtight container.

Preparation time: 15 minutes
Baking time: 30 minutes
Servings: 3 to 4

Hot Water Cornbread Pones

**2 c. white cornmeal, medium
  ground**
1/2 tsp. salt (optional)
1 3/4 c. boiling water

In medium bowl, mix cornmeal
and salt.

Add boiling water all at once;
stir until well mixed. Dough will
be very stiff.

As soon as it is cool enough to
handle, with your hands, form it
into small pones about 1/2 inch
thick and about 3 inches long;
or divide it into 3 equal
parts and form into 3 large
pones about 1/2 inch thick.

Have a small bowl with a little
water handy for dampening
your fingers and hands for
handling the dough so it will
not stick to your hands.

To bake in oven, place pones on
sprayed shallow baking pans
and bake at 400 degrees for 50
to 60 minutes until lightly
browned.

To bake on top of stove, place
in a sprayed 8 or 9-inch heavy
skillet and bake over medium
heat with loose-fitting lid for 50
to 60 minutes.

Turn once with spatula after
baking about 30 minutes, or
when bottom side is lightly
browned.

Preparation time: 20 minutes
Baking time: 1 hour
Servings: 6 to 8

SWEET
BREADS

Prevention

Dr. Alabaster said, "Preventive measures are really the way of the future. They have also been the way of the past. A hundred years ago, half the population was dead before the age of forty, mainly because of infection. Now that number is down to three percent, entirely due to preventive measures: better sanitation, better hygiene, vaccinations, and to a very small extent, direct therapy. This is a dramatic change produced by preventive measures.

Apple Bread

2 3/4 c. whole wheat flour
2 tsp. cinnamon
1 tsp. baking soda
1/2 tsp. baking powder
1/4 tsp. salt (optional)
1/4 c. applesauce
1/4 c. corn syrup
1 1/2 c. sugar
4 egg whites or 1 Tbsp. egg
    replacer mixed with 1/4 c. +
    2 Tbsp. water
1/2 tsp. vanilla
3 c. apples, peeled, cored,
    coarsely chopped

In a large bowl, combine flour, cinnamon, baking soda, baking powder and salt.

In a medium bowl, combine applesauce, corn syrup, sugar, egg whites or egg replacer, vanilla and apples; stir into flour mixture.

Divide mixture between two 8 x 4-inch bread pans that have been sprayed with nonstick spray.

Bake at 350 degrees for 40 to 45 minutes or until bread tests done.

Cool for 10 minutes on wire racks before removing from pans.

Preparation time: 20 minutes
Baking time: 45 minutes
Servings: 2 loaves—about 24 slices

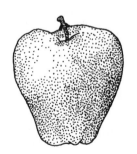

Carrot Spice Bread

2 c. whole wheat flour
1 1/4 c. + 3 Tbsp. oatmeal,
quick or old fashioned,
uncooked
1/2 c. brown sugar
1/2 c. chopped dates or raisins
4 tsp. baking powder
1/2 tsp. baking soda
1/2 tsp. cinnamon
1/4 tsp. ginger (optional)
1/8 tsp. cloves (optional)
1/4 tsp. salt (optional)
1/2 c. frozen apple juice
concentrate, thawed
2 Tbsp. applesauce
1/4 c. corn syrup
1/4 c. water
4 egg whites or 1 Tbsp. egg
replacer mixed in 1/4 c. +
2 Tbsp. water
1 c. shredded carrots (about 2
medium)

Heat oven to 350 degrees.

Spray an 8 x 4 or 9 x 5-inch loaf pan with nonstick spray.

In a medium bowl, combine dry ingredients except 3 tablespoons oats; mix well.

Add liquid ingredients that have been combined in a small bowl; mix just until moistened.

Fold in carrots. Spread evenly in prepared pan.

Sprinkle with remaining 3 tablespoons oatmeal.

Bake 1 hour and 10 minutes, or until it tests done. Cool 10 minutes; remove from pan.

Cool completely. Store tightly covered.

Preparation time: 20 minutes
Baking time: 1 hour and 10 minutes
Servings: 1 load—12 slices each

Oatmeal Pumpkin Bread

1 c. oatmeal, uncooked
1 1/4 c. skim soy milk, room
    temperature
3/4 c. pumpkin puree
4 egg whites or 1 Tbsp. egg
    replacer mixed in 1/4 c. +
    2 Tbsp. water
2 Tbsp. corn syrup
1/2 c. sugar (optional)
2 Tbsp. applesauce
2 c. whole wheat flour
1 Tbsp. baking powder
1/4 tsp. salt (optional)
1 tsp. cinnamon
1/4 tsp. nutmeg
1/2 c. golden raisins

Heat oven to 350 degrees. Spray a 9 x 5 inch loaf pan with nonstick spray.

In a large bowl, mix oatmeal and milk. Let sit a few minutes.

Beat in next 5 ingredients. In a medium bowl, mix flour, baking powder, salt and spices.

Stir into pumpkin mixture until well combined. Stir in raisins.

Pour into prepared loaf pan; bake 55 to 60 minutes or until a toothpick comes out clean.

Let cool 20 minutes before removing from pan.

Preparation time: 20 minutes
Baking time: 1 hour
Servings: 1 loaf—about 12 slices

Ginger-bread

Delicious served with lemon sauce (see recipe).

2 c. whole wheat flour
2 tsp. baking powder
1/2 tsp. baking soda
2 tsp. ginger
1 tsp. cinnamon
1/2 tsp. salt (optional)
1/4 c. applesauce
2 Tbsp. corn syrup
2 egg whites or 1 1/2 tsp. egg
    replacer mixed in 3 Tbsp.
    water
2/3 c. molasses
1 c. fat-free soy milk with
    1 Tbsp. vinegar

In a small bowl, mix flour, baking powder, baking soda, ginger, cinnamon and salt. In a medium bowl, combine applesauce, corn syrup, egg whites or egg replacer and molasses.

Alternately add dry ingredients and skim soy milk, a little at a time, beating until smooth after each addition.

Pour batter into an 8-inch square pan that has been sprayed with nonstick spray.

Bake in a 350 degree oven 50 minutes or until it tests done.

Preparation time: 20 minutes
Baking time: 50 minutes
Servings: 9

BREAKFAST

Prevention The Best Cure

In his 1990 book, *The Power of Your Plate*, Neal D. Barnard, M.D., has emphasized that cancer prevention is all important. "From my own prospective, an optimal diet for cancer prevention means cutting back or eliminating meats and dairy products, which are devoid of fiber and frequently much too high in fat and protein. It means avoiding fried foods and added oils. And it means having generous amounts of whole grains, legumes, and vegetables. Any shift toward this optimal diet is a shift toward health," he said.

Breakfast is the most important meal of the day. Eat a large portion of whole grain hot cereal daily.

CEREALS

Whole grains are essential to health. They are made up of starch, complex carbohydrate, (fiber), B & E vitamins, zinc, selenium and other nutrients for the best posible health.

The Miracle Diet

The Miracle Diet is a plant-centered diet program that allows your body to seek its ideal weight with natural, high energy. It is based upon plants, not vegetables. The five basic starches are the basis of the diet.

- **Grain**   (wheat, oats, and barley)
- **Rice**   (a basic grain)
- **Corn**   (a basic grain)
- **Legumes**   (beans, peas, and lentils)
- **Potatoes**   (the only vegetable)

The National Physicians Committee for Responsible Medicine said: "The tools used to teach Americans good nutrition should be changed to reflect the mounting evidence that diets high in fat and low in fiber increase the risk of heart disease, cancer, obesity and diabetes."

Granola Mix

5 c. old-fashioned oatmeal,
  uncooked
1 c. raisins
1/2 c. wheat bran
1/4 c. firmly packed brown
  sugar
1 tsp. cinnamon
1/2 tsp. salt (optional)
1/2 c. water
1/2 c. corn syrup
1/4 c. honey
1/4 c. molasses
1 tsp. vanilla

Combine first 4 ingredients in a large bowl.

Combine remaining ingredients in a small saucepan; place over medium heat and cook, stirring often, until sugar dissolves.

Pour hot mixture over cereal mixture; stir until thoroughly blended. (Mixture will appear wet.)

Spread evenly in a sprayed, large, shallow pan.

Bake at 300 degrees for 1 hour, stirring every 15 minutes.

Cool; store in an airtight container.

Preparation time: 20 minutes
Baking time: 1 hour
Servings: 9 1/2 cups

Hot Mixed Cereals

(Super Healthy)

4 c. water
1 c. dry mixed cereals: equal parts Wheatena, oats, oat bran
Raisins or other fruit (optional)

Options:
Use any other grains in any combination for variety.
Millett
Rye
Rice
Cornmeal
Cracked Wheat
Wheat Bran
Steel cut oats
Crushed Wheat
Bulgur Wheat

Bring the water to a boil in a medium saucepan.

Add the premixed cereal slowly, stirring constantly; reduce heat to medium low, cover and cook about 15 minutes.

Stir occasionally. For smoother cereal, cook longer; turn to low heat if you want to cook it longer than 15 minutes.

Add water to thin mixture if needed. Add fruit if desired.

For variety, this is delicious served with a little unsweet-ened applesauce and a little cinnamon or apple pie spice sprinkled over the top.

Also, try using all or part apple juice instead of all water.

Keep a combination of your favorite cereals premixed in a large covered container.

Preparation time: 5 minutes
Cooking time: 10 to 20 minutes
Servings: 4 to 6

Whole Wheat Berries

2 c. boiling water
1 tsp. salt (optional)
1 c. whole wheat berries

Wash wheat berries in water until water is clear. Place wheat berries in pan and cover with boiling water. Let stand overnight. Pour off water, saving 2 cups for cooking.

If cooking in pressure cooker, place soaked wheat berries, water in which wheat berries have been soaked, and salt in pressure cooker and follow cooking directions.

To cook in medium saucepan, place soaked wheat berries, water in which wheat berries have been soaked, and salt in saucepan. Bring almost to boiling, reduce heat, cover tightly and keep just below boiling point about 2 hours. Chewy and delicious. It has to be very nourishing because it is made from whole grain, which also adds to its taste.

Preparation time: 10 minutes
Soaking time: overnight
Cooking time: 2 hours
Servings: 5 to 8

Cornmeal Mush

Cornmeal mush has helped sustain Americans since the country's beginning. It was one of the staple foods of pioneer families and has since become a popular stick-to-the-ribs southern dish. There is a trick for preparing this simple dish without lumps.

1 1/2 c. yellow or white cornmeal
1 tsp. salt (optional)
3 Tbsp. white flour
1 1/2 c. cold water
4 1/2 c. boiling water

Mix together the cornmeal, salt, and flour. Stir in cold water and mix thoroughly. Immediately dump this cold batter mixture into the boiling water and stir. Bring to a boil and cook until it thickens. Put a lid on the pan and lower the heat to simmer; allow to cook an additional 10 minutes.

Serve as a hearty breakfast cereal with skim soy milk and/or fruit, if desired. If you have any mush left over, place it in a pan that has been lightly sprayed with nonstick spray and refrigerate overnight. Cut the firm mush into 1/4-inch thick slices, place on a cookie sheet that has been lightly sprayed with nonstick spray and brush with the following, which has been beaten:

1 egg white or 1 1/2 tsp. egg replacer mixed with 2 T. water
1 Tbsp. water
Or, cut mush slices can be brushed with liquid Butter Buds before baking.

Mix in a cup:
4 tsp. Butter Buds (1/2 packet)
1/4 c. hot tap water
(or proportions as needed)

Bake in oven that has been preheated to 450 degrees for 10 to 15 minutes or until lightly browned. Delicious served with maple syrup or all-fruit jam or jelly. Or, sprinkle with Mrs. Dash before baking and eat with fork as a bread with cooked vegetable dishes.

MUFFINS

**All grain is good for the food of man because we are
Plantarians by Nature.**

Dr. Oliver Alabaster M.D., world-wide authority on cancer prevention says: "The three major killer diseases that now account for
premature mortality are cancer, heart disease and stroke. They
account for four out of five deaths. Yet these three diseases are
largely untreatable and almost entirely preventable if we make the
right decisions. So the three major killer diseases which will
otherwise be with us well into the next century could be abolished
if we take the right steps."

"Plantarianism"
It's truly a miracle!

- Prevent heart-artery disease
- Reverse adult diabetes
- Lower blood pressure
- Prevent many cancers

- Reverse heart disease
- Prevent adult diabetes
- Lose weight permanently
- Prevent Osteoporosis

Breakfast Muffins

2 c. whole wheat flour
2 tsp. baking powder
1/2 tsp. salt (optional)
1/4 c. corn syrup
1 1/2 c. fat-free soy milk
2 egg whites or 1 1/2 tsp. egg
    replacer mixed in 3 Tbsp.
    water
2 Tbsp. applesauce

For a different taste, use 1 cup cornmeal in place of 1 cup flour. Or, try 1/2 cup raisins, 1/2 teaspoon cinnamon or 1/4 teaspoon nutmeg, ginger or allspice.

In a medium mixing bowl, combine dry ingredients.

In a small mixing bowl, combine remaining ingredients; add to flour mixture, stirring only until moistened.

Spoon into 12 nonstick muffin cups that have been lightly sprayed.

Bake at 400 degrees for 18 to 20 minutes until lightly browned and firm to touch.

Preparation time: 10 minutes
Baking time: 18 to 20 minutes
Servings: 12 muffins

Apple Oat Muffins

1 c. whole wheat flour

1 c. quick-cooking oats, uncooked

2 Tbsp. sugar

2 tsp. baking powder

1/2 tsp. salt (optional)

1/4 tsp. cinnamon

1/8 tsp. nutmeg

3/4 tsp. lemon rind, grated

2 egg whites or 1 1/2 tsp. egg replacer mixed in 3 Tbsp. water

1/2 c. unsweetened apple juice

1/4 c. fat-free soy milk

2 Tbsp. applesauce or corn syrup

Use a nonstick muffin tin.

Combine first 8 ingredients in medium size mixing bowl; make well in center of mixture.

In a small bowl, combine egg whites or egg replacer, apple juice, milk and applesauce or corn syrup; add to dry ingredients, stirring just until moistened.

Spoon into muffin pans, filling 2/3 full.

Bake at 425 degrees for 15 minutes.

Preparation time: 20 minutes
Baking time: 15 minutes
Servings: 12 muffins

Apple Streusel Muffins

1 c. whole wheat flour
1/2 c. oat bran cereal
1/3 c. sugar
2 tsp. baking powder
1 tsp. cinnamon
1/4 tsp. salt (optional)
1/2 c. fat-free soy milk
2 Tbsp. applesauce
2 Tbsp. corn syrup
2 egg whites or 1 1/2 tsp. egg
　　replacer mixed in 3 Tbsp.
　　water
1 tsp. vanilla
1 1/2 c. unpeeled apples, cored
　　and chopped
1/4 c. whole wheat flour
1/4 c. sugar
1 tsp. cinnamon

In a medium bowl, combine all dry ingredients.

In a small bowl, mix milk, applesauce, corn syrup, egg whites or egg replacer and vanilla.

Add to flour mixture, stirring just until moistened.

Fold in apples gently.

Fill 12 paper-lined muffin cups 2/3 full. Sprinkle with mixture of remaining flour, sugar and cinnamon, mixed in a small bowl.

Bake at 350 degrees for 20 minutes or until muffins test done.

Preparation time: 20 minutes
Baking time: 20 minutes
Servings: 12 muffins

Banana Muffins

1 1/2 c. whole wheat flour
1/4 c. wheat bran
2 tsp. baking powder
1/2 tsp. baking soda
1/2 tsp. salt (optional)
1/2 tsp. cinnamon
2 egg whites or 1 1/2 tsp. egg replacer mixed in 3 Tbsp. water
2 large, ripe bananas, mashed
2/3 c. fat-free soy milk
1/3 c. light or dark corn syrup
1 tsp. vanilla

Variation: For Blueberry Muffins, substitute 1/4 cup sugar for wheat bran, reduce milk to 1/2 cup, and use 1 cup fresh blueberries instead of the bananas. Bake 20 to 25 minutes.

In a large bowl, combine all dry ingredients.

In a medium bowl, beat egg whites or egg replacer with a fork or wire whisk.

Stir in remaining ingredients. Add to flour mixture, stirring just until moistened.

Spoon into 12 nonstick muffin cups.

Bake at 400 degrees for 18 to 20 minutes or until firm to touch.

Cool in muffin tin 5 minutes.

Remove to wire rack to cool completely.

Preparation time: 20 minutes
Baking time: 18 to 20 minutes
Servings: 12 muffins

Cranberry Muffins

2 1/2 c. whole wheat flour
1/4 c. sugar
3/4 tsp. baking soda
1 tsp. baking powder
1/4 tsp. salt (optional)
2 egg whites or 1 1/2 tsp. egg
** replacer mixed with**
** 3 Tbsp. water**
3/4 c. fat-free soy milk
2 Tbsp. corn syrup
2 Tbsp. applesauce
1 c. cranberries, chopped
1/4 c. sugar

Mix together flour, 1/4 cup sugar, baking soda, baking powder and salt in medium mixing bowl.

Combine egg whites or egg replacer, skim soy milk, corn syrup and applesauce in small bowl; blend well.

Add all at once to dry ingredients, stirring just enough to moisten.

Combine cranberries and other 1/4 cup sugar; stir into batter.

Spoon the batter into a 12-muffin nonstick pan, filling 2/3 full.

Bake in 400 degree oven 20 to 25 minutes.

Preparation time: 20 minutes
Baking time: 25 minutes
Servings: 12 muffins

Pineapple Muffins

2 1/2 c. whole wheat flour
2 tsp. baking powder
1/4 tsp. salt (optional)
1/4 c. sugar
2 egg whites or 1 1/2 tsp. egg
** replacer mixed in 3 Tbsp.**
** water**
1 can (8 oz.) crushed
pineapple, undrained
1/4 c. applesauce
1/4 c. corn syrup
1/4 c. plus 1 Tbsp. fat-free
** soy milk**
1 tsp. vanilla

Combine first 4 ingredients in large bowl; make well in center of mixture.

In a small bowl, combine egg whites or egg replacer with remaining ingredients.

Add to dry ingredients, stirring just until moistened.

Spoon batter into 1 1/2 dozen paper cup-lined muffin cups, filling 2/3 full.

Bake at 400 degrees for 20 to 22 minutes.

Remove from pans immediately.

Preparation time: 20 minutes
Baking time: 22 minutes
Servings: 18 muffins

Bran Muffins

1 3/4 c. unprocessed bran
1/4 c. brown sugar
2 1/2 c. whole wheat flour
2 1/2 tsp. baking soda
1/2 tsp. salt (optional)
1 Tbsp. orange peel, grated
4 egg whites or 1 Tbsp. egg
   replacer mixed in 6 Tbsp.
   water
1/2 c. honey
1/4 c. molasses
1/4 c. applesauce
1/4 c. corn syrup (or increase
   applesauce)
2 c. fat-free soy milk
1 c. boiling water

In a large bowl, combine bran, sugar, flour, baking soda, salt and orange peel; set aside.

In a small bowl, combine egg whites or egg replacer, honey, molasses, applesauce, corn syrup, skim soy milk and boiling water; mix well with dry ingredients.

Spoon batter into two nonstick muffin tins for 12, filling 2/3 full.

Bake at 350 degrees for 20 to 25 minutes. (Batter may be made ahead and stored in refrigerator for up to 1 month to be used as needed.)

Preparation time: 25 minutes
Baking time: 20 to 25 minutes
Servings: 24 muffins

Oat Bran Muffins

2 c. whole wheat flour
2 c. oat bran or oat bran cereal
4 tsp. baking powder
1 tsp. cinnamon
1/2 c. raisins (optional)
2 c. apple juice
1 Tbsp. corn syrup
2 egg whites or 1 1/2 tsp. egg
    replacer mixed in 3 Tbsp.
    water

Use nonstick muffin tins.

In a large mixing bowl, sift dry ingredients together; add raisins.

In a medium bowl, combine apple juice, corn syrup and egg whites or egg replacer.

Add to dry ingredients and stir until just mixed.

Spoon into muffin cups.

Bake at 425 degrees for 17 minutes.

Preparation time: 20 minutes
Baking time: 17 minutes
Servings: 18 muffins

Maple Bran Muffins

3/4 c. natural wheat bran
1/2 c. fat-free soy milk
1/2 c. maple syrup
2 egg whites or 1 1/2 tsp. egg
   replacer mixed in 3 Tbsp.
   water
1/4 c. corn syrup or applesauce
1 1/4 c. whole wheat flour
3 tsp. baking powder
1/2 tsp. salt (optional)

In a small bowl, combine bran, milk and maple syrup.

Mix in egg whites or egg replacer and corn syrup or applesauce.

Combine remaining ingredients in a medium bowl.

Add bran mixture, stirring until just moistened.

Divide batter in a 12-muffin nonstick pan.

Bake at 400 degrees for 18 to 20 minutes.

Preparation time: 20 minutes
Baking time: 20 minutes
Servings: 12 muffins

Whole Wheat Bran Muffins

1 c. wheat bran
1 c. fat-free soy milk
2 egg whites or 1 1/2 tsp. egg
   replacer mixed in 3 Tbsp.
   water
1/4 c. corn syrup (or part
   applesauce)
1/4 c. honey
1 1/4 c. whole wheat flour,
   unsifted
2 tsp. baking powder
1/4 tsp. baking soda
1/2 tsp. salt (optional)

*Variations: For Raisin Bran Muffins,
add 3/4 cup raisins to above recipe.
For Banana Bran Muffins, add 1/2 cup
mashed ripe banana (about 1 medium.)
For Prune Muffins, add 1 cup prunes,
pitted and chopped.*

Stir bran and milk together in a large mixing bowl.

Let stand 2 minutes. Add egg whites or egg replacer, corn syrup and honey and beat well.

Stir together in small bowl, flour, baking powder, baking soda and salt.

Add this to liquid mixture and stir only until mixed.

Spoon into a nonstick 12-muffin pan, filling 2/3 full.

Bake in preheated 400 degree oven 20 to 25 minutes.

Preparation time: 20 minutes
Baking time: 25 minutes
Servings: 12 muffins

Brown Rice Muffins

1 1/2 c. whole wheat flour
2 tsp. baking powder
1/4 tsp. salt (optional)
2 Tbsp. sugar (optional)
3 Tbsp. applesauce
2 egg whites or 1 1/2 tsp. egg replacer mixed in 3 Tbsp. water
1 c. fat-free soy milk
1 c. cold, cooked brown rice

In a medium bowl, stir together the flour, baking powder, salt and sugar. In a small bowl, beat egg whites or egg replacer until foamy; add applesauce and milk, and mix well.

Add rice and add to flour mixture.

Stir only until dry ingredients are moistened.

Spoon into a nonstick muffin tin for 12, filling 1/2 to 2/3 full.

Bake at 425 degrees for 20 minutes, or until done. Remove from pans immediately and serve hot.

Tops will be rounded, but muffins will be only about an inch high.

Preparation time: 20 minutes
Baking time: 20 minutes
Servings: 12 muffins

Cornmeal Muffins

1 c. plain cornmeal
1 c. whole wheat flour or
   1/2 c. whole wheat flour and
      1/2 c. oatmeal
1/2 tsp. salt (optional)
2 tsp. baking powder
4 egg whites or 1 Tbsp. egg
   replacer mixed in 6 Tbsp.
   water
1 1/2 c. fat-free soy milk

In a medium bowl, combine cornmeal, flour, salt and baking powder; set aside.

In a small bowl, combine egg whites or egg replacer and skim soy milk; stir into dry ingredients.

Fill 1 1/2 dozen muffin cups 2/3 full.

Bake at 425 degrees for 15 to 20 minutes.

Preparation time: 20 minutes
Baking time: 15 to 20 minutes
Servings: 18 muffins

Country Corn Muffins

1 c. yellow cornmeal
1 c. whole wheat flour
1 Tbsp. plus 2 tsp. baking
   powder
1/4 tsp. salt (optional)
1/2 tsp. baking soda
2 egg whites or 1 1/2 tsp. egg
   replacer mixed in 3 Tbsp.
   water
1 can (8.5 oz.) cream-style corn
1 c. fat-free soy milk

Combine cornmeal, flour, baking powder, salt and baking soda in a large mixing bowl; make a well in center of mixture.

In a small bowl, combine remaining ingredients; add to dry ingredients, stirring just until moistened.

Spoon into two nonstick muffin tins for 12.

Bake at 400 degrees for 12 to 15 minutes or until browned.

Preparation time: 20 minutes
Baking time: 12 to 15 minutes
Servings: 24 muffins

Oatmeal Muffins

2 c. whole wheat flour
2 c. quick-cooking oatmeal, uncooked
1/2 c. brown sugar (optional)
2 tsp. baking powder
1/2 tsp. salt (optional)
1 tsp. soda
2 tsp. cinnamon
4 egg whites or 1 Tbsp. egg replacer mixed in 6 Tbsp. water
2 c. fat-free soy milk
1/3 c. applesauce
1/3 c. corn syrup (or increase applesauce)

Combine dry ingredients in large bowl and mix well.

In a medium bowl, stir together egg whites or egg replacer, soy milk, applesauce.

Add to dry ingredients, stirring just until moistened.

Spoon into two nonstick muffin tins for 12.

Bake at 400 degrees for 18 to 20 minutes.

Preparation time: 20 minutes
Baking time: 18 to 20 minutes
Servings: 24 muffins

Variations: For Oatmeal Apple Raisins Muffins, add 1 cup raisins, 1 cored and peeled apple, and 1 teaspoon nutmeg. For Oatmeal Blueberry Muffins, use 1/3 cup honey for the corn syrup and add 1 cup frozen blueberries, thawed.

Ginger Spiced Muffins

2 1/2 c. whole wheat flour
1 1/2 tsp. baking powder
1 tsp. cinnamon
1 tsp. ginger
1/4 tsp. nutmeg
1/2 tsp. salt (optional)
2 egg whites or 1 1/2 tsp. egg
**   replacer mixed in 3 Tbsp.**
**   water**
1/2 c. molasses
1 c. fat-free soy milk
1/4 c. applesauce
1/4 c. corn syrup (or increase
**   applesauce)**

Lightly spray 24 muffin tin cups (2 1/2-inch size); set aside.

Preheat oven to 375 degrees. In large mixing bowl, combine dry ingredients.

In medium size mixing bowl, mix egg whites or egg replacer, molasses, soy milk, applesauce, and corn syrup.

Add moist ingredients to dry ingredients and beat 2 minutes.

Spoon into muffin cups.

Bake 20 to 25 minutes or until toothpick come out clean.

Preparation time: 20 minutes
Baking time: 20 to 25 minutes
Servings: 24 muffins

Microwave Pumpkin Muffins

1 c. coarsely crushed graham
  crackers
1/2 c. whole wheat bread
  crumbs
1 1/2 tsp. baking soda
1 tsp. ginger
3/4 tsp. allspice
1/2 tsp. nutmeg
1/2 c. pumpkin puree
1/4 c. fat-free soy milk
2 egg whites, lightly beaten, or
  1 1/2 tsp. egg replacer
  mixed with 3 Tbsp. water
1 Tbsp. molasses

In a medium bowl, combine the crackers, bread crumbs, baking soda, ginger, allspice and nutmeg.

In a small bowl, combine the pumpkin, milk, egg whites or egg replacer and molasses.

Pour the liquid ingredients over the flour mixture. Stir lightly with a fork just to mix.

Divide the batter evenly among six 1/2-cup ramekins or custard cups.

Place in the microwave in a circle on a carousel or directly on the bottom of the microwave.

Cook, uncovered, on High (100 percent) for 7 1/2 minutes.

Remove from oven. Turn out onto serving dish and serve warm or at room temperature.

Preparation time: 20 minutes
Baking time: 7 1/2 minutes
Servings: 6 muffins

Pumpkin Bran Muffins

1 1/2 c. whole wheat flour
1 c. wheat bran
2 tsp. baking powder
1/2 tsp. baking soda
1/2 tsp. salt (optional)
1 tsp. cinnamon
2 egg whites or 1 1/2 tsp. egg
   replacer mixed in 3 Tbsp.
   water
1 c. canned pumpkin
3/4 c. fat-free soy milk
1/2 c. corn syrup
1 tsp. vanilla

In a large bowl, combine dry ingredients. In a medium bowl, with a fork or wire whisk, beat egg whites or egg replacer lightly.

Stir in remaining ingredients; add to flour mixture, stirring only until moistened.

Spoon into 12 nonstick muffin cups.

Bake in a 400 degree oven for 18 to 20 minutes until firm to touch. Cool in pan 5 minutes; remove to wire rack.

Can be frozen for future use.

Preparation time: 20 minutes
Baking time: 18 to 20 minutes
Servings: 12 muffins

Yam Muffins

1 1/2 c. whole wheat flour, unsifted
1/2 c. brown sugar
2 tsp. baking powder
1/2 tsp. salt (optional)
1/2 c. oatmeal, quick or old fashioned, uncooked
2 egg whites or 1 1/2 tsp. egg replacer mixed in 3 Tbsp. water
1 c. fat-free soy milk
1/2 c. cold cooked yam*, mashed
2 Tbsp. applesauce
2 Tbsp. corn syrup

*Prepare yam by baking in a 400 degree oven 40 minutes or boiling in water for 20 minutes, until soft. Cool, peel and mash until smooth.

Mix flour, brown sugar, baking powder, salt and oatmeal in large bowl.

In a medium bowl, beat egg whites or egg replacer and milk.

Add mashed yam, applesauce and corn syrup to liquid mixture; mix well.

Add to flour mixture. Stir briskly just until flour is moistened.

Spoon batter into 1 1/2 dozen nonstick muffin pan cups, filling each cup about 2/3 full.

Bake in a 400 degree oven for 25 minutes.

Preparation time: 20 minutes
Baking time: 25 minutes
Servings: 18 muffins

Onion Chive Muffins

3/4 c. Vidalia or mild onions,
   chopped
1/4 c. water
1 1/2 c. whole wheat flour
1/4 c. fresh chives or green
   onion tops, chopped
2 tsp. baking powder
1/2 tsp. salt (optional)
1/4 tsp. baking soda
1 c. fat-free soy milk
1/4 c. corn syrup or applesauce
2 egg whites or 1 1/2 tsp. egg
   replacer mixed in 3 Tbsp.
   water

Lightly spray 12 muffin cups with nonstick spray.

In small skillet over medium heat, saute onions in water until tender; set aside.

In large bowl, combine flour, chives or onion tops, baking powder, salt and baking soda.

In a small bowl, combine cooked onions, soy milk, corn syrup or applesauce, and egg whites or egg replacer; mix well.

Add to dry ingredients; stir just until dry ingredients are moistened.

Fill muffin cups about 3/4 full.

Bake at 375 degrees for 12 to 14 minutes or until toothpick inserted in center comes out clean. Immediately remove from pan.

Preparation time: 20 minutes
Baking time: 14 minutes
Servings: 12 muffins

PANCAKES, FRENCH TOAST AND WAFFLES

HINTS AND HELPS

#1 Make your favorite pancake recipe, using fruit juice instead of milk. Add 1 tablespoon baking powder with the juice, stir the batter thoroughly, then let stand for 15 to 20 minutes before stirring lightly and baking as for pancakes. Orange, lemon, peach, pineapple and apple juices are good flavors.

#2 Club soda with 1 tablespoon of carob or 1 1/2 teaspoons vanilla, lemon, almond or mint extract are also very good instead of milk.

#3 Try substituting applesauce or corn syrup for the oil in your favorite recipes.

"Teaching" The New Four Food Groups

The Physicians Committee for Responsible Medicine, a national based group of 3,000 doctors announced to the world on April 8, 1991, that meat and dairy products should be dropped from the "Basic Four Food Groups."

Banana Applesauce Pancakes

1 c. whole wheat flour
1 1/2 tsp. baking powder
1 1/4 c. fat-free soy milk or apple juice
2 Tbsp. applesauce
1 tsp. honey
1/2 tsp. vanilla
1 medium banana, finely chopped

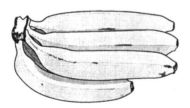

In a medium bowl, combine flour and baking powder. In a small bowl, mix all remaining ingredients except banana.

Add to flour mixture, stirring until just moistened.

Fold in banana. For each pancake, pour 1/4 cup batter onto a nonstick griddle that has been preheated over medium heat.

Turn cakes when bubbly on top. Serve with topping of your choice.

Preparation time: 10 minutes
Cooking time: 15 to 20 minutes
Servings: 12 pancakes

Blueberry Cornmeal Pancakes

1 1/2 c. yellow cornmeal
1/4 c. whole wheat flour
2 tsp. baking powder
1/2 tsp. salt (optional)
1 Tbsp. honey
2 Tbsp. applesauce
2 c. fat-free soy milk
2 egg whites or 1 1/2 tsp. egg
  replacer mixed in 3 Tbsp.
  water
1 1/2 c. blueberries

Combine the cornmeal, flour, baking powder and salt in a medium bowl.

In a small bowl, combine the honey, applesauce, skim soy milk and egg whites or egg replacer.

Stir well and quickly mix into the dry ingredients.

Let stand 10 minutes to soften the cornmeal.

Gently stir in the blueberries.

Spoon the batter onto a nonstick griddle that has been heated over medium heat.

Allow about 1/4 cup batter for each pancake.

Turn cakes when bubbles appear and cook until golden brown.

Preparation time: 20 minutes
Cooking time: 15 minutes
Servings: 8 to 10 pancakes

Brown Rice Pancakes

1 c. whole wheat flour
1/2 tsp. salt (optional)
2 tsp. baking powder
4 egg whites or 1 Tbsp. egg
  replacer mixed with
  6 Tbsp. water
1 c. fat-free soy milk
2 Tbsp. applesauce
2 c. cooked brown rice

Variation: Brown Rice Raisin Pancakes Use ingredients in above recipe and add 1/2 cup raisins with rice.

In a medium mixing bowl, stir together flour, salt and baking powder.

In another medium bowl, combine egg whites or egg replacer, milk and applesauce; mix until smooth.

Stir in rice and add to flour mixture.

Spoon onto a nonstick griddle that has been preheated over medium heat, using 1/4 cup batter for each pancake.

Cook, turning once when bubbles appear.

Preparation time: 15 minutes
Cooking time: 25 minutes
Servings: 16 5-inch pancakes

Whole Wheat Oat Bran Pancakes

2 egg whites or 1 1/2 tsp. egg replacer mixed in 3 Tbsp. water

1 c. fat-free soy milk

2 Tbsp. applesauce or corn syrup

1 c. whole wheat flour

1/4 c. wheat bran

1/4 c. oat bran cereal

2 tsp. baking powder

1/2 tsp. salt (optional)

In a small bowl, blend egg whites or egg replacer, milk and applesauce (or substitute).

In a medium bowl, combine flour, wheat bran, oat bran cereal, baking powder and salt.

Add liquid ingredients to flour mixture; mix well, adding a small amount of milk or water if batter is too stiff.

Pour onto nonstick griddle that has been preheated over medium heat, using 1/4 cup batter for each pancake.

Preparation time: 15 minutes
Cooking time: 15 minutes
Servings: 8 to 10 pancakes

Oatmeal Pancakes

1 c. flour, half whole wheat, half white
1/2 c. uncooked oats, quick or old-fashioned
1 tsp. baking powder
1/2 tsp. salt (optional)
1 c. fat-free soy milk
2 egg whites or 1 1/2 tsp. egg replacer mixed in 3 Tbsp. water
2 Tbsp. applesauce or corn syrup

In medium bowl, combine the flour, oats, baking powder and salt.

In a small bowl, mix milk, egg whites or egg replacer and applesauce (or substitute); add to dry ingredients.

Stir until just moistened. Let the batter stand while you heat a nonstick griddle over medium-high heat (375 degrees for an electric frying pan).

For each pancake, pour about 1/4 cup batter onto the griddle.

Turn when the top is covered with bubbles and the edges are golden brown.

Turn only once. Serve with topping of your choice.

Preparation time: 15 minutes
Cooking time: 15 minutes
Servings: 10 to 12 pancakes

Orange Juice Pancakes

2 egg whites or 1 1/2 tsp. egg replacer mixed in 3 Tbsp. water
1 tsp. vanilla
1/2 tsp. almond extract
1 1/2 c. orange juice
1/4 c. applesauce
1 3/4 c. whole wheat flour
1/2 tsp. soda
1/2 tsp. salt (optional)

In medium bowl, mix together egg whites or egg replacer, vanilla, almond, orange juice and applesauce.

In separate medium bowl, mix flour, soda and salt; add to liquid mixture.

If batter is too thick, add more orange juice; if too thin, add more flour.

Pour onto nonstick griddle that has been preheated over medium heat, using 1/4 cup batter for each pancake.

Turn when bubbly.

Preparation time: 15 minutes
Cooking time: 15 minutes
Servings: about 10 pancakes

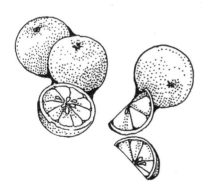

Apple Pie Waffles or Pancakes

1 3/4 c. whole wheat flour
1/2 c. wheat bran
1/2 tsp. salt (optional)
1 tsp. apple pie spice
3/4 c. warm water (115 to 120 degrees)
2 tsp. yeast (dry)
1 tsp. honey
2 apples
3 Tbsp. applesauce
1 c. fat-free soy milk
2 egg whites or 1 1/2 tsp. egg replacer mixed in 3 Tbsp. water

In a 2-quart measuring bowl or other utensil that will pour easily, mix flour, bran, salt and spice; set aside. In a medium bowl, combine water, yeast, and honey; let rest 5 minutes while peeling, coring and grating apples.

Add grated apples, applesauce, milk and egg whites to yeast mixture; mix well.

Stir into dry ingredients.

Cover batter and let rest for 15 minutes.

Pour about 1 c. of batter into hot waffle iron and cook for 7 to 8 minutes, or until the lid lifts easily.

For pancakes; pour about 1/2 cup of batter onto a nonstick griddle that has been preheated over med. heat. Cook about 10 minutes on first side, about 6 to 8 minutes on the other. Turn when bubbles have formed on top. These cakes are thicker than regular pancakes and will take longer to cook.

Preparation time: 30 min.
Resting time: 15 minutes
Waffle cooking time: 30 min.
Pancake cooking time: 1 hour
Servings: 4 waffles or 8 to 10 pancakes

Whole Wheat Waffles or Pancakes

1 c. whole wheat berries
1 c. fat-free soy milk
2 Tbsp. applesauce
4 egg whites or 1 Tbsp. egg
   replacer mixed in 6 Tbsp.
   water
1/2 tsp. salt (optional)
4 tsp. baking powder
1 Tbsp. sugar

Put wheat berries and milk in blender; blend until smooth.

Place in a 4-cup glass measuring cup and add applesauce, egg whites or egg replacer, salt, baking powder, and sugar.

Blend all ingredients. Pour about 1 cup batter into hot waffle iron and bake about 8 minutes.

For pancakes, use only 2 egg whites or 1 1/2 teaspoons egg replacer mixed in 3 tablespoons water.

Pour 1/3 cup of batter onto hot griddle. Turn when bubbly on top.

Preparation time: 15 minutes
Baking time: waffles 25 min.
pancakes 35 min.
Servings: 3 waffles, or 6 to 8

Oatmeal Waffles

3/4 c. whole wheat flour
1/2 c. quick-cooking oatmeal, uncooked
1 1/2 tsp. baking powder
1/4 tsp. cinnamon
1/8 tsp. salt (optional)
2 egg whites or 1 1/2 tsp. egg replacer mixed in 3 Tbsp. water
3/4 c. fat-free soy milk
2 Tbsp. applesauce or corn syrup
1 Tbsp. brown sugar (optional)

In a medium mixing bowl, stir together flour, oatmeal, baking powder, cinnamon and salt.

In a small mixing bowl, stir together egg whites or egg replacer, milk, applesauce (or substitute) and brown sugar.

Add to flour mixture; stir until blended. (If too stiff, add a little more milk or water.)

Pour batter onto preheated nonstick waffle iron (amount will vary according to size of waffle iron).

Close lid quickly; do not open during baking.

Use fork to remove baked waffle.

Preparation time: 15 minutes
Servings: 12 waffles (4-inch square each), about 6 servings

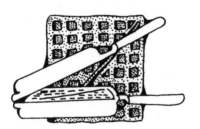

Whole Wheat Pancakes

1 c. Whole Wheat Flour
1 tsp. baking powder
2/3 c. water or fat-free soy milk
2 egg whites or 1 1/2 tsp. egg
    replacer mixed in 3 Tbsp.
    water
3 Tbsp. corn syrup or
    applesauce
1/4 tsp. salt (optional)

In a small bowl, combine water, egg whites or egg replacer and corn syrup or applesauce and mix into dry ingredients which have been placed in a medium bowl.

For each pancake, spoon 2 tablespoons batter onto a nonstick griddle that has been preheated over medium heat.

Turn when top is covered with bubbles.

Preparation time: 5 minutes
Cooking time: 15 to 20 minutes
Servings: 11 (3-inch) pancakes

Whole Wheat Waffles

1 c. Whole Wheat Flour
1 tsp. baking powder
3/4 c. fat-free soy milk or water
2 egg whites or 1 1/2 tsp. egg replacer mixed in 3 Tbsp. water
3 Tbsp. corn syrup or applesauce

In a small bowl, combine corn syrup or applesauce, egg whites or egg replacer and milk or water, mixing well.

Add to dry ingredients in another small bowl and mix well.

Bake in a preheated, nonstick waffle iron.

Preparation time: 10 minutes
Servings: 2 (8-inch) waffles

French Toast

2 egg whites or 1 1/2 tsp. egg
  replacer mixed in 3 Tbsp.
  water
1/4 tsp. vanilla
1 tsp. cinnamon
1/4 c. fat-free soy milk
1/4 c. frozen orange juice,
  thawed
2 slices whole grain bread

In a 1-quart casserole dish, combine first 6 ingredients.

Soak bread in blended mixture.

Cook on nonstick griddle over medium heat or in a 350 degree oven on a nonstick pan for 10 minutes on each side.

Serve hot with topping of your choice.

Preparation time: 10 minutes
Baking time: 20 minutes
Servings: 1 to 2

For a complete explanation of the cause of degenerative diseases and how to change your lifestyle to prevent or reverse disease — read Earl Updike's companion book (with the bright yellow cover).

"THE MIRACLE DIET — 14 DAYS TO NEW VIGOR AND HEALTH."

DESSERTS
Without Guilt

"Let food be thy medicine."
—Hippocrates, about 431 B.C.

*"If we eat wrongly, no doctor can cure us;
if we eat rightly, no doctor is needed."*
—Dr. Victor G. Rocine, about 1930

This is a "plantarian," not vegetarian program.
plan•tar´•i•an (plan tar´ ian) n. [plant + arian] a person whose basic diet revolves around plants (starches), supplemented with vegetables and fruit.

Sliced Fruit Plate

2 firm apples
2 firm pears
3 Tbsp. lemon or lime juice
2 kiwi fruit, peeled
Strawberries or mint leaves for
   garnish

Dressing:
6 Tbsp. corn syrup
3 Tbsp. lemon or lime juice
1 Tbsp. honey
1/2 tsp. ginger

Halve and core apples and pears.

Place cut side against feed tube wall of Presto Salad Shooter™ slicer-shredder and slice directly into a large bowl.

Toss with lemon or lime juice to prevent browning.

Place kiwi fruit in Salad Shooter and slice.

Arrange overlapping fruit slices on individual plates and garnish with mint leaves or strawberries sliced in Salad Shooter.

In a small bowl stir or whisk all dressing ingredients together to blend.

Spoon dressing over each arrangement. Serve.

Preparation time: 20 minutes
Servings: 4

Cantaloupe and Raspberry Melba

1/2 c. cranberry juice cocktail
1 Tbsp. sugar
2 tsp. cornstarch
1/4 tsp. almond extract
3 c. cantaloupe cubes or balls
1 c. raspberries
Mint leaves (optional)

In a small saucepan, blend juice, sugar and cornstarch.

Cook and stir over medium heat until mixture thickens.

Stir in extract. Cool.

When ready to serve, combine cantaloupe and raspberries in individual bowls.

Top with cranberry sauce and mint garnish, if desired.

Preparation time: 25 minutes
Cooking time: 10 minutes
Servings: 4 to 6

Banana Grape Cup

4 bananas, sliced
24 seedless green grapes
1 c. orange juice
Dash of nutmeg

Combine the sliced banana and the grapes in a large dessert dish.

Pour the orange juice over the fruit and sprinkle with nutmeg. Chill the fruit until ready to serve.

Preparation time: 15 minutes
Chilling time: 1 hour or more
Servings: 4

Baked Apples

4 apples, peeled
Apple pie seasoning, sprinkle
4 tsp. seedless raisins
4 Tbsp. undiluted frozen apple juice concentrate, thawed

Core the apples and place in a 1-quart baking dish; sprinkle the apple pie seasoning into the core cavity.

Put 1 teaspoon raisins in each apple core cavity.

Pour apple juice in dish.

Bake in 350 degree oven for 1 hour or until the apples are fork tender.

Preparation time: 20 minutes
Baking time: 1 hour
Servings: 4

Junior Apple Crisp
(*can be baked in toaster oven*)

2 apples
1 Tbsp. flour
1 heaping Tbsp. brown sugar
1 tsp. cinnamon
Dash of salt (optional)
2 to 4 tsp. water
Butter Buds, sprinkle

Peel and core apples. Then slice them directly into toaster oven baking tray or small cookie sheet.

In a small bowl, blend flour, brown sugar, cinnamon and salt.

Scatter flour mixture over apples.

Sprinkle water over all ingredients (use more water if apples are not very juicy); sprinkle Butter Buds over all.

Place tray in toaster oven, or cookie sheet in stove oven, and bake at 375 degrees for 30 minutes.

Preparation time: 20 minutes
Baking time: 30 minutes
Servings: 2

Peach Blueberry Crisp

1/2 c. wheat bran
1/3 c. flour
1/3 c. brown sugar
1 tsp. cinnamon
2 Tbsp. white corn syrup
6 c. fresh or 2 (16 oz.) packages
   frozen, thawed sliced
   peaches
1 c. fresh or frozen blueberries

In a small bowl, combine wheat bran, 1/4 cup flour, brown sugar and cinnamon.

Stir in corn syrup with a fork; set aside.

In a large bowl, combine fruit and remaining 4 teaspoons flour, tossing to coat evenly.

Spoon into 8-inch square baking dish.

Top with wheat bran mixture.

Bake in a 375 degree oven 30 to 35 minutes or until fruit is tender.

Preparation time: 20 minutes
Baking time: 35 minutes
Servings: 6

Apple-Apricot Bake

1 c. dried apricots, chopped

1/2 c. apple juice

1 c. oats

2 Tbsp. applesauce

3 Tbsp. brown sugar

1/2 tsp. cinnamon

1/4 tsp. allspice

3-4 large tart apples (Granny Smith are good)

Place apricots and apple juice in a glass pitcher and microwave on high for 2 minutes.

Cover with foil and set aside.

Measure into a medium sized bowl the oats, applesauce, brown sugar, cinnamon, allspice.

Add the hot apricot/apple juice mixture and stir; set aside.

Wash and slice apples into a 9" square pan. top with the oat mixture and cover with foil.

Bake at 400 degrees, covered, for 25 minutes.

Remove foil and place in broiler for a minute or two, just until the oats are browned. Serve warm.

Preparation time: 20 minutes
Baking time: 30 minutes

Baked Fruit Salad Supreme

1 can (16 oz.) pineapple chunks
in natural juice, drained
4 Tbsp. frozen pineapple juice
concentrate
1 Tbsp. minute tapioca
1 fresh apple, diced
1 orange, peeled and diced
2 egg whites
1/8 tsp. cream of tarter
4 tsp. sugar
1/2 tsp. vanilla

In a small saucepan, combine drained pineapple juice and pineapple juice concentrate with tapioca. Let stand 5 minutes.

Bring to a boil over medium heat, stirring often. Cool.

Combine the apple, pineapple chunks, orange and pineapple juice mixture.

Mix well to coat the fruits with the juice.

Spoon fruit into 4 individual soufflé baking dishes.

Beat the egg whites until soft peaks form; add the cream of tarter and sugar and continue beating until stiff peaks form.

Add the vanilla. Swirl the egg whites to top of the fruit salad, heaping it thick and spreading it to edges of dishes.

Place in preheated 450 degree oven for 4 to 5 minutes until meringue is lightly browned.

Preparation time: 25 minutes
Baking time: 5 minutes
Servings: 4

Apple Pizza

Note: delicious for a treat at breakfast, a snack or a "not too sweet" dessert.

Pizza crust (see recipe on page 251)

4 medium apples, peeled and thinly sliced

1/3 c. brown sugar

1 tsp. cinnamon

Pat pizza dough onto a pizza pan or a baking sheet.

Crimp edges as for a pizza.

Spread apples over dough and sprinkle brown sugar and cinnamon over apples.

Bake at 350 degrees for 30 minutes.

Preparation time: 45 minutes
Baking time: 30 minutes
Servings: 12

Green 'n Gold Holiday Fruit Bowl

1/3 c. melon juice or orange
  juice
1/4 c. corn syrup
Grated peel of 1/2 lemon
Juice of 1 lemon
2 Tbsp. fresh mint leaves,
  chopped
4 oranges, peeled, cut in half
  cartwheel slices
2 c. green seedless grapes
2 green-skinned pears or
apples, unpeeled, cored, sliced
2 kiwis, peeled, sliced

In a large bowl, combine juice
and corn syrup, lemon peel,
lemon juice and mint.

Gently stir in remaining
ingredients.

Cover and chill 2 hours or
longer to blend flavors, stirring
occasionally. (Or, marinate in a
tightly sealed bag, turning
occasionally.)

Garnish with whole fresh mint
leaves, if desired.

Preparation time: 30 minutes
Chilling time: 2 hours or longer
Servings: 10 to 12

Fresh Fruit

1 1/2 c. fresh raspberries

2 kiwi fruit, peeled and sliced

2 bananas, sliced

1 pint fresh strawberries,
   hulled and sliced

1/4 c. orange juice

Pour orange juice over mixed
fruit.

Chill until ready to serve.

(If making a day ahead,
substitute another seasonal fruit
for bananas. Or, you may use
any combination of fruits in
season according to your taste.)

Preparation time: 20 minutes
Servings: 6 to 8

Apple Crisp

2 cans (16 oz.) sliced apples,
     water-packed
1 c. pitted dates, chopped
1 c. pineapple juice
Apple pie spice to taste
1 1/2 c. whole wheat flour
1/2 c. wheat flakes or quick
     oats
1 tsp. cinnamon
1/2 c. frozen apple juice
     concentrate, undiluted
1 Tbsp. lemon juice
1/4 c. honey

Arrange apple slices, including liquid, in a 2-quart casserole.

Sprinkle with chopped dates; add pineapple juice.

Sprinkle with apple pie spice to taste.

In a medium bowl, mix flour, cinnamon, and wheat flakes or oats.

In a small bowl, mix apple juice, lemon juice and honey.

Add a little at a time to flour mixture and toss with a fork.

Sprinkle mixture over apples.

Bake in 350 degree oven for 15 to 30 minutes.

Preparation time: 20 minutes
Baking time: 30 minutes
Servings: 8 to 10

Cherry Cobbler

1/2 c. Grape-Nuts™ cereal
4 Tbsp. fruit juice
2 1/2 Tbsp. minute tapioca
1/8 tsp. mace
1/2 c. concentrated orange
    juice
4 c. sweet cherries
1/4 tsp. almond extract

Crust:
1 c. Grape-Nuts cereal,
    crushed
1 c. quick oatmeal

In a small bowl, combine
Grape-Nuts and fruit juice; set
aside for 1 hour.

In a large bowl, blend together
the tapioca, mace, orange juice,
and let stand.

Stir in the cherries and the
almond extract after 15
minutes.

In a small bowl, mix cereal and
oatmeal; sprinkle into the
bottom of a 2-quart casserole
dish.

Add cherry mixture and top
with soaked Grape-Nuts and
fruit juice mixture.

Bake in a preheated 350 degree
oven for about 40 minutes.

Preparation time: 20 minutes
Soaking time: 1 hour
Baking time: 40 minutes
Servings: 6 to 8

Fruit Cobbler

1 c. flour
1 c. sugar
1 c. fat-free soy milk
1 tsp. baking powder
Butter Buds, sprinkle
1 qt. canned fruit with juice
(cherries, blueberries, etc.)

Mix first 4 ingredients together and pour into a 9 x 13-inch nonstick baking dish.

Sprinkle with Butter Buds and pour fruit and juice on top of batter.

Bake at 350 to 375 degrees for 45 minutes.

To use unsweetened pie cherries, use 1/4 to 1/2 c. sugar dissolved in the cherries before adding to batter.

Preparation time: 15 minutes
Baking time: 45 minutes
Servings: 12 to 15

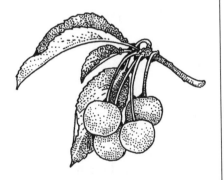

Blueberry Betty

4 c. fresh blueberries, or frozen
2 c. whole wheat bread crumbs
1/4 c. liquid Butter Buds (mix
4 tsp.—1/2 packet—Butter
Buds in 1/4 c. hot tap water)
1/2 c. brown sugar
1 tsp. cinnamon
1 Tbsp. grated lemon rind
2 Tbsp. lemon juice
1/4 c. hot water

Wash and pick blueberries.

Drain well. In a small bowl, toss bread crumbs with liquid Butter Buds.

In another small bowl, combine sugar, cinnamon and lemon rind.

Sprinkle 1/3 bread crumbs in bottom of a nonstick 8-inch square baking pan.

Cover with half the berries and half the sugar mixture.

Repeat crumbs, berries and sugar mixture.

Top with last 1/3 of crumbs. In a cup, combine lemon juice and water and pour evenly over top.

Bake in a 350 degree oven for 30 minutes.

Serve warm with nonfat topping of your choice.

Preparation time: 30 minutes
Baking time: 30 minutes
Servings: 6

PIES
Fat-Free / Healthy / Guiltless

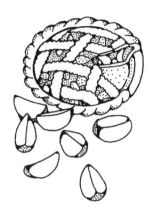

"If we eat wrongly, no doctor can cure us;
if we eat rightly, no doctor is needed."
—Dr. Victor G. Rocine, about 1930

It's truly a miracle!

- Prevent heart-artery disease
- Reverse adult diabetes
- Lower blood pressure
- Prevent many cancers

- Reverse heart disease
- Prevent adult diabetes
- Lose weight permanently
- Prevent Osteoporosis

Grape-Nuts Pie Crust

1 c. Grape-Nuts cereal, crushed

1/4 c. apple juice concentrate

Combine Grape-Nuts and apple juice concentrate.

Pat this into a 9-inch pie pan.

Pour in your favorite pie filling; then bake.

Preparation time: 15 minutes
Servings: 1 pie crust

PASTRIES
FOR PIES
(Additional)

"You can have your pie and eat it too while losing weight."

"Let food be thy medicine."
—Hippocrates, about 431 B.C.

Rice Krispies Pastry

1 1/2 c. Rice Krispies, crushed
2 egg whites, beaten well

Mix well and press into pie pan.

Bake at 400 degrees for about 8 minutes or until dry.

Pour in your favorite pie filling.

Preparation time: 10 minutes
Yield: 1 pie crust

Corn Flakes Pastry

2 c. corn flakes, crushed
2 egg whites, well beaten

Variation: Use 5-6 Tbsp. apple juice concentrate instead of egg whites; bake at 350 degrees for 15 minutes or until crisp.

Mix together and press into pie pan.

Bake at 400 degrees for 8 minutes or until dry.

Preparation time: 15 minutes
Yield: 1 large or 2 small pie crusts

Apple Pie

Grape-Nuts pie crust (see recipe)

1 can apples, water-packed
1/2 c. apple juice concentrate
1 Tbsp. tapioca
2 Tbsp. honey
1 Tbsp. lemon juice
1 1/2 tsp. apple pie spice, or
1 tsp. cinnamon,
1/2 tsp. nutmeg, and
1/4 tsp. allspice

Place apples, concentrate and tapioca in a medium saucepan and bring to a boil.

Boil about 2 minutes; add remaining ingredients.

Place in pie crust. Sprinkle a few crushed Grape-Nuts over top. cover with foil and bake 1/2 hour at 350 degrees.

Preparation time: 10 minutes
Cooking time: 5 minutes
Baking time: 30 minutes
Servings: 6

Mince Pie

Grape-Nuts pie crust (see recipe)

1 orange, juiced, rind reserved
1/2 c. raisins
4 medium apples, unpeeled, cored, and chopped in 1/2 inch pieces
1/3 c. apple juice
1 Tbsp. minute tapioca
1/2 c. honey
1/2 tsp. cinnamon
1/2 tsp. cloves
1/2 tsp. rum extract

Mince the orange rind and raisins in a food processor.

In a medium saucepan, combine chopped apples, orange juice, raisin mixture, apple juice and tapioca.

Cover and cook until apples are very soft.

Stir in remaining ingredients. Pour into pie crust.

Bake at 350 degrees for 30 minutes.

Preparation time: 15 minutes
Cooking time: 20 minutes
Baking time: 30 minutes
Servings: 6

Light Mincemeat Pie

Grape-Nuts pie crust (see recipe)

3 c. cooking apples, peeled and cubed

1 1/2 c. raisins

6 Tbsp. sugar or equivalent amount low calorie sweetener

3 Tbsp. orange juice

2 Tbsp. apple juice

2 Tbsp. whole wheat bread crumbs, fine

1 tsp. cider vinegar

1 tsp. grated orange rind

1/2 tsp. cinnamon

1/2 tsp. salt (optional)

1/4 tsp. cloves

First, combine the following for pie topping:

1/2 c. Grape-Nuts cereal

1/2 c. apple juice concentrate

Combine mincemeat ingredients and fill pie crust.

Sprinkle topping over mincemeat filling and bake in a 375 degree oven for 35 to 45 minutes or until golden brown.

Serve warm or cool.

Filling can also be baked in custard cups to be served with cookies.

Preparation time: 30 minutes
Baking time: 45 minutes
Servings: 6 to 8

Raspberry Pie

Grape-Nuts pie crust (see recipe)

1/2 c. Grape-Nuts cereal
1/4 c. fruit juice
2 1/2 Tbsp. minute tapioca
1/8 tsp. mace
1/2 c. frozen orange juice concentrate
4 c. raspberries
1/4 tsp. almond extract

In a small bowl, combine Grape-Nuts cereal with fruit juice; set aside for 1 hour.

In medium bowl, blend together the tapioca, mace, orange juice, and let stand 15 minutes.

Stir in the raspberries and the almond extract.

Pour into prepared pie crust.

Top with Grape Nuts cereal-fruit juice mixture.

Bake in a preheated 350 degree oven for about 40 minutes.

Soaking time: 1 hour
Preparation time: 20 minutes
Baking time: 40 minutes
Servings: 6

FAT-FREE PUDDINGS
Satisfying and Healthful

"Nature cures when given the opportunity."
—Dr. Bernard Jensen

This is a "plantarian," not vegetarian program.
plan•tar´•i•an (plan tar´ ian) n. [plant + arian] a person whose basic diet revolves around plants (starches), supplemented with vegetables and fruit.

Baked Rice Pudding

May be served hot or cold.

2 c. cooked brown rice
1 1/2 c. fat-free soy milk
1 Tbsp. minute tapioca
1 c. raisins
3 Tbsp. honey
1 tsp. vanilla
1 tsp. cinnamon
1/2 tsp. nutmeg

Combine all ingredients.

Pour into a 1 1/2-quart casserole, cover and bake at 325 degrees for 45 minutes.

Preparation time: 15 minutes
Baking time: 45 minutes
Servings: 4

Carrot Pudding

2 c. cooked carrots
1 can (15 oz.) crushed
   pineapple
5 slices whole wheat bread,
   broken in small pieces
1/2 c. raisins
2 tsp. grated orange rind
1 tsp. cinnamon
1/4 tsp. allspice
1/4 tsp. nutmeg
4 egg whites or 1 Tbsp. egg
   replacer mixed in 6 Tbsp.
   water

In a blender, puree carrots and pineapple.

Place broken bread in a large mixing bowl; add carrot-pineapple puree, raisins, orange rind, and spices; mix lightly.

In a medium bowl, beat egg whites or egg replacer until stiff peaks form.

Fold into carrot mixture.

Pour into an 8 x 10-inch nonstick baking pan.

Bake at 350 degrees for 45 minutes, or until a knife inserted in center comes out clean.

Preparation time: 25 minutes
Baking time: 45 minutes
Servings: 6

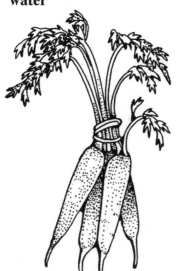

Date and Rice Pudding

This recipe is sweetened primarily with dates, a Middle Eastern favorite. It's delicious warm or cold.

2 c. cooked brown rice

15 pitted dates, finely chopped

2 c. fat-free soy milk

3 Tbsp. sugar

In a blender or food processor, process rice until coarse.

Transfer rice to a large saucepan; add dates, milk and sugar.

Cook, covered, on low heat until dates are tender, about 15 to 20 minutes.

Preparation time: 15 minutes
Cooking time: 20 minutes
Servings: 6

Microwave Pudding

3 Tbsp. cornstarch

1/3 c. granulated sugar

2 c. fat-free soy milk

1 Tbsp. vanilla

In a 4-cup glass measuring cup or a 2-quart microwave-safe casserole, combine cornstarch and sugar. Stir in milk and vanilla.

Cook on high (100 percent power) in the microwave for 3 minutes. Stir.

Continue cooking on high for 2 to 8 minutes more, or until the pudding comes to a full boil and is thickened, stirring each minute to keep smooth.

Pour the pudding into individual serving dishes or a bowl and let cool before serving.

Refrigerate if the pudding will not be served for an hour or more.

Chocolate Pudding Variation:

Add 1/4 to 1/3 cup carob powder (depending on how much chocolate flavor you like) to the sugar and cornstarch.

Reduce the vanilla to 1 teaspoon.

Tapioca Pudding Variation:

You can make Tapioca Pudding in exactly the same way by substituting 3 tablespoons instant tapioca for the cornstarch, and adding 1 egg white with the milk.

For light and fluffy tapioca, fold in 1 stiffly beaten egg white into the pudding immediately after removing from the microwave oven while it is still hot.

Sugar may be reduced slightly.

Preparation time: 5 minutes
Cooking time: 10 minutes
Servings: 3 to 4

COOKIES AND BROWNIES

The Miracle Diet

The Miracle Diet is a plant-centered diet program that allows your body to seek its ideal weight with natural, high energy. It is based upon plants, not vegetables. The five basic starches are the basis of the diet.

- **Grain**   (wheat, oats, and barley)
- **Rice**   (a basic grain)
- **Corn**   (a basic grain)
- **Legumes**   (beans, peas, and lentils)
- **Potatoes**   (the only vegetable)

Oatmeal Banana Cookies

1 c. whole wheat flour
1/2 tsp. baking powder
1/2 tsp. baking soda
1/4 tsp. cream of tartar
1 tsp. cinnamon
1 c. quick oatmeal
2 medium ripe bananas,
    mashed
3 Tbsp. applesauce
1/3 c. raisins
1/2 c. pitted dates, chopped
    (optional)
1/2 c. apple juice concentrate
2 Tbsp. honey
1 tsp. vanilla

In a medium mixing bowl, combine first six ingredients.

In a small bowl, mix remaining ingredients. Add to flour mixture.

Drop by teaspoons on nonstick cookie sheets.

Bake in a 350 degree oven 10 to 15 minutes until set.

Cool on wire racks.

If desired, substitute 3/4 cup carob chips for raisins and dates.

Preparation time: 20 minutes
Baking time: 10 to 15 minutes
Servings: 24 cookies

Oatmeal Fruit Cookies

Sift together into large mixing bowl:
1 c. whole wheat flour
1/2 tsp. baking soda
1/2 tsp. baking powder
1/4 tsp. cream of tartar
1 tsp. cinnamon

Add:
2 mashed ripe bananas
1 1/4 c. oatmeal
1/2 c. raisins
3/4 c. pitted dates, chopped
1 tsp. vanilla
1/2 c. apple juice concentrate
2 Tbsp. honey

Drop by teaspoonfuls on nonstick cookie sheets.

Bake 15 minutes at 350 degrees.

Preparation time: 25 minutes
Baking time: 15 minutes
Servings: 3 dozen cookies

Oatmeal ✓ Raisin Cookies

1 1/2 c. whole wheat flour
1 3/4 c. oatmeal
1 tsp. baking powder
1 tsp. cinnamon
1/2 c. raisins
1 1/2 tsp. egg replacer mixed in
   3 Tbsp. water or 2 egg
   whites
1/2 c. honey
1 c. applesauce

In a large mixing bowl, combine flour, oats, baking powder, cinnamon, and raisins. Mix well.

In a small bowl, beat the egg replacer or egg whites until frothy.

Add honey and applesauce and stir well to mix.

Add this mixture to the flour-oat mixture, again mixing well.

Drop by tablespoons onto a nonstick baking sheets.

Flatten slightly with a fork.

Bake at 375 degrees for 10 to 12 minutes, until lightly browned.

Preparation time: 25 minutes
Baking time: 12 minutes
Servings: about 30 cookies

Brownie Oat Cookies

2/3 c. whole wheat flour
1/3 c. sugar
1 c. quick oats
1/4 c. carob powder
1 tsp. baking powder
1/4 tsp. salt (optional)
2 egg whites or 1 1/2 tsp. egg replacer mixed in 3 Tbsp. water
1/3 c. light or dark corn syrup
1 tsp. vanilla

In a medium bowl, combine dry ingredients.

In a small bowl, mix egg whites or egg replacer, corn syrup and vanilla.

Add to dry ingredients, stirring just until moistened.

Drop by teaspoons onto nonstick cookie sheets.

Bake in 350 degree oven 10 minutes until set.

Cool 5 minutes on cookie sheets. Remove to wire rack to complete cooling.

Note: Carob contains less than 9% fat)

Preparation time: 15 minutes
Baking time: 10 minutes
Servings: 2 dozen cookies

CAKES

"Now you can have your cake and eat it too, while losing weight."

For the greatest and fastest weight loss you should severely limit fine ground flours and simple carbohydrates (sugars).

If you find your cakes or muffins sticking in the pan you may prefer to very lightly spray your pans with cooking spray.

- **Eat to live . . . Don't live to eat**
- **Think of food as fuel**
- **Treat yourself with preventive medicine**

Fat-Free Chocolate Cake

Good with Rocky Mountain Frosting (see recipe).

1 1/4 c. flour
1/2 c. sugar
1/4 c. carob powder
1/4 c. cornstarch
1/2 tsp. baking soda
1/2 tsp. salt (optional)
4 egg whites or 1 Tbsp. egg replacer mixed in 6 Tbsp. water
1 c. water
1/2 c. light or dark corn syrup
Confectioners sugar, sprinkle (optional)

Preheat oven to 350 degrees.

Use 9-inch square nonstick baking pan.

In large bowl combine dry ingredients until well mixed.

In medium bowl, whisk egg whites, water, and corn syrup; stir into dry ingredients until smooth.

Pour into prepared pan.

Bake 30 minutes or until cake springs back when lightly touched.

Cool on wire rack 10 minutes.

Note: Carob powder is less than 10% fat.)

Preparation time: 20 minutes
Baking time: 30 minutes
Servings: 9 to 16

Easy Eggless Carob Cake

1 1/2 c. flour
1/2 c. sugar
2 or 3 Tbsp. carob powder
1/4 c. cornstarch
1 tsp. baking soda
1/4 tsp. salt (optional)
1 c. water
1/4 c. corn syrup
1 Tbsp. vinegar
1 tsp. vanilla

In a medium bowl, combine flour, sugar, carob, cornstarch, soda and salt.

Add water, corn syrup, vinegar and vanilla; stir until smooth.

Pour into a nonstick 8-inch square pan.

Bake in a preheated 350 degree oven for 35 to 40 minutes or until it tests done. Cool.

Dust with powdered sugar, if desired.

Preparation time: 15 minutes
Baking time: 40 minutes
Servings: 9

Blueberry Oatmeal Cake

Serve warm or cool.

1 c. blueberries

1/4 c. plus 2 Tbsp. sugar

1/3 c. corn syrup

2 egg whites or 1 1/2 tsp. egg replacer mixed in 3 Tbsp. water

3/4 c. all-purpose flour

2 Tbsp. cornstarch

1 tsp. baking powder

1/4 tsp. baking soda

1/3 c. quick or old-fashioned oatmeal, uncooked

1/2 tsp. lemon rind, grated

1/4 tsp. nutmeg

1/8 tsp. cardamon

1/2 c. nonfat mayonnaise

Use a nonstick 9-inch layer cake pan. Line bottom with wax paper.

In small bowl, combine blueberries and 2 tablespoons of sugar. Spoon into pan.

In large bowl, mix corn syrup and remaining sugar. Add egg whites or egg replacer; beat until light and fluffy.

Combine dry ingredients and lemon rind. Stir into egg mixture, alternating with mayonnaise.

Carefully spoon over berries in pan.

Bake in a 350 degree oven for 30 to 45 minutes or until top springs back when touched.

Remove from oven; let stand 5 minutes. Loosen sides with metal spatula. Invert on cooling rack and remove wax paper.

Preparation time: 25 minutes
Baking time: 45 minutes
Servings: 8

Blueberry Upside Down Cake

Other fruits can be used for variety. This is a delectable dessert which is low in calories, fat free and cholesterol free.

1/4 c. brown sugar
2 Tbsp. light corn syrup
1 Tbsp. lemon juice
1 c. fresh or frozen blueberries
White Cake batter (recipe
    follows)

Use a nonstick 9-inch round cake pan.

Add brown sugar, corn syrup and lemon juice; stir to combine.

Place pan in a 350 degree oven 3 minutes. Remove.

Add blueberries.

Prepare White Cake batter.

Carefully spoon batter over blueberries; smooth top.

Bake 35 to 40 minutes or until toothpick inserted in center comes out clean. (Do not underbake.) Immediately run spatula around edge of pan and invert cake onto serving plate.

Preparation time: 20 minutes
Baking time: 35 to 40 minutes
Servings: 12

White Cake

1 c. flour
1/3 c. sugar
1/3 c. cornstarch
2 tsp. baking powder
1/2 tsp. salt (optional)
2 egg whites or 1 1/2 tsp. egg
   replacer mixed in 3 Tbsp.
   water
2/3 c. fat-free soy milk
1/3 c. light corn syrup
1 tsp. vanilla

In a medium bowl, combine dry ingredients.

In a small bowl, using fork or wire whisk, mix egg whites or egg replacer, milk, corn syrup and vanilla. Add to flour mixture; stir until smooth.

Pour into a nonstick 9 x 9-inch baking pan.

Bake in 350 degree oven 20 to 25 minutes, or until toothpick inserted in center comes out clean.

Cool in pan on wire rack.

Preparation time: 20 minutes
Baking time: 20 to 25 minutes
Servings: 16

No Fat ✓
Carrot Cake

2 c. flour
2 c. sugar *add / Cup + ck for*
2 tsp. baking soda *sweetner*
add Sugar
1 tsp. cinnamon *last*
1 tsp. allspice
1 tsp. nutmeg
2 c. grated carrots
3 egg whites or 2 1/4 tsp. egg
    replacer mixed in 1/4 c.
    water
1 can (20 oz.) crushed
pineapple, with juice
1 can (8 oz.) crushed
pineapple, drained

In large mixing bowl, mix all ingredients together and pour into 9 x 13-inch nonstick pan.

Bake at 350 degrees for 40 to 45 minutes.

Preparation time: 20 minutes
Baking time: 45 minutes
Servings: 12 to 15

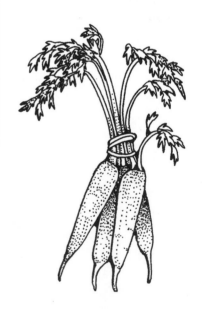

Fruit Cake
(Mexican Style)

2 c. flour
2 c. sugar
2 tsp. baking soda
3 egg whites or 2 1/4 tsp. egg
**   replacer mixed in 1/4 c.**
**   water**
1 can (20 oz.) crushed
pineapple, with juice
1 can (8 oz.) crushed
pineapple, drained

In large mixing bowl, mix all ingredients together and pour in 9 x 13-inch nonstick pan.

Bake at 350 degrees for 40 to 45 minutes.

Preparation time: 20 minutes
Baking time: 45 minutes
Servings: 12 to 15

Spice Cake

1 c. whole wheat flour
1/3 c. brown sugar
1/3 c. cornstarch
2 tsp. baking powder
1/2 tsp. salt (optional)
1/2 tsp. cinnamon
1/8 tsp. ginger
1/8 tsp. nutmeg
2 egg whites or 1 1/2 tsp. egg
   replacer mixed in 3 Tbsp.
   water
2/3 c. fat-free soy milk
1/3 c. dark corn syrup
1 tsp. vanilla

In a medium bowl, combine dry ingredients.

In a small bowl, using a fork or wire whisk, mix egg whites or egg replacer, milk, corn syrup and vanilla.

Add to flour mixture; stir until smooth.

Pour into a nonstick 9-inch square pan and bake in a 350 degree oven 25 to 30 minutes, or until a toothpick inserted in center comes out clean.

Cool in pan on wire rack.

Serve with applesauce for an old-fashioned treat.

Preparation time: 20 minutes
Baking time: 25 to 30 minutes
Servings: 16

Sugarless Spice Cake

2 c. raisins
2 c. water
1 c. unsweetened applesauce
4 egg whites or 1 Tbsp. egg replacer mixed in 1/3 c. water
1 Tbsp. liquid artificial sweetener
1/2 c. corn syrup
1 tsp. baking soda
1/3 c. cornstarch
2 c. all-purpose flour
1 1/2 tsp. cinnamon
1/2 tsp. nutmeg
1 tsp. vanilla

In a medium saucepan, cook raisins in water until water evaporates.

Add applesauce, egg whites or egg replacer, sweetener and corn syrup; mix well.

In a small bowl, combine baking soda, cornstarch, flour and spices.

Blend in flour mixture; stir in vanilla.

Pour into a nonstick 8-inch square baking pan.

Bake at 350 degrees for 25 minutes.

Preparation time: 30 minutes
Baking time: 25 minutes
Servings: 16

FROZEN DESSERTS

Take your tongue for
a sleigh ride while becoming
more attractive and healthy.

It's truly a miracle!

- Prevent heart-artery disease
- Reverse adult diabetes
- Lower blood pressure
- Prevent many cancers

- Reverse heart disease
- Prevent adult diabetes
- Lose weight permanently
- Prevent Osteoporosis

Raspberry Ice

2 c. fresh raspberries
1/4 c. sugar
1/2 c. water
2 Tbsp. orange juice
2 egg whites or 1 1/2 tsp. egg
  replacer mixed in 3 Tbsp.
  water
1/4 tsp. cream of tartar
Pinch of salt (optional)
Fresh mint leaves to garnish
\

In blender container, combine raspberries, sugar, water and orange juice. Process until smooth.

Pour mixture into small saucepan; cook on low heat for 5 minutes, stirring occasionally.

Let cool.

Pour into medium mixing bowl; cover and freeze 45 minutes.

Meanwhile, in a small bowl, combine egg whites or egg replacer, cream of tartar and salt.

Beat until stiff peaks form; set aside.

Beat partially frozen raspberry mixture until fluffy; fold in egg mixture.

Freeze until firm.

Garnish with mint leaves when serving, if desired.

Preparation time: 25 minutes
Freezing time: 2 hours 45 minutes
Servings: 6

Low-Cal Ice Cream

1 pkg. (10 oz.) unsweetened frozen strawberries, partially thawed
1 large banana
1/4 c. orange juice
1/2 c. sugar

In mixer bowl, combine above ingredients.

Beat until smooth and thick, about 10 minutes.

Pour into serving cups, parfait glasses or soufflé cups that have been chilled, cover and freeze.

Preparation time: 15 minutes
Freezing time: 3 or more hours
Servings: 2 to 4

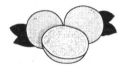

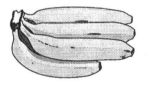

Frozen Fruit Ice

1 can (16 oz.) grapefruit sections
1 can (16 or 20 oz.) crushed pineapple
Juice of 1 or more lemons
1 c. sugar
1/2 c. water
Orange juice

In medium bowl, break grapefruit into small bits and mix all fruit and lemon juice.

Make a syrup of sugar and water; cool and add to fruit mixture.

Freeze in 2 ice cube trays.

To serve, remove desired number of cubes from trays; place in serving dishes.

Break cubes with fork and pour orange juice over all.

Garnish with fresh strawberry, mint leaves or other fruit of choice.

Preparation time: 15 minutes
Freezing time: 4 or more hours
Servings: 7 to 9

Banana Strawberry Freeze

8 bananas, sliced and frozen

1 c. frozen strawberries, unsweetened

1 c. cold water

Place bananas in blender.

Blend, adding a little water at a time.

Use only enough water to give the consistency of ice cream.

Use less water if using a food processor.

Break up frozen strawberries and blend into banana mixture until smooth.

Serve immediately.

To freeze bananas, peel, slice, place in a plastic bag and freeze about 12 hours.

Preparation time: 10 minutes
Servings: 4 to 6

Frozen Fruit Dessert

1 1/2 c. canned unsweetened crushed pineapple with juice

3 bananas, sliced and frozen for at least 12 hours

3 c. frozen raspberries (16 oz. bag, low sugar

Place pineapple in blender.

Add bananas and raspberries a little at a time and blend well.

Put 1/2 cup of mixture into each of 8 dessert dishes and freeze 15 to 30 minutes.

If frozen for a longer period of time, remove from freezer for a short time before serving.

Preparation time: 10 minutes
Freezing time: 15 to 30 minutes
Servings: 8

CONGEALED
DESSERTS

In this *Miracle Diet Cookbook* you will find a whole new world of exciting tastes and aromas. Recipes using the herbs, spices, and flavors will delight your senses. Experience the joy of the best possible health! Eliminate the harmful fat and salt from your food. Use instead the ravishing reds of tomatoes and peppers; the garnishing greens of spinach and salads; the yummy yellows and oranges of citrus and carrots; all combined to make dining a rich, colorful delight.

Fruit Delight

1 can (8 3/4 oz.) fruit cocktail

1 pkg. (3 oz.) fruit gelatin, any flavor

1 1/2 c. crushed ice

Drain fruit; measure liquid.

Add water to liquid to make 3/4 cup; bring to boil in small saucepan.

Combine boiling liquid and gelatin in blender.

Cover and blend at low speed for 30 seconds or until gelatin dissolves.

Add crushed ice.

Blend at high speed until ice melts, about 30 seconds.

Pour into glasses.

Add drained fruit.

Chill until set, 30 minutes or longer.

Dessert forms 2 layers as it chills.

Preparation time: 15 minutes
Chilling time: 30 minutes or longer.
Servings: 6

Gelatin Fruit Delight

This is quick and easy to make. Your whole family will be delighted.

1 large pkg. gelatin (same flavor as fruit)

1 pkg. (16 oz.) frozen fruit, partially thawed

1/2 angel food cake

In a 2-quart bowl, prepare gelatin as per directions using fruit juice as part of the liquid.

Pour partially thawed frozen fruit with its juice into gelatin mixture; stir well.

Refrigerate until syrupy.

Tear angel food cake into bite-size pieces and place in a 2 1/2-quart casserole dish.

Pour gelatin and fruit mixture over cake pieces and refrigerate.

Preparation time: 5 to 10 minutes
Chilling time: 3 or more hours
Servings: 8

Fruit Parfaits

1 pkg. (3 oz.) fruit gelatin, any flavor
1 c. boiling water
1 c. cold water
2 c. fresh strawberries, sliced

Dissolve gelatin in boiling water in small pan; add cold water.

Chill until firm.

Alternately layer gelatin and strawberries in parfait glasses. Chill.

Garnish as desired.

Preparation time: 15 minutes
Chilling time: 2 hours or more
Servings: 6 to 8

BEVERAGES
Tasty and Satisfying

Apple Cider or "Wassail" for a Party

5 gallons apple juice or apple cider
1/4 c. whole allspice
1/4 c. whole cloves
24 sticks cinnamon
1 tsp. mace

In a large kettle, heat the apple juice or cider until it is simmering.

Put all the spices into a cloth bag or cheese cloth, tying it securely.

Put the bag into the cider and let the spices simmer in the cider for 15 minutes.

Remove spices and serve the cider hot.

Preparation time: 10 minutes
Cooking time: 25 minutes
Servings: 40

Frozen Pineapple and Berry Fruit Drink

1 can (6 oz.) frozen
   juice
1 box (10 oz.) frozen
   raspberries or strawberries
6 oz. water
2 c. crushed ice

Combine all ingredients in an electric blender.

Process until thick and smooth.

Makes approximately 6 servings.

Preparation time: 10 minutes
Servings: 6

Natural Sodas

2 1/2 c. sparkling spring water
1 1/2 c. fruit juice (grape, apple, etc.)

Mix.

Makes 1 quart.

Serve with a piece of fresh fruit in each glass.

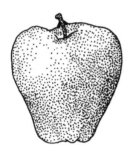

Herbal Punch

2 c. water
4 herbal tea bags (peppermint, raspberry, etc.)
2 c. fruit juice (apple, etc.)

Boil water and add tea bags; let steep for 4 to 6 minutes.

Add fruit juice.

Makes 1 quart.

Variation:
For a punch with fizz, use lemon, lime, cherry or orange sparkling spring water instead of juice.

Pineapple Grape Juice

1/2 c. unsweetened pineapple juice
1/2 c. white grape juice

Stir together.

Serve over ice.

If a more festive, fizzy drink is desired, use sparkling white grape juice.

Servings: 1

Cranberry Fizz

3/4 c. cranberry juice cocktail
1/4 c. plain seltzer water

Stir together.

Serve over ice.

Servings: 1

Strawberry Apple Slush

1 c. frozen strawberries

1/2 c. apple juice

Blend together.

Pour into a glass, garnish with fresh mint.

Servings: 1

DRESSINGS
DIPS
SAUCES
AND
SALSAS

Fat-Free and Healthy
Fit for a King

- **Eat to live . . . Don't live to eat**
- **Think of food as fuel**
- **Treat yourself with preventive medicine**

Brown Gravy

2 Tbsp. water
1 small onion, finely chopped
1/2 c. whole wheat flour
2 1/2 c. water
1/4 c. low sodium soy sauce
1/4 lb. sliced mushrooms, or
    4 oz. canned mushrooms

Variations: Omit mushrooms, add garlic powder, and substitute onion flakes and/or onion powder for onion.

Heat 2 tablespoons water in a large saucepan over medium heat and saute onion for 5 minutes, or until translucent.

Blend in the flour, stirring constantly until lightly browned.

Add rest of water and soy sauce.

Stir until blended well and gravy thickens.

Add mushrooms and cook 5 to 10 minutes longer.

Add more water if too thick.

Preparation time: 15 minutes
Cooking time: 25 minutes
Servings: 4 (about 3 cups)

Coleslaw Dressing

1/3 c. honey
1 tsp. dry mustard
1 tsp. paprika
1/4 tsp. salt (optional)
1 Tbsp. lemon juice
2/3 c. rice vinegar
1/4 tsp. onion powder
1/3 c. water
1 tsp. celery seed
1/4 tsp. pepper

Combine all ingredients in a jar.

Cover; shake vigorously until blended.

Store in refrigerator.

Shake before dressing coleslaw.

Preparation time: 10 minutes
Servings: 1 1/3 cups

Dressing for Green Beans or Salad

1/4 c. tomato juice

1 Tbsp. apple cider vinegar

1 Tbsp. fat free Italian dressing seasoning:

Italian seasoning, basil, onion and/or garlic powder

In a small bowl, blend ingredients.

Place in covered jar and store in refrigerator if not used immediately.

Preparation time: 10 minutes
Servings: about 1/3 cup dressing

Onion Dill Vinaigrette

2/3 c. apple cider vinegar
1/4 c. green onions, chopped
2 tsp. dried dill weed
1/2 to 1 tsp. salt (optional)
1 tsp. dry mustard

Combine all ingredients in a jar.

Cover; shake vigorously.

Chill to blend flavors.

Shake again before serving with mixed garden salad.

Preparation time: 10 minutes
Servings: about 1 cup

Lentil Butter or Dip

This savory appetizer can be spread on whole grain crackers or bread or used as a vegetable dip.

1 c. uncooked lentils
1/2 tsp. salt (optional)
2 1/4 c. water
1/4 c. water
6 green onions, sliced, green
    part only
1 small garlic clove, minced
1 1/2 Tbsp. dried parsley
Dash cayenne pepper or to
    taste
Dash tumeric or to taste
1/4 to 1/2 cup water, as needed

Combine lentils, salt and 2 1/4 cups water in a medium saucepan and cook until soft, about 35 minutes.

Reserve cooking water. Heat 1/4 cup water in a small skillet and saute onions and garlic until onions are translucent.

Add parsley and spices; cook another minute. Set aside.

Combine lentils, cooking water and onion mixture in a food processor.

Process, adding more water as needed, a tablespoon at a time, until mixture reaches a spreadable consistency.

Cover and refrigerate a few hours before serving.

Preparation time: 10 minutes
Cooking time: 35 minutes
Processing time: 10 minutes
Chilling time: 2 to 3 hours
Servings: 6

Apple Butter

1 qt. applesauce
1 1/2 tsp. cinnamon
1/4 tsp. ground cloves
1/2 tsp. allspice
2 tsp. sugar (optional)

Note: About 2 teaspoons apple pie seasoning may be substituted for the separate spices.

Combine all ingredients in a medium saucepan and simmer over low heat for 1 hour.

Can be used as spread on bread, toast, muffins, pancakes and waffles, etc., instead of butter, margarine, peanut butter, etc.

Preparation time: 5 minutes
Cooking time: 1 hour
Servings: 6 to 8

Blueberry Sauce

Serve warm or chilled over pancakes, cakes, puddings and frozen desserts.

2 c. fresh or frozen blueberries
1/3 c. water
1/2 c. sugar
1 Tbsp. cornstarch
1 Tbsp. lemon juice

In a small saucepan, combine all ingredients except lemon juice; heat to boiling, stirring frequently, until thickened.

Cook 2 minutes more over medium heat, stirring occasionally.

Stir in lemon juice.

Preparation time: 10 minutes
Cooking time: 15 minutes
Servings: 2 cups sauce

Raisin Sauce

Use as dressing on grated carrot salad or cabbage and carrot salad.

1 1/2 c. raisins

1 c. water

1/3 c. brown sugar

1/4 c. vinegar

Put raisins and water in small saucepan.

Heat slowly about 10 minutes to plump raisins.

Add sugar and vinegar.

Boil slowly about 15 minutes until thickened.

Preparation time: 10 minutes
Cooking time: 25 minutes
Servings: 2 cups

Strawberry Breakfast Spread

1 tsp. unflavored gelatin
1/4 c. orange juice
1 c. mashed or pureed fresh or frozen unsweetened strawberries
2 Tbsp. sugar (optional)
1 Tbsp. orange peel slivers
1/4 tsp. coriander

In a small saucepan, sprinkle gelatin over orange juice. Let stand 1 minute.

Heat over low heat until gelatin is dissolved and mixture comes to a boil.

Remove from heat and stir into strawberries that have been placed in a small bowl.

Add remaining ingredients and stir to blend.

Pour into a pint jar, cover and refrigerate until firm, 3 to 4 hours.

Best when used within 1 week.

Preparation time: 15 minutes
Cooking time: 5 minutes
Servings: 1 1/4 cups

Mushroom Sauce
(creamed)

Serve on grains, potatoes or vegetables.

1/2 lb. mushrooms, sliced
1 onion, chopped
1/2 c. water
2 c. fat-free soy milk
1/8 tsp. white pepper
1/8 tsp. garlic powder
1 Tbsp. low sodium soy sauce
2 Tbsp. cornstarch

In a medium saucepan, saute the mushrooms and onion in 1/4 cup water for 5 minutes.

Add milk, pepper, garlic powder, and soy sauce.

In a small covered jar, mix cornstarch with remaining 1/4 cup water by shaking vigorously.

Add to mushroom mixture.

Stir and cook over medium heat until mixture thickens.

Preparation time: 15 minutes
Cooking time: 25 minutes
Servings: 3 cups

Fresh Celery and Tomato Sauce

1/4 c. water
1 c. onion, chopped
3/4 c. water
2 c. celery, finely diced
2 c. tomatoes, diced
1 1/2 tsp. basil leaves, crushed
1/8 tsp. freshly ground black
  pepper
1 Tbsp. lemon juice

In a medium saucepan, heat 1/4 cup water and saute onion until transparent, about 5 minutes.

Add 3/4 cup water; bring to a boil.

Add celery, reduce heat and simmer, covered, for 5 minutes.

Add tomatoes, basil, black pepper and lemon juice; simmer, covered, until vegetables are very soft and flavors blended, about 10 minutes.

Stir frequently and add more water if needed. Serve on baked potatoes.

Preparation time: 15 minutes
Cooking time: 20 minutes
Servings: 3 cups, or 4 to 6
  portions

Mustard Sauce

1/2 c. Dijon-style mustard
1/4 c. sugar
1 Tbsp. white rice vinegar
1/2 c. fresh dill, finely chopped,
   or 2 Tbsp. dry dill

Combine all ingredients and mix well.

Let stand 15 minutes before serving.

Preparation time: 10 minutes
Servings: 2/3 cup

Spaghetti Sauce

75 plum tomatoes or 50
　　medium-sized regular
　　tomatoes, washed, cored
　　and chopped

1/4 c. brown sugar

1 to 2 Tbsp. salt (optional)

1/2 tsp. pepper

3 large onions, chopped

6 garlic cloves, minced

3/4 c. fresh parsley, chopped,
　　or 1/4 c. dried parsley

1 Tbsp. dried basil or 3 Tbsp.
　　fresh, chopped

1 Tbsp. dried oregano leaves
　　or 3 Tbsp. fresh, chopped

1 Tbsp. dried thyme or
　3 Tbsp. fresh, chopped

3 bay leaves

*Note: One tablespoon
cornstarch, diluted in a little
water, added to 1 quart of sauce
before reheating will thicken
sauce perfectly.*

In a 12-quart kettle, combine tomatoes, brown sugar, salt and pepper. Bring to a boil, stirring occasionally.

Reduce heat and boil gently, uncovered, stirring occasionally for 1 hour.

Add remaining ingredients; boil gently, stirring occasionally for 1 hour or until the sauce is the desired consistency.

Remove bay leaves.

Puree hot sauce through food mill.

Pour hot sauce into sterilized hot pint jars, leaving 1-inch head space. Adjust lids.

Process in pressure canner at 10 pounds for 35 minutes (adjust for altitude differences) or, sauce can be frozen.

Preparation time: 30 to 40 min.
Cooking time: 2 1/2 hours, if frozen 3 1/4 hours, if canned

Home-made Spaghetti Sauce
(in 10-Minutes)

1 can (14 1/2 oz.) stewed tomatoes

1 can (6 oz.) tomato paste

3 oz. (6 Tbsp.) water

Combine ingredients in a small saucepan; bring to a boil.

Reduce heat; simmer 5 minutes, or until desired thickness.

Preparation time: 5 minutes
Cooking time: 5 minutes
Servings: 2 cups

Spaghetti Sauce
(made easy)

1/2 c. onions, chopped
1/4 c. green pepper, chopped
1 large garlic clove, crushed
1 1/4 c. water
1 can (6 oz.) tomato paste
2 cans (8 oz.) tomato sauce
1/4 tsp. basil leaves
1 tsp. oregano leaves
1 bay leaf
1/2 tsp. salt (optional)
1/8 tsp. pepper
1 tsp. sugar

Saute onion, green pepper and garlic in 1/4 cup water in medium saucepan.

Stir in remaining water and other ingredients.

Heat to boiling; reduce heat and boil gently, uncovered, for 30 minutes.

Remove bay leaf.

Preparation time: 15 minutes
Cooking time: 35 minutes
Servings: about 2 1/2 cups
  sauce

Creole Seasoning

2 1/2 Tbsp. paprika
2 Tbsp. dried minced garlic or
    garlic powder
2 Tbsp. ground black pepper
1 Tbsp. dried minced onion or
    onion powder
1 Tbsp. ground red pepper
1 Tbsp. dried thyme
1 Tbsp. dried oregano

In small bowl, mix together all ingredients.

Transfer to a small jar, seal tightly and store in a cool, dry place.

This is great for making creole rice, bean and salad dishes.

Preparation time: 10 minutes

Picante Sauce

4 c. tomatoes, peeled and chopped
1 c. onion, chopped
1 garlic clove, minced
2 or 3 jalapeno peppers, finely chopped
1 Tbsp. fresh or canned green chilies, chopped
2 tsp. sugar
2 Tbsp. apple cider vinegar
1 tsp. salt (optional)
1/4 tsp. ground cumin
1/4 tsp. ground coriander

Combine all ingredients in a large saucepan.

Bring to a boil over medium heat; reduce heat and simmer, uncovered, 25 minutes.

Preparation time: 20 minutes
Cooking time: 30 minutes
Servings: 3 cups

Salsa

*Delicious with homemade
Tortilla Chips or Cornmeal Oat
Pones (see recipes).*

**1 can (16 oz.) tomatoes,
    drained and chopped fine**

1/2 onion, chopped

1 can (7 oz.) diced green chilies

1 Tbsp. wine vinegar

1/2 tsp. basil

1 tsp. parsley flakes

1/2 tsp. minced garlic

1/2 tsp. seasoned pepper

1 tsp. original blend Mrs. Dash

1/4 tsp. Tabasco sauce

In a small bowl, combine all ingredients, stirring well.

Can be used as a dip, relish, or baked potato topping.

If you use a blender, use 2 of the tomatoes, blend well with onion and green chilies; add remaining ingredients and mix lightly.

Preparation time: 15 minutes
Servings:

Salsa Dip
(Made Fresh)

2 cans (4 oz.) minced green
  chilies
1 c. mushrooms, chopped
3 green onions, tops included,
  finely chopped
4 firm red tomatoes, finely
  cubed
2 to 3 Tbsp. bottled nonfat
  Italian dressing
2 Tbsp. fresh cilantro, finely
  chopped

Combine chilies, onions,
tomatoes and dressing.

Chill overnight.

Top with cilantro; mix gently.

Preparation time: 15 minutes
Chilling time: overnight
Servings: 6 cups

Salsa
(Fresh California Style)

1 pint canned tomatoes, chopped

2 medium size fresh tomatoes, diced

1 can (4 oz.) green chilies, diced

1 bunch green onions, diced

1/2 bunch fresh cilantro leaves, minced

2 Tbsp. cider vinegar

1 tsp. salt (optional)

Combine all ingredients; mix well.

Refrigerate, covered, a minimum of 1 hour.

Preparation time: 20 minutes
Chilling time: 1 hour
Servings: 5 to 6 cups

Mexican Hot Sauce or Dip

5 c. tomato puree

1/2 tsp. oregano

1/2 tsp. Tabasco sauce

2 Tbsp. lemon juice

1 1/2 tsp. sugar

1/2 tsp. black pepper

1 3/4 tsp. chili powder

1 tsp. garlic powder

1/2 tsp. cumin

1/2 tsp. salt (optional)

1/2 tsp. cayenne pepper

2 tsp. red wine vinegar

In a medium bowl, combine all ingredients.

Store, covered, in refrigerator.

Keeps well; also freezes well.

Preparation time: 15 minutes
Servings: 5 cups sauce

Barbecue Sauce

2 c. catsup
Juice of 2 lemons
4 garlic cloves, crushed
1 or 2 dashes Tabasco
2 Tbsp. brown sugar
2 Tbsp. corn syrup
2 tsp. smoke flavor

Combine all ingredients; bring to a boil.

Simmer 5 minutes.

Preparation time: 10 minutes
Cooking time: 5 minutes
Servings: 2 1/4 cups

Sweet and Sour Sauce

Good served over cooked brown rice.

1/2 c. unsweetened pineapple juice

2 c. apples, peeled and chopped

2 Tbsp. cider vinegar

2 Tbsp. honey

1 tsp. low sodium soy sauce

1 Tbsp. cornstarch, if thicker sauce is desired

Combine all ingredients in a small saucepan.

Cover and cook until fruit is tender, about 20 minutes.

Mash with a hand masher.

If you want a thicker sauce, add 1 Tbsp. cornstarch to the liquid before cooking and stir well until thick.

Serve hot or cold.

Preparation time: 10 minutes
Cooking time: 20 minutes
Servings: 2 cups sauce

Lemon Glaze

Pour over freshly baked cakes.

1/2 c. sugar
1/2 c. water
1 tsp. lemon rind, grated
1/4 c. lemon juice

Combine all ingredients in a small bowl, stirring until sugar dissolves.

Preparation time: 10 minutes
Servings: 1 1/4 cups

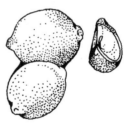

Lemon Sauce

Serve on gingerbread or plain cake.

1/2 c. sugar
1 1/2 Tbsp. flour
1/16 tsp. salt (optional)
1 c. boiling water
3 Tbsp. lemon juice

In a small saucepan, mix the sugar, flour and salt; add the boiling water and cook until mixture thickens.

Stir in lemon juice.

Remove from heat, cool and store in a covered jar in refrigerator.

Preparation time: 10 minutes
Cooking time: 10 minutes
Servings: 1 1/4 cups

Orange Sauce

1/4 c. sugar
1/3 c. orange juice
1 Tbsp. cornstarch
1 tsp. grated orange peel

In a small saucepan mix sugar and cornstarch; add orange juice and orange peel.

Cook over medium heat, stirring constantly, until mixture thickens and begins to boil.

Makes enough to dress 3 cups of cooked, drained sliced beets.

Preparation time: 10 minutes
Cooking time: 10 minutes
Servings: 1/3 cup

Caramel Sauce

3 Tbsp. cornstarch
1/2 c. brown sugar
1/4 c. liquid Butter Buds (mix
    1/2 packet Butter Buds in
    1/4 c. hot tap water)
2 c. fat-free soy milk
1 tsp. vanilla

In a small saucepan, mix cornstarch and brown sugar.

Add liquid Butter Buds and milk.

Cook, stirring constantly, until thickened.

Remove from heat and add vanilla.

Preparation time: 10 minutes
Cooking time: 10 minutes
Servings: 2 cups sauce

Vanilla Sauce

Serve hot over spice cake or other pastries.

2 c. fat-free soy milk
3 Tbsp. cornstarch
1/2 c. brown sugar
1 tsp. vanilla

In small saucepan, cook first three ingredients together until thickened.

Remove and add vanilla.

Preparation time: 5 minutes
Cooking time: 10 minutes
Servings: sauce for 9 servings of spice cake, about 2 1/2 cups.

Frosting
(made easy in 7-Minutes)

This makes enough to frost 2 layers of an 8 or 9-inch cake.

1/2 c. sugar
1/2 c. light corn syrup
1/8 tsp. salt (optional)
2 egg whites
1 tsp. vanilla

Place water in lower part of double boiler up to level of bottom of top saucepan when in place, and bring water to boil.

In top of double boiler, combine sugar, corn syrup, salt and egg whites.

Place over boiling water.

Cook, beating constantly with portable electric mixer at medium speed, about 7 minutes, or until mixture will stand in peaks having curved tops.

Remove from heat and beat 1 minute longer at high speed until thick enough to spread.

Add flavoring and blend.

Preparation time: 10 minutes
Cooking time: 7 minutes
Servings: frosting for 2 layers
of 8 or 9-inch cake

Rocky Mountain Frosting

1 c. sugar
1 tsp. cream of tartar
1/2 c. water
2 eggs whites
1 tsp. vanilla

In a small saucepan, cook together first 3 ingredients until hard ball forms when dropped in water.

Meanwhile, in a medium bowl beat egg whites until stiff.

Beat hot syrup into egg whites until stiff peaks form. Add vanilla.

Preparation time: 15 minutes
Cooking time: 7 to 10 minutes
Servings: frosting for 2-layer cake

APPETIZERS
RELISHES
AND
SNACKS

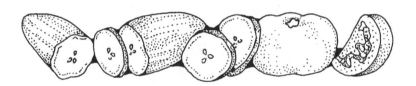

Daniel's Training in Babylon

"Please test your servants for ten days: Give us nothing but vegetables to eat and water to drink. Then compare our appearance with that of the young men who eat the royal food, and treat your servants in accordance with what you see."

So he agreed to this and tested them for ten days.

At the end of the ten days they looked healthier and better nourished than any of the young men who ate the royal food.

So the guard took away their choice food and the wine they were to drink and gave them vegetables instead.

Daniel 1:12-16 New International Version (1984)

For a complete explanation of the cause of degenerative diseases and how to change your lifestyle to prevent or reverse disease — read Earl Updike's companion book (with the bright yellow cover).

"THE MIRACLE DIET — 14 DAYS TO NEW VIGOR AND HEALTH."

APPETIZERS

The Miracle Diet

The Miracle Diet is a plant-centered diet program that allows your body to seek its ideal weight with natural, high energy. It is based upon plants, not vegetables. The five basic starches are the basis of the diet.

- **Grain**   (wheat, oats, and barley)
- **Rice**   (a basic grain)
- **Corn**   (a basic grain)
- **Legumes**   (beans, peas, and lentils)
- **Potatoes**   (the only vegetable)

Eggplant Appetizer

Serve at room temperature spooned onto wedges of pita bread.

1 Tbsp. garlic, minced
1 Tbsp. oregano
1/4 c. water
1 medium eggplant, trimmed
    and chopped
2 ripe tomatoes, chopped
1 zucchini, trimmed and
    chopped
Salt to taste (optional)
Freshly ground pepper to taste

In a large skillet, over medium heat, saute garlic and oregano in water until garlic is soft. Do not brown.

Add vegetables and cook over medium heat, stirring occasionally, until very soft, about 25 minutes.

Season with salt and pepper.

Preparation time: 15 minutes
Cooking time: 30 minutes
Servings: 4 to 6

Pickled Mushrooms

2 lb. fresh button mushrooms

Dressing:
1/2 c. lemon juice
1/2 c. water
1 tsp. garlic, minced
3/4 tsp. salt (optional)
1/2 tsp. pepper
1/3 c. fresh parsley, chopped
1/4 c. red bell pepper, diced

Place mushrooms in a pretty glass bowl; set aside.

Mix lemon juice, water, garlic, salt and pepper in a small saucepan and bring to a boil.

Pour over mushrooms, Cover; refrigerate for at least 2 hours.

Add the parsley and red pepper, stirring to blend.

Preparation time: 15 minutes
Marinating time: at least 2 hours
Servings: 10 appetizer servings

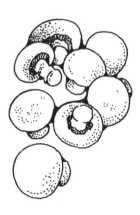

Croutons
(Zesty Italian Style)

Use croutons to garnish salads, soups and casseroles, or as a snack.

1/4 c. nonfat Italian salad
    dressing
1 1/2 tsp. oregano leaves
1 1/2 tsp. basil leaves
1/2 tsp. garlic powder
4 c. Nabisco™ Shredded
    Wheat 'N Bran

In bowl, combine salad dressing, oregano, basil and garlic powder; stir in cereal, tossing to coat well.

Spread on 15 1/2 x 10 1/2 x 1-inch baking pan.

Bake at 325 degrees for 20 minutes, stirring after 10 minutes.

Spread on absorbent paper to cool.

Store in airtight container.

Preparation time: 15 minutes
Baking time: 20 minutes
Servings: 4 to 6

Creole Seasoning

This is great for making creole rice, bean and salad dishes.

2 1/2 Tbsp. paprika
2 Tbsp. dried garlic or garlic
**   powder**
2 Tbsp. ground black pepper
1 Tbsp. dried onions or onion
**   powder**
1 Tbsp. ground red pepper
1 Tbsp. dried thyme
1 Tbsp. dried oregano

In small bowl, mix together all ingredients.

Transfer to a small jar, seal tightly and store in a cool, dry place.

Preparation time: 10 minutes

Corn Tortilla Chips

Several companies now make fat free baked corn chips and baked potato chips.

Cut tortillas in eighths. Place on a nonstick cookie sheet and bake about 30 minutes at 350 degrees, stirring once.

Or, brush lightly with water, sprinkle with Butter Buds, onion powder and/or garlic powder. Cut in eighths. Place on nonstick cookie sheet and bake about 15 minutes at 350 degrees, stirring once.

Preparation time: 10 to 20 minutes
Baking time: 15 minutes
Servings: variable

Baked Commercial Corn Chips found in Supermarkets:
Tostitos by Frito-Lay
Guiltless Gourmet
Others found in health food stores.

Fat Free Potato Chips found in Supermarkets:
Louise's Fat Free Potato Chips
Others found in health food stores.

RELISHES
Spice Up Your Life

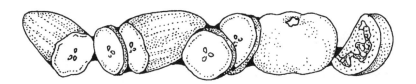

It's truly a miracle!

- Prevent heart-artery disease
- Reverse adult diabetes
- Lower blood pressure
- Prevent many cancers

- Reverse heart disease
- Prevent adult diabetes
- Lose weight permanently
- Prevent Osteoporosis

Cranberry Plus Relish

**4 c. (1 lb.) fresh or frozen
cranberries**
**4 oranges, peeled, sectioned
and seeded**
2 c. sugar, or less for tart taste
**1 apple, unpeeled, cut up,
cored**
1/2 tsp. almond flavoring
**1 can (8 1/2 oz.) undrained
crushed pineapple**

Chop cranberries in a food processor, then add oranges and chop.

Add remaining ingredients; pulse for several seconds to blend.

Chill several hours before serving.

Preparation time: 25 minutes
Chilling time: several hours
Servings: 7 1/2 cups relish

Sunshine Pepper Relish

1 large sweet yellow pepper, seeded and diced
1 large red bell pepper, seeded and diced
1 medium onion, diced
1 tsp. salt (optional)
2 Tbsp. sugar
2 Tbsp. Balsamic vinegar

Coat small saucepan with nonstick spray.

Add all ingredients.

Simmer 30 minutes or until thoroughly blended.

Serve cold.

Preparation time: 15 minutes
Cooking time: 30 minutes
Servings: 3/4 to 1 cup

Stewed Tomato Relish

1 can (16 oz.) stewed tomatoes
1 pkg. (3 oz.) lemon or
strawberry gelatin
1/2 tsp. salt (optional)
1 Tbsp. vinegar

Pour tomatoes into medium saucepan, saving can.

Bring tomatoes to a boil.

Reduce heat; simmer 2 minutes.

Add gelatin, salt and vinegar; stir until gelatin dissolves.

Pour into can.

Chill until firm.

Puncture bottom of can, dip in warm water and unmold onto serving dish and slice.

Preparation time: 5 minutes
Cooking time: 10 minutes
Chilling time: several hours
Servings: 6

Minty Pineapple Relish

1 pkg. (3 oz.) lime gelatin
Dash of salt (optional)
3/4 c. boiling water
1 can (13 to 16 oz.) crushed
   pineapple
4 drops mint or peppermint
   extract
2 1/2 tsp. vinegar

Dissolve gelatin and salt in boiling water in a medium pan.

Stir in remaining ingredients.

Chill until thickened.

Pour into a 1-quart serving dish.

Chill until firm, at least 3 hours.

Preparation time: 15 minutes
Chilling time: 3 hours or more
Servings: 8 to 10

SNACKS

- If you want salted popcorn, fill a pump spray-bottle with plain water. As the air-popped corn comes out into a bowl spray lightly with water and shake on some salt. It works great!

- Air-popped popcorn is a fat-free food. Delight anytime of the day or night. Buy an air popcorn popper, they are inexpensive.

- Baked cornchips are now in every supermarket. A real healthy treat. Tostitos, by Frito Lay Inc., contain only the natural fat in corn.

- **Eat to live ... Don't live to eat**
- **Think of food as fuel**
- **Treat yourself with preventive**

Popcorn Crunch

1/2 c. unpopped popcorn, airpopped
1/2 c. light corn syrup
1 1/2 c. sugar
1/4 c. boiling water
1 1/2 tsp. baking soda

Pop corn and place in large mixing bowl.

In a medium sized saucepan over medium heat, combine corn syrup, sugar and boiling water.

Bring to a boil, add soda and stir until color changes and the mixture rises.

Remove from heat and pour over popcorn.

Mix with a wooden spoon.

Spread on a lightly sprayed cookie sheet.

When cool, break into small pieces.

Store in airtight container.

Preparation time: 30 minutes
Servings: 14 to 18

Popcorn Balls
(made Quick and Easy)

3 qts. air-popped popcorn
1 c. light corn syrup
1 c. sugar
1/2 tsp. salt (optional)
1 tsp. vanilla
**1/4 tsp. red or green food
    coloring (optional)**

Keep popcorn in a 250 degree oven.

In a 2-quart saucepan mix together the corn syrup, sugar and salt.

Cook over medium heat until mixture comes to a boil.

Cook without stirring 4 minutes.

Remove from heat. Stir in vanilla and food coloring.

Pour syrup slowly over popcorn, mix thoroughly with sprayed fork or spoon.

When cool enough to handle, shape into balls.

Let stand in warm, dry place until cool and balls lose stickiness.

Wrap in plastic wrap and place in plastic bag. Store in tightly covered container.

Preparation time: 45 minutes
Servings: 15 to 20

SANDWICHES

In addition to *these* great sandwich recipes, invent a few of your own. Plant foods with no added fat provide the ingredients for an endless variety of tasty and satisfying sandwiches.

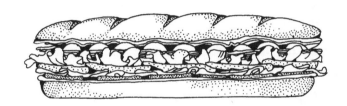

The Miracle Diet

The Miracle Diet is a plant-centered diet program that allows your body to seek its ideal weight with natural, high energy. It is based upon plants, not vegetables. The five basic starches are the basis of the diet.

- **Grain** (wheat, oats, and barley)
- **Rice** (a basic grain)
- **Corn** (a basic grain)
- **Legumes** (beans, peas, and lentils)
- **Potatoes** (the only vegetable)

Tomato Burger

1 to 4 tomato slices
1 onion slice
1 lettuce leaf
5 pickle slices
Fat free mayonnaise and/or
    mustard

Note: Order this at your
favorite Fast Food Chain.
Wendy's **seems best. Average**
price is about 80¢.

Spread mayonnaise and/or
mustard on bun; arrange other
ingredients and enjoy!

Preparation time: 2 minutes
Yield: 1 burger

Bean Delight Sandwich

1 c. mashed pinto beans
Red onion slice
Red and green chili
Lettuce
Fat free mayonnaise or
**   mustard to taste**
Salt to taste (optional)

Note: Many canned beans
without added fat are now
available including no fat
refried beans.

Spread on 9 grain or whole
wheat bread.

Preparation time: 10 minutes
Yield: 1 cup

Black Bean Supreme Sandwich

1 c. mashed black beans, cooked
3/4 tsp. cumin
1 1/2 tsp. garlic powder
Onion slice
Tomato slice
Alfalfa and clover sprouts
Lettuce
Fat free mayonnaise or mustard to taste
Salt to taste (optional)

Mix well and spread on 9 grain or whole wheat bread.

Preparation time: 15 minutes
Yield: 1 cup

Kidney Bean Sandwich

1 1/2 c. kidney beans, cooked and drained
1 garlic clove, crushed
1/2 tsp. cumin seeds
1/2 tsp. Tabasco sauce
1/2 Tbsp. cider vinegar
2 Tbsp. water
2 Tbsp. fresh parsley

Place all the ingredients in food processor or blender and process until smooth.
Spread on bread.

Yield: 1 1/2 cups

Use your imagination. Invent a variety of sandwiches. Great as a bean dip.

Boca Burger (Fat-Free)

A delicious alternative to the high-cholesterol, high-fat animal-food hamburger.

1 soybean pattie
1 slice tomato
1 lettuce leaf
1 slice onion
1 burger bun
Garnish with pickles

Brown pattie in a non-stick skillet.

Assemble like a hamburger.

Preparation time: 10 minutes
Cooking time: 5 minutes
Servings: 1 burger per person

Note: Fat-Free Boca Burgers can be purchased in most health food stores. If they don't carry this item, ask them to order the product for you. This is a frozen product from Boca Raton, Florida.

Bean Sandwich
(Hot and Spicy)

1 1/2 c. kidney or pinto beans,
    cooked and drained
1/2 medium onion, chopped
1 tomato, chopped
1 garlic clove, chopped
1 Tbsp. low sodium soy sauce
1/2 Tbsp. chili powder
1/2 Tbsp. ground cumin
1/2 tsp. paprika
1/2 tsp. dried oregano

Process all ingredients in a food processor or blender until smooth; add a little water if necessary during processing. Spread on bread.

Preparation time: 15 minutes
Yield: 2 cups

Bean Sandwich

1 small onion, finely chopped
1 garlic clove, crushed
2 Tbsp. chopped green chilies
1/8 tsp. cayenne pepper
1 1/2 c. white beans, cooked and drained
1 Tbsp. low sodium soy sauce
2 Tbsp. apple juice

Note: A great variety of canned beans are available without added fat.

Place the onion, garlic and green chilies in a saucepan with a small amount of water.

Cook and stir until the onion is soft.

Add the cayenne and mix well.

Add the beans and cook, mashing beans as they cook.

Add soy sauce.

Cook and stir for several minutes.

Transfer to bowl, cover and refrigerate for at least 2 hours. Spread on bread.

Preparation time: 20 minutes
Chilling time: 2 hours
Yield: 2 cups

Carrot Spread

1 c. carrot, grated
6 Tbsp. crushed pineapple, drained
2 Tbsp. fat free Miracle Whip™

Mix well and spread on bread.

Preparation time: 10 minutes
Yield: 1 cup

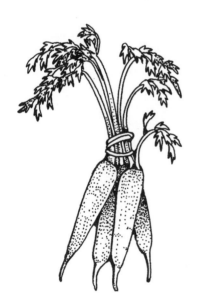

Cucumber Spread

**2 medium cucumbers, grated
or chopped fine
1 Tbsp. sweet onion, grated
2 Tbsp. fat free mayonnaise
1/8 tsp. salt (optional)**

For different flavors you may add fat free mayonnaise, dill weed, or fat free ranch or Italian dressing to the above.

Mix and spread on bread for a great sandwich.

Preparation time: 15 minutes
Yield: 1 cup

HERBS AND SPICES

Fresh herbs and spices, more than any other single element in cooking, give life and sparkle to food. They can transform an ordinary dish into something special. Below are some suggested uses for various herbs and spices.

Food	Herbs and Spices
apples, baked	caraway seed, cinnamon, cloves
apple pie or apple cake	aniseed, cinnamon, cloves, coriander, nutmeg
apples, stewed	allspice, aniseed, cinnamon, cloves
asparagus	mustard seed, sesame seed, tarragon
bananas	cinnamon
beets	allspice, bay leaf, caraway seed, cloves, dill, ginger, mustard, savory, thyme
bread, fruit	allspice, aniseed, cinnamon, cloves, coriander, ginger, sesame
bread, rye	caraway, cumin
breads,	sweet curry

Food	Herbs and Spices
broccoli	caraway seed, dill, mustard, oregano, tarragon
brussel sprouts	basil, caraway seed, dill, mustard, nutmeg, sage, thyme
buns	allspice, garlic, paprika
cabbage, green	caraway seed, celery seed, cumin, curry powder, dill, fennel, mustard, nutmeg, savory, tarragon
cabbage, red	aniseed (plus above herbs)
cake, fruit	allspice, cinnamon, cloves, ginger, nutmeg, sesame, vanilla
carrots	allspice, aniseed, bay leaf, cinnamon, cumin, curry powder, dill, fennel, ginger, mace, marjoram, mint, nutmeg, poppy seed (topping), thyme
carrot soup	coriander, tarragon leaves, watercress, leeks
cauliflower	caraway seed, cayenne, celery seed, chili powder, dill, mace, mustard powder (for sauce), nutmeg, paprika, rosemary, tarragon
celery	lovage, paprika , parsley
coleslaw	caraway seed, mustard seed
cookies	allspice, aniseed, cardamom, cinnamon, cloves, ginger, mace, nutmeg, sesame, vanilla

Food	Herbs and Spices
corn	basil, cayenne, celery seed, chili powder, cilantro, curry powder, garlic, mint, paprika, parsley, safflower
cucumbers	dill, fennel seed, parsley
eggplant	allspice, bay leaf, chili powder, garlic, marjoram, oregano
egg-white dishes (with fruits, grains, etc.)	allspice, cinnamon, cloves, cream of tarter (beaten egg whites), ginger, nutmeg, saffron
egg-white dishes (with veg, grains, etc.)	basil, chives, curry powder, marjoram, mustard powder, nutmeg, oregano, paprika (garnish), parsley, pepper (black or white), poppy seed, saffron, tumeric
fruits, dried, mixed, stewed	cinnamon, cloves, ginger, nutmeg
fruits, pickled	cloves, dill
green beans	basil, dill, marjoram, mint, mustard, nutmeg, oregano, savory, tarragon, thyme
lentil soup	basil, bay leaves, coriander, dill seed, parsley, sorrel
lima beans	marjoram, nutmeg, oregano, sage, savory, tarragon, thyme
macaroni salad	mace, parsley, thyme

Food	Herbs and Spices
mushrooms	garlic, marjoram, mint, parsley, pepper
onions	bay leaf, caraway, mustard, nutmeg, oregano, paprika, sage, thyme
parsnips	aniseed, chives, parsley, poppy seed
peaches	aniseed, basil, cinnamon
pears	allspice, chervil leaves, cinnamon
peas	basil, chili powder, dill, marjoram, miny, oregano, poppy seed, rosemary, sage, savory
pea soup	coriander, parsley
pickles	allspice, cumin, dill, fenugreek, juniper
pickling vegetables	caraway seed, cardamom, cloves, ginger, pepper (black or white)
pie, fruit	allspice, aniseed, cinnamon, cloves, cumin (sparingly), ginger, mace (cherry), nutmeg
potatoes	basil, bay leaves, caraway seed, celery seed, chives, dill, fennel, mustard seed, oregano, paprika, pepper, poppy seed, sesame seed, thyme
puddings	allspice, cinnamon, cloves, ginger, mace, nutmeg
rhubarb	allspice, cinnamon, ginger

Food	Herbs and Spices
rice	basil, cardamom, cilantro, cinnamon, fenugreek, garlic, parsley, saffron (changes rice color), sage, tumeric
salad dressings	aniseed, black pepper, paprika, parsley
salads, vegetable	anise (chopped leaves), basil leaves, chives, dill, paprika, parsley, pepper
soup, creamed	chilies, cinnamon, cloves, curry (garnish), sorrel
soup, vegetable	basil, cardamom, cilantro, marjoram, parsley, poppy seeds (whole as garnish), rosemary (sparingly), sage
spinach	allspice, cinnamon, nutmeg, oregano, rosemary, sesame seed
squash	allspice, basil, bay leaves, cinnamon, cloves, fennel, ginger, mustard seed, nutmeg, paprika, rosemary
stewed fruits	cardamom
stuffings	parsley, sage
sweet potatoes	allspice, caldamona, cardamom seed, cinnamon, cloves, ginger, nutmeg, paprika, sage, sesame seed, tarragon, thyme
sweet-and-sour sauces	cloves, cumin, ginger
toast	cinnamon, garlic, mace

Food	Herbs and Spices
tomatoes	basil, bay leaves, celery seed, chili powder, cilantro, cumin, curry powder, garlic, marjoram, oregano, parsley, sage, sesame, tarragon, thyme
turnips	allspice, celery seed, curry powder, dill, oregano, parsley, thyme
vegetable curries	cinnamon, curry powder, tamarind, tumeric
vegetable dishes	basil, black pepper, parsley
vegetable sauces	paprika (garnish)
vinegar	tarragon (steep 1 Tbsp. per pint vinegar)
waffles	allspice, cinnamon, cloves, ginger, nutmeg, poppy seed, sage

GENERAL INFORMATION INDEX

RECIPE INDEX

(Index entries in all capital letters *represent section headings*)

ABOUT THE AUTHORS

Ethel Crosby Updike

Ethel Updike originated the idea that a cookbook was the best way to show people how tasty and appealing healthful plant food can be. She believed that if everyone ate a plant-centered diet, very few people would suffer from the life-threatening, devastating, painful and miserable degenerative diseases of breast cancer, multiple sclerosis, heart disease, diabetes, osteoporosis and many others.

Ethel has always loved to plan and cook meals, unfortunately for many years she followed the standard American diet (mostly animal foods and added fat) which is the wrong fuel for man. Then she became convinced that what was necessary was to change to the correct fuel (plant-centered) for the best possible health.

Ethel felt that she would never have suffered from Multiple Sclerosis or breast cancer if she had followed a plant-based diet from childhood.

Earl F. Updike

Author Earl F. Updike is a businessman, writer, and a student of nutrition for 50 years. He believes that the healthier you are, the better you can serve others.

He has taught for many years that everyone should follow a plant-centered food plan if you want to be thin and attractive. He also says that happiness and health are synonymous.

For over fifty years medical science has been proving by irrefutable evidence that the correct fuel for humans is plant food, as it is for all primates. Primates are herbivores by nature, and man is classified by science as a primate.

Updike says, "If you want the 'Best Possible Health' you must eat a (starch) plant-based diet."